Exit, Miss Saigon

An American Memoir

David Mura

MINNESOTA

UNIVERSITY OF MINNESOTA PRESS
MINNEAPOLIS
LONDON

I want a home here not only for the Negro, the mulatto and the Latin races; but I want the Asiatic to find a home here in the United States, and feel at home here, both for his sake and for ours. The outspread wings of the American Eagle are broad enough to shelter all who are likely to come.

—Frederick Douglass

Building community is to the collective as spiritual practice is to the individual.

—Grace Lee Boggs, Asian American activist

Contents

Introduction

A Surrealist Asian in Minnesota

I

In 1974, I came to Minneapolis, for the Ph.D. program in English literature at the University of Minnesota. At the time there were very few Asian Americans here. But back then I didn't think of myself as an Asian American or even as a Sansei, a third-generation Japanese American—much less a person of color. Yes, my parents and their families had been imprisoned by the U.S. government in World War II for their race and ethnicity, but when I was growing up, the adults never talked to us kids about the internment camps or their experiences during the war: the "camps" were quarantined in a zone of silence. As my father later said, "We didn't want you to grow up with a chip on your shoulder."

So in 1974, the issues of race weren't on my mind. Certainly they weren't in the courses I was taking for my Ph.D. In my five years in the program, all the authors I read were white, except a few poems by Amiri Baraka. When my fellow Ph.D. student, the African American poet Marilyn Nelson, handed me the anthology of Asian American writers *Aiiieeeee!* I put it on my bookshelf and did not look at it for a couple of years. For me, to read such an anthology meant I'd be somehow grouped with the writers within it, and I'd already learned implicitly and explicitly from my white professors that "minority literature" was called that for a reason: it was minor, secondary. To view myself as a writer of color would be to relegate myself to a literary ghetto, to attempt to enter literature through a sort of back-door affirmative action program. It meant I couldn't cut it and make it legitimately through the front door.

And oh, I so wanted to enter through that front door. I worshiped poets like Robert Lowell, Randall Jarrell, and John Berryman (who'd taught at the University of Minnesota and committed suicide by jumping off the Washington Avenue Bridge). These were all Ivy League–educated white male poets, wreathed in prestige, learning, and tradition, tortured artists but tortured not by anything political but by personal demons, by their families, by their sensitivity, by their fight against a barbarian mass culture. I was less enamored with the more Bohemian Beats and what was regarded as their less disciplined, less artistic debasings and departures from the traditional canon.

At the time, the meager poems I was writing were less like Lowell or Berryman and more minimal and surrealist, what my poet friend Garrett Hongo has dubbed "Caucasian haiku," describing the poems in his graduate workshop. I was influenced by Minnesota's Robert Bly and the quiet prairie surrealism he and James Wright helped make famous; I studied how they were influenced by the surrealism of Latin American poets like César Vallejo and Pablo Neruda, by the Spanish poets Federico García Lorca, Antonio Machado, and Juan Jiménez.

But if the literary world I dwelt in was all white, where I couldn't avoid racial issues was in the bars and nightclubs I frequented back then—the Cabooze, where live bands played, and later disco clubs like Scottie's on Seventh and Chi-Chi's out on 494 in suburban Bloomington. In clubs where people go in part to mingle with the opposite sex, the body is always present, whereas in situations like the classroom the racial body can be a bit more hidden or unremarked on.

Back then I understood that there were Black bars like the Tempo. But at the same time I barely understood that there was something going on between the handful of Black men who'd show up at the Cabooze and the white women there; I'd even overheard a white woman talking to her friend about the sexual prowess of Black men, and I didn't understand exactly what that meant. I just knew I was not a part of that, just as I was not white.[1] I had no knowledge of Black

1 Whatever was happening on the sexual down-low, the racism against Blacks in the Twin Cities at that time was still strongly in force and enforced; my friend, the writer and scholar Frank Wilderson, writes in his memoir *Incognegro* about when his family in the early seventies was the first Black family to move into Kenwood—the Mary Tyler

life or Black culture, no Black friends; to identify with the Blacks in the club or to interact with them was not a possibility I entertained. I was too white identified.

On the other hand, there were no Asian or Asian American men in those clubs.[2] If there was an occasional Asian American woman, usually a Filipina, she never paid any attention to me, never reacted to me as having any connection to her. If she was there, it was obvious she was looking for white guys. The white guys knew this. They'd ask me if she was my sister, if I knew her, obviously hoping I might serve as some sort of sexual conduit.

Let me be clear: I did meet women in these bars, just as I did meet women at the university, and almost all these women were white. And I was not unsuccessful. But clearly, in those places of sexual exchange, I was an anomaly. I didn't have a place. As much as I wanted to think of myself as white, as much as I could pretend in grad school or in my little surrealistic imitations of James Wright that I wasn't a person of color, things were different every time I entered a bar or club. There I could never completely erase my awareness I was not white. Oh, I could hide my face, my body when I was studying Johnson's *Lives of the Poets,* but asking a white, often working-class woman to dance as the Lamont Cranston Band admonished, "Don't roll your bloodshot eyes at me" or James Brown screeched, "Please please please"? No, that was different.

In the bars and clubs, I was what I didn't want to be: a yellow man (here, track Randy Newman crooning, "Got to have a yellow woman if you're a yellow man"); I was a Jap, a Chink, a gook, someone associated with Peter the cranky houseboy on *Bachelor Father,* or screaming soldiers being mowed down by John Wayne at Iwo Jima, or Hop Sing the cook in *Bonanza,* or the buck-toothed thick-glassed

Moore neighborhood. They were greeted with a petition with five hundred names demanding that Frank's family be kept out of the neighborhood; Wilderson later relates how his attempt to date the white daughter of a former mayor was blocked by her family.

2 This was before the waves of Asian immigrants to the Twin Cities—Vietnamese, Cambodian, Hmong, Tibetan, South Asian, Karen from Myanmar, and adoptees from Korea and China.

farcical Japanese played by a yellow-face Mickey Rooney in *Breakfast at Tiffany's.* I was a weird incongruity, carrying the weight of stereotypes I'd been aware of since childhood, constantly sensing that people didn't quite know what to make of me, knowing that people's reactions to me, especially those of the white women, were filtered through a lens I couldn't escape or quite deny.

Looking back now, I find my presence in bars and nightclubs then could be viewed as a true example of surrealism, what Bly called "leaping poetry"—where an image from some distant or unassociated realm suddenly appears within the world of the familiar. But writing about that surrealism rather than Bly's *Silence in the Snowy Fields* or James Wright's poem about horses in a field outside Rochester? My mind simply didn't go there. I had no context for the surrealism that was my actual life.

When I think of myself as the only Asian American man at those bars and nightclubs, I'm struck by the sheer chutzpah I evinced then, the audacity, and in some ways the blindness, that allowed me to stroll into those places and try to act as if I was no different from anyone else there, as if I were part of the norm and not an alien presence.

I look back at that twenty-three, twenty-four-year-old third-generation Japanese American English Ph.D. would-be-poet grad student at the Cabooze, some rhythm and blues band riffing on the stage, as I wove through a crowd of mainly white young people and a handful of young Black men, and this image now comes up: one night, I spotted the young Bonnie Raitt, the red-haired singer and great guitarist, who was then only a Minnesota luminary, standing on some risers by the wall. For a few moments, I thought of going up to talk to her and asking her to dance. In the end, I chickened out, probably because she was locally famous then.

In the annals of the Cabooze, still a Twin Cities institution, who but me would even imagine such an encounter? It's unthinkable. Couldn't be part of Minnesota history. Back then we were the land of Mary Tyler Moore, of Lake Wobegon and its white Scandinavian Lutherans and occasional Catholics.

And if I'd had a little more guts and talked to Bonnie Raitt? I have no idea what she would have made of me. My guess is that she would have politely turned me down. But what she would have been thinking about me specifically—as opposed to what she might have thought about any random white guy who could have approached her that night ("I'm just here to listen to the music, pal. Why don't you leave me alone.")—I don't know. My guess is she wouldn't have known either.

An Asian man walks up to Bonnie Raitt in a bar—that's the surrealistic image I should have been writing about back then.

After five years in the English Ph.D. program, I was asked to leave and my teaching assistantship was taken away. Mired in bouts of depression, I had racked up seven incompletes. At the time, this felt like a devastating failure. (Certainly, it completely ripped apart the image of Asian American academic success for me—so much for stereotypes.)

I never returned to English grad school. But one day in a bookstore, I picked up *Black Skin, White Masks* by the Black Martinique psychiatrist and revolutionary Frantz Fanon, author of *The Wretched of the Earth.* In *Black Skin, White Masks,* Fanon explores the psychological effects of racism on both whites and Blacks. In one passage he describes the Black schoolchildren in the Martinique French colonial school system; these Black students were reading history texts about "our ancestors" the Gauls and how the great white hunters and explorers conquered and colonized Africa and brought civilization to the savages there. What is the Black schoolchild learning, observes Fanon, but self-alienation, self-hatred, and an identification with their colonial ruler?

When I read that passage in my late twenties, I experienced an immediate epiphany: "Oh shit, that's what I've been doing." I realized that I had been in denial about my racial identity: I was not white and I would never be white. So who the hell was I?

II

There is no typical Asian American, even remotely so. Nor does any specific breakdown of this group constitute a defining majority—not ethnicity, not geography, not religion, not class, not generation, not language, not immigrant status.

We Asian Americans have immigrant roots, but we don't share a common immigration history. Some of us arrived from Asia in the past few years, but for some, our American roots go back three, four, or even seven or eight generations for some Chinese Americans.[3] So we come from a myriad of countries, with different languages, cultures, histories, and ethnicities and for varied reasons. We or someone in our family came from Asia to America for economic advantages or because of war or famine or political oppression or love or marriage or family ties.[4]

And yet Asian American scholars do write Asian American history books, political science books, ethnic studies books, just as Asian American authors like me contribute to the growing field of Asian American literature.

So, as my old community activist colleague Valerie Lee used to ask when we started an Asian American arts organization, "What do we have in common other than racism and rice?"

The label *Asian American* is said to have been coined during the founding of the Asian American Political Alliance by historian Yuji Ichioka and Emma Gee in 1968. They viewed the term as a tool to connect Asians from different ethnic groups into a self-defining political entity.[5]

3 And there are Pacific Islanders, as in Hawai'i, who are indigenous.

4 Though there are professional Asian Americans who seemingly might be considered part of the spurious "model minority," there are also Asian American refugee communities like the Vietnamese and the Hmong or more recently the Karen, refugees who have fled from war or persecution, and many of whom came to America with nothing and are still fighting economic marginalization. Even within one seeming ethnic Asian grouping there's a wide variety: a person whose genetics might be mainly Chinese who immigrated from the Philippines or Vietnam derives their identity from a very different background and history from that of a recent Chinese immigrant from Shanghai, and both will be very different—linguistically, culturally, historically—from a Chinese American whose family has been living in the Bay Area for five generations. And what do any of these individuals share in common with, say, a Muslim Indian American from the South Bay whose parents immigrated to the United States from Tanzania?

5 In an interview with Yen Espiritu in *Asian Pan-Ethnicity,* Ichioka explains that the term was at first a political tool, a way of placing Asian Americans more prominently within the activism of the 1960s: "There were so many Asians out in the political demonstrations but we had no effectiveness. Everyone was lost in the larger rally. We figured

The unwieldiness and recent vintage of this coinage are part of what Korean American writer Jay Caspian Kang negatively references in a 2009 *New York Times Magazine* article, "What a Fraternity Hazing Death Revealed about the Painful Search for Asian American Identity," which gave the title to his book *The Loneliest Americans.* For Kang, the label is artificial, a forced inorganic grouping and a failed attempt to mirror the experiences and politics of other racial groups. In Kang's article, many aspects of the death of the Chinese American Psi Delta Psi student Chun Hsien (Michael) Deng resembled hazing deaths on campuses across the country—drinking gone too far, peer pressure, an accident, a cover-up. But Kang also explores the fact that Psi Delta Psi was a Chinese American fraternity and thus reflected a distinctly Asian American version of young college men gone awry:

> Asians are the loneliest Americans. The collective political consciousness of the '80s has been replaced by the quiet, unaddressed isolation that comes with knowing that you can be born in this country, excel in its schools and find a comfortable place in its economy and still feel no stake in the national conversation. The current vision of solidarity among Asian-Americans is cartoonish and blurry and relegated to conversations at family picnics, in drunken exchanges over food that reminds everyone at the table of how their mom used to make it. Everything else is the confusion of never knowing what side to choose because choosing our own side has so rarely been an option. Asian pride is a laughable concept to most Americans. Racist incidents pass without prompting any real outcry and claims of racism are quickly dismissed. A common past can be accessed only through dusty, dug-up things: the murder of Vincent Chin, Korematsu v. United States, the Bataan Death March and the illusion that we are going through all these things together. The Asian-American fraternity is not much more than a clumsy step toward finding an identity in a country where there are no more reference points for how we should act, how we should think about ourselves.

that if we rallied behind our own banner, behind an Asian American banner, we would have an effect on the larger public. We could extend the influence beyond ourselves to other Asian Americans."

I have problems with Kang's statement, starting with the first sentence: are the Chinese in LA's Monterey Park or the Koreans in Koreatown lonelier than whites in rural Montana or Alaska? And, really, Bataan Death March? As for *Korematsu v. United States,* my parents and grandparents, like Korematsu, were incarcerated by the U.S. government during World War II, so that history for me is neither dusty nor dug up.[6]

Kang pictures Asian Americans as confused as to who we are and mere victims to the laughter and scorn of other Americans. He seems ignorant of any collective activism, organization building, and art in the Asian American community since the 1980s or any of the ways Asian Americans have forged coalitions with other BIPOC groups—all subjects this book will explore. He doesn't see that there are principles of justice, equity, fairness, and mutual support that can guide our actions with each other and other communities (and yes, a fraternity *can* adopt such values). He seems to think we Asian Americans are

6 The suspension of the writ of habeas corpus, which is at the heart of *Korematsu,* is again occurring today in Trump's America in immigrant communities, and if there arise clashes between an Asian country and the United States, I have no doubt all Asian Americans, immigrants or not, will be eyed with suspicion. With Trump's rejection of diversity and DEI, he is reinvoking certain principles of Whiteness that have shaped this country. According to these principles, white knowledge is always valid, objective, true, and official; in direct contrast, the knowledge of people of color is always invalid, subjective, false, or suspicious and unofficial—unless whites decree otherwise. Whiteness and white people determine what America is and control the narratives we tell about our history. This supremacy has always guided the backlash against any racial progress and the laws and policies designed to establish that progress, whether after the Civil War or the civil rights movement or the Obama presidency or the Black Lives Matter movement.

Within this context, this book on Asian Americans presents a different history, a different set of narratives and experiences that many are still unaware of or try to ignore. Trump and his minions have cited the un-Constitutional imprisonment of Japanese Americans as a precedence and justification for any number of anti-Muslim and anti-immigrant measures. Despite the apology by Congress and President Ronald Reagan to our community in 1988, despite the government's declaration that there was no military necessity for the camps, despite the fact that after that apology many Japanese Americans thought, *Good, this will never happen again,* we are again faced with a backlash to take away the rights of immigrants like my grandparents and American citizens like my parents. The struggle continues.

helpless, that we can't use the tools of community building, activism, and art to bring people together.

As to being confused over what side to choose, I can understand this, especially since I grew up wanting to be thought of as white. But as the reader will see, the more I learned about race in America and the more contact I had with other BIPOC communities, the choices I've made to ally myself with their causes became very clear to me.

Still, I do think Kang should be taken seriously on his main point: he calls out the seemingly quixotic attempts at forging an Asian American solidarity in any aspect of our lives—political, cultural, social, personal.[7]

On a conceptual or political level, I understand what Kang is getting at: the term *Asian American* is, in various ways, inorganic, a faulty or unwieldy concept that conceives of a unity that doesn't quite exist. And for many recent immigrants, life can indeed be quite lonely, especially if they are in a place with few other Asians—as opposed to, say, the Hmong in the Twin Cities where I live.

But I also understand what he's saying here on a personal level. Part of me too resonates with his assertion that Asian Americans are the loneliest Americans. Of course, the loneliness and angst I experienced in my adolescence and twenties derived in part from psychological issues that, seen through one lens, were not that different from those of many young Americans, no matter their race—issues having to do with family systems, self-doubt, self-criticism, and depression. Yet even back when I rejected the labels *Japanese American* or *Asian American,* I knew deep inside that some aspect of my loneliness and alienation was distinctly racial and derived from my being Asian American.

7 Though he doesn't say this explicitly, Kang implies his experience too has been less one of Asian American solidarity than of blurriness and inchoateness, a lack of connection. He sees something similar in the attempts of Psi Delta Psi to form an organization based on an Asian American brotherhood. What specifically should an Asian American fraternity stand for? What forms the basis of its social identity that makes it different from, say, a white fraternity, or, conversely, makes it perhaps like a black fraternity (see Spike Lee's satire *School Daze*)? Or is it only an Asian American fraternity that is laughable or cartoonish or clumsy in its attempts at bonding while a Black or Jewish fraternity—or an all-white fraternity—is not?

If there is no typical Asian American, there is no ideal or essential Asian American identity; thus someone like Kang might conclude that the term therefore is useless or meaningless, at least for him. But in my life as an artist and activist, the term has served as a field of inquiry, as a launching space for the arts and political organizing, as a way of combating the loneliness and alienation Asian Americans often feel in American society. It has helped me to analyze not just the ways Whiteness and the dominant culture have affected my life and my community; it has enabled me to see more clearly the struggles of other communities of color and learn from them.

As a writer, I explore how our racial histories have shaped our psychologies and our sense of who we are. In this book I am trying to discover language to uncover the complexities and contradictions of my life and those of other Asian Americans, a language the surrounding culture has not created. Certain formulations or even lived experiences of being Asian American may strike others, as they do Kang, as cartoonish, but that is exactly what I am writing against—the propensity to stereotype, belittle, and simplify—the inability of the mainstream culture to recognize us as an essential and complex element of America.

Asian Americans who grow up in America and go to American schools learn and absorb white culture and history. Eventually we come to grasp the ideology of Whiteness and what being white means in America (though we may not recognize it as an ideology).[8] But so often Asian Americans don't learn to interrogate their own identities—or they begin to do so almost by chance, say, from a course in college or a few books of Asian American literature. Many start out learning by themselves, as I first did, autodidactically.

8 When I use the term *Whiteness,* I am referring to a system of beliefs, rules, and practices that have established white supremacy in America since 1619. This ideology manifests itself not simply in a "few bad apples" but instead structures our social interactions, our politics, our laws, our cultural products, both in conscious and unconscious ways. But to be clear, this ideology is not something inherent to white people; many white Americans do not subscribe to this ideology, at least consciously. Certainly, in other countries that have experienced a very different racial history and makeup, white people do not subscribe to the specific American ideology of Whiteness.

It's my hope that after reading this book, all Americans, no matter their race, will see themselves in a more nuanced dialectic, one where the multiplicity of the American experiment must be acknowledged and articulated. As I frequently tell Asian American audiences: *Yes, we Asian Americans lead far more complex lives than those outside our communities realize. But our lives are often more complex than even we ourselves understand or possess the language to acknowledge.*

III

In this book, I examine a variety of issues affecting Asian Americans—the anti-Asian hate crimes during Covid, the Harvard admissions case and affirmative action, racial and sexual stereotypes in the media and on Tinder and Grindr, Asian-Black and interracial relationships, the legacy of the Japanese American internment, Asian Americans and mental health. With this last topic, this book can be seen as a psychological self-help manual for Asian Americans and other BIPOC to help them heal from the damaging effects of American racism, particularly internalized racism and the lack of adequate tools to investigate our identities and our experiences. I am delineating various ways we can fend off the labels and stereotypes Whiteness thrusts upon us, how we can find a more authentic path to defining ourselves for ourselves.

As I've gathered these essays together, written over the past thirty years, I see they tell a story. Recounting "the education of David Mura," this book tells how I transformed from what could be termed a "banana"—yellow on the outside, white on the inside—into an Asian American writer.

At age seventy-one looking back, I can hardly take in how quickly time has passed. The writer of the earliest essay included here, "Raising a Multicultural Daughter in a Multicultural World," feels to me distant and still unformed, even though he was forty at the time. In 1992, he and his white wife had moved into their first home in St. Paul; he had a young daughter, he had published one poetry book and a memoir about a year spent living in Japan. The memoir *Turning Japanese* examined his Japanese cultural "roots" and how that led him to explore his parents' imprisonment by the American government during World War II.

But rereading that 1992 *Mother Jones* essay now, I think less of how I was a young father or an author just establishing himself and exploring his Japanese American past. Instead, I'm aware of how, up until the controversies and protests by the Asian American community over the musical *Miss Saigon,* I had thought myself firmly ensconced in the white writing community of the Twin Cities; that I was surrounded by white artist friends whom I believed loved and supported me. Yes, I had begun to explore race and ethnicity in my writing. But I was yet to learn that such explorations would exact a price, that claiming my Asian American identity would eventually lead me to leave—or to be expelled by—the white writing community I thought myself so much a part of.

Today yellow face casting—as in the original production of *Miss Saigon*—is recognized as a vile practice similar to black face; none of my former white friends would get up in public today and defend that practice as they privately did to me back in the early 1990s. More broadly, in recent years, as in Viet Thanh Nguyen's Pulitzer Prize–winning novel *The Sympathizer* and the HBO series, there's been more and more criticism of the Orientalist stereotypes that undergird *Miss Saigon.*[9] But back in the day, to many of my white friends I seemed

9 The Orientalist garbage of *Miss Saigon* is now being replaced by the work of a slew of Southeast Asian artists, such as Bao Phi, Ocean Vuong, Bich Minh Nguyen, Monique Truong, Lan Cao, Thi Bui, Eric Nguyen, Mai C. Doan, Kao Kalia Yang, and Saymoukda Vongsay. Viet Thanh Nguyen's Pulitzer Prize–winning novel *The Sympathizer* is now an HBO miniseries.

These Southeast Asian American artists not only abandon, critique, and mock colonialist tropes, but they present a complex and three-dimensional portrait of the Asian people on both sides of that war. Their work articulates a viewpoint that most white Americans have never even acknowledged existed. Indeed, part of *The Sympathizer* involves a satiric take on the racism embedded in movies like *The Deer Hunter* and *Apocalypse Now;* both in the novel and miniseries, the joke often centers on the ignorance and racism of white Americans—CIA operatives, military, politicians, academics, filmmakers. In so many ways, these Asian American writers are putting the nail on the coffin of *Miss Saigon,* exposing it for the Orientalist trash it is. It is no longer the place of white culture to tell us who we are or what our story is; we are doing that for ourselves, thank you. A similar take occurs in Qui Nguyen's play *Vietgone,* about the first Vietnamese refugees who came to America in 1975. This comedy focuses on a love story between two Vietnamese rather than a white GI and an underage Vietnamese prostitute. In the play, the Vietnamese characters rap and speak in sharp, colloquial American English, while the whites speak nonsense syllables with occasional recognizable words like "cheeseburger" and "waffle fries"—exactly the opposite of what

to have transmogrified into the crazy, angry man of color, someone dangerous and uncontrolled. Even a racial separatist. Part of this characterization resulted from my bringing up issues of race and arguing with these white friends. But then, first and foremost, came my writing about those arguments and *Miss Saigon* in *Mother Jones*—which freaked out almost all my white artist friends.

Some of this backlash, I now believe, derived from a common response to any racial anger or even racial arguments from Asian Americans: *Why are you so angry? We treat you so well. You're the model minority. You're not Black or Native American; how can you be speaking about race, much less be angry about race?*

As I began to change my identity and my understanding of race in America, that journey involved multiple paths: it led to my breaking with white artist friends who could not countenance whom I was becoming, who felt threatened by my questioning not only my identity but *their* identity. It involved encountering other Asian Americans artists across the country and, at the same time, trying to build a local Asian American community and arts organization. It involved learning from Black artist friends and other BIPOC communities, diversifying my life in ways I could not have imagined when I was growing up in an all-white suburb of Chicago. It involved analyzing and critiquing the

happened in the first Broadway production of *Miss Saigon* or in American films about the war.

In a 2019 *New York Times* op-ed critiquing the musical, Nguyen's reaction to seeing the musical is almost exactly the same as mine: "I saw the musical in New York City in 1996, paying for tickets in the fourth row, an extravagant expenditure for a graduate student on a minimal fellowship. In my earnest idealism, I believed that I should see a work before I criticized it. But sometimes things are as they appear on their yellowface. All around me, audience members sobbed at the tragic love story. I was disgusted. I could not help but think of how 'Miss Saigon' was based on Puccini's opera 'Madama Butterfly,' set in Japan. In Puccini's by-now universal story, two star-crossed lovers, a Japanese woman and a white man, together embody Rudyard Kipling's dictum, 'East is East and West is West and never the twain shall meet.' Because East and West are fundamentally opposed, the lovers are doomed, or, to put it more accurately, one lover is doomed—the Japanese woman. Happy to see that her child will live a better life in the West, she takes her own worthless life."

stereotypes surrounding Asian Americans in works like *Miss Saigon* and then learning to exorcise them from my own psyche.

After rejecting the rules of Whiteness and being ostracized from the local white writing community, I began to make connections with ever-widening circles of BIPOC artists and communities. In this process, I was constantly encountering different narratives, different perspectives, different histories, and thus constantly changing my sense of identity and place in the world. Encountering stranger after stranger and engaging with them transformed them into friends, colleagues, part of my tale.

I often tell audiences that I am part of the first fully integrated generation of American writers. This book explores what that has meant to my own artistic and personal development. My story may be singular, but it does not stand alone; it was not created by me alone. Instead, my Asian American voice is one of many changing the possibilities of who we are as a country and the myriad voices great within us.

As an aid to readers, there is a timeline of the events in Exit, Miss Saigon. *There are also footnotes everywhere in this book. If Asian Americans were more prominent in our society, some of the information in the footnotes would be more common knowledge, or the analysis in the footnotes, often addressed more specifically to Asian American readers, would be part of the text. All this is a compromise part of me would rather not make. If it turns out these footnotes will be criticized as a compromise by later Asian Americans, that would make me happy; it would mean our importance to American culture has become more assumed. At any rate, readers can choose to either read the footnotes or not.*

Timeline of Events

Here is an autobiographical timeline of events alluded to in these essays, written over thirty years.

1979 Reads Fanon's *Black Skin, White Masks*; leads to epiphany on his identity as a Japanese American.

1985 Awarded U.S. Japan Exchange Fellowship, which enables living in Tokyo during 1985–86.

1989 Publishes first poetry book, *After We Lost Our Way*; meets Japanese American writer Garrett Hongo; attends Broadway performance of David Henry Hwang's *M. Butterfly*.

1990 Meets African American writer Alexs Pate.

1991 Publishes *Turning Japanese,* about his trip to Japan; tours West Coast and begins meeting other Asian American artists.

1992 With activist Valerie Lee and Asian American community members creates the Asian American Renaissance, a community arts organization, which presents the first AAR conference with Asian American artists from around the country; artistic and development director until 1997.

1992 First local protest against the St. Paul Ordway Theater's presentation of *Miss Saigon.*

1992 Publishes "Secrets and Anger" in *Mother Jones* that recounts arguments about *Miss Saigon* with white artist friends; the article leads to the dissolution of friendships with his white artist friends and his ostracism from local white writing community.

1993 Creates with Alexs Pate *Secret Colors,* a performance piece on the Rodney King beating and the violence in Los Angeles.

1995 Film *Slowly This*, directed by Arthur Jaffa, written and performed by Alexs Pate and David Mura; broadcast on PBS series *Alive* TV.

2001 Starts teaching at VONA, a BIPOC summer writers' conference; meets Junot Díaz, Elmaz Abinader, Suheir Hammad, and other BIPOC writers from around the country.

2010 Plays King in *The King and I* at the Bloomington Theater Company.

2013 St. Paul's Ordway Theater brings back *Miss Saigon* a third time; local Asian Americans organize the Don't Buy *Miss Saigon* Coalition to protest the musical's racism and stereotypes.

2014 Ordway Theater writes a letter apologizing to the Asian American community and promising never to present *Miss Saigon* again.

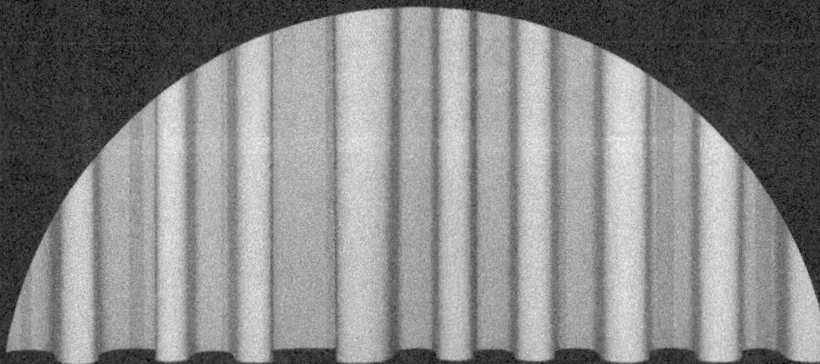

PART I

Do I Belong Here?

In 2020, while the pandemic was still spreading, I was walking through the Mall of America. A reporter from the *Minneapolis Star Tribune* approached me. She wanted to interview me for an article: "How are your relatives in China responding to the Corona-19 virus?"

I explained I was not Chinese, but Japanese *American.*

"Well, how do your relatives in Japan feel about the virus?"

In case the egregiousness of this questioning isn't clear to the reader, imagine the same reporter going up to random white people at the Mall and asking, "How are your relatives in Russia responding to the invasion of Ukraine?" Or "How are your relatives in Finland responding to the closing of the border with Russia?" Or "How are your relatives in England reacting to the fall of the Tory government?" Such questions would never be asked; to do so would be absurd.

But the connections between Asian Americans and any country in Asia? Well, that connection can never be severed, no matter how long and how many generations your family has been in America, no matter if you have any connections with that country or not.

As an Asian American, growing up I was constantly trying to fit into the white Jewish Chicago suburban world around me. But in subtle or not so subtle ways, the messages I received there and from American society can be summed up in a single cut: "You don't belong here." This message was there despite the fact that I hardly ever heard openly racial insults or epithets growing up. For the message I heard wasn't said very often directly to me. No, it was said indirectly to me growing up within the American culture of the fifties, sixties, and seventies—and in recent years, with the rise in anti-immigrant attacks, this message has in some ways gotten stronger. The message is familiar to all Asian Americans, whether we are immigrants or not, whatever our class background, whether we seemingly conform to the model minority stereotype or not.

We know it from looks, from assumptions people make about us, from open or implied declarations, from the myriad stereotypes about us:

"You're not an American, you're not from here, you're not part of our community."
"You're strange, foreign. You look funny."
"You look like the enemy in films about World War II, the Korean War, the war in Vietnam—or Kim Jong Il or Xi Jinping."
"Chinese, Japanese, Vietnamese, it's all the same—you're all the same."
"You're not a potential romantic or sexual partner, not someone I would ever think of dating, much less marrying."
"Your sister must be hot . . . *Me so horny . . . me love you longtime.*"
"You must speak with an accent."
"You speak English well—for an immigrant, for someone who wasn't born here."
"You're not athletic, you not a baller, you don't got game."
"You must eat funny food at home, things real Americans don't eat."
"You don't know anything about American culture."
"You know kung fu. You know samurai and yakuza . . . ancient Asian stuff."
"You, your relatives caused the pandemic. Didn't Trump call it the Kung Flu?"
"You're sexist."
"You're not a leader."
"You're a nerd, quiet, socially awkward, bumbling."
"You're either a cook or an engineer or scientist."
"You're good at math and science, you aren't creative."
"You're a joke, easy to make fun of. We can mock you and no one's going to cry racist."
"You're sneaky, inscrutable, you can't be trusted."
"You're stealing our auto industry, our industrial secrets, our technology, our social media, even our own data with your stealthy TikTok."

"You're a spy."
"You all look alike. . . . You're some other Asian I know."
"You're dull and robot-like, you have no personality."
"You can never be President, a lead actor, a rock and roll singer, an R&B singer, head of an American corporation, a real American writer, a Minnesota writer."
"You're not leadership material."

And if you're South Asian? You're Muslim even if you're a Hindu or Sikh or Christian. You're an Arab even if you're Indian, Sri Lankan, or Pakistani. (Never underestimate the stupidity and ignorance of American racism.) And these mistaken associations lead to stereotypes far worse than many of the above: "You're a terrorist." "You people were responsible for 9/11." "You look like Osama Bin Laden." "You're a jihadist." "You're Hamas." "You're a threat to our country, absolutely un-American."

Of course, such reactions and perceptions have led to violence against South Asians, just as the Covid-19 virus has led to violence against East Asians and a 150 percent rise in attacks against us. Google anti-Asian hate crimes. Here's what comes up: "Attacks on Asian-Americans in New York Stoke Fear, Anxiety and Anger," "A Rise in Hate Crimes Against Asian-Americans and Others," "A Tense Lunar New Year for the Bay Area after Attacks on Asian-Americans," "He Came from Thailand to Care for Family. Then Came a Brutal Attack," "Why Has There Been a Spike of Anti-Asian Hate Crimes?" "Spit on, Yelled At, Attacked: Chinese Americans Fear for Their Safety." There's even a guide for teachers: "Lesson of the Day: A Rise in Attacks on Asian-Americans."

In short, the message America so often sends to Asian Americans is, "What the hell are you doing here?"[1]

1 In her book *Space-Time Colonialism: Alaska's Indigenous and Asian Entanglements,* my friend, the scholar Juliana Pegues argues that the first Asian Americans to come to America must be seen against an intersectional history: in one of the many compromises over slavery, Texas was admitted to the union as a slave state and California as a free state. After the war, white elites in California needed a labor force that could be exploited. But Blacks were now citizens and could supposedly vote and own land and

As Asian Americans, we are perpetual outsiders. Even our successes can be held against us, as when Steve Bannon complained there were too many Asians running Silicon Valley tech companies—meaning we're always a potential fifth column element (an accusation we Japanese Americans know quite well).

Our assumed foreignness is something Asian Americans face, not just from blatant racists but in everyday encounters with seemingly friendly or well-meaning non-Asians.

To choose one of many personal examples, I golf, and on the golf course I'm constantly meeting strangers. Often, I'll be asked by white strangers where I am from. Or, as one middle-aged white man from South Minneapolis put it last week, "What nationality are you?"

"What nationality are you?" I asked.

He looked surprised. "Well, I'm Irish-German. But you know what I mean."

Of course, I knew what he meant. His ethnic background isn't a question, much less a problem. Mine is.

And here I went into my prepared statement: "My grandfather came here from Japan in 1898."

Why do I say this particular phrase? I know this white guy didn't perceive all I intended, but here's what that phrase means to me. It was my grandparents who came from Japan and thus were Japanese. My father was born in LA in 1926, my mother in Seattle in 1931, so they are natural-born American citizens—and yet at ages fifteen and eleven, respectively, they were imprisoned unjustly by the U.S. government in World War II as fifth column threats to the country. When my paternal grandfather came here in 1898, William McKinley was President, Henry James and Mark Twain were still alive, ragtime was in vogue, Babe Ruth was three years old, and Louis Armstrong wasn't even born. My uncles served in World War II, two in the famed 442nd regiment,

could reproduce. Mexicans had a previous claim to the land and could reproduce. Native Americans were being forced from the land and exterminated. So Asian laborers were brought in because they were forbidden from becoming citizens, could not own land, and since Chinese women were forbidden entry, the Chinese laborers could not reproduce. And because they did not speak English, they could be more easily controlled and exploited.

the most decorated unit in the European theater, and another as a linguist in the Military Intelligence Service, where the Nisei (second generation) soldiers served in the Pacific theater as battlefield guides, interrogators, and translators of captured documents and messages. My father's an ex-GI from the time of the Korean War, and as a reporter he interviewed Louis Armstrong, Conrad Hilton, and the murderers Sacco and Vanzetti. My Aunt Sachi was the first Japanese American woman to graduate from the University of Washington back in the 1930s. Living in the Village in the late 1940s and '50s, my Aunt Ruth went to parties with e. e. cummings, Frank O'Hara, and Paul Robeson; while working for a Broadway producer, she met Katharine Hepburn and watched Eugene O'Neill direct *The Iceman Cometh.* I went with my father to the 1959 World Series and can still name that White Sox lineup; in Addison Park I watched George Halas run the Bears through drills and got their autographs; in 1963, at Wrigley Field, in the freezing cold, my father and I cheered their win in the NFL title game against the New York Giants and the balding Y.A. Title.

In short, my family has been here for a century and quarter and yet you're still asking me where I'm from?

But I don't say all this. I simply add, "I didn't grow up speaking any Japanese or knowing much about Japanese culture." Meaning: "I'm two generations removed from Japan. I was born here. I'm an American, man. That's my nationality."

Of course, my interlocutor doesn't hear my anger behind my answers to his questions. I hide that. In a way he's just trying to be friendly, and so I don't talk about anything I'm going into in this essay. He doesn't realize that, like the reporter from the *Star Tribune,* he's making racist assumptions about who I am.

Today, running in the snow along the Mississippi River, I thought I needed to complicate the portrait I've given here: I obviously think about my racial and ethnic identity far more than most Asian Americans, certainly far more than my parents or my siblings. It's part of my task as a writer, searching for a language to describe my life and the lives of Asian Americans.

There are, of course, times when I'm not thinking about race or ethnicity. Sometimes I wonder if I am mired in stereotype threat. I question whether my vision is too myopic. If I had grown up in Japan as a Japanese, would I even have become a writer, would I have felt this need to explore my identity? When I was in Japan, my focus on my identity in my writing seemed surprising to my Japanese friends. They never wondered about who they were. They were Japanese. Their ethnicity or race wasn't a question or a problem.

Many first-generation Asian immigrants feel something similar; they're Vietnamese or Indian, even if they're living in America. They might think about how whites regard them from time to time, but that question isn't at the core of who they are. They know who they are. When I talk with them, I'm often aware of how much more I think about being a so-called hyphenated American than they do. I grew up here. It's the only country I truly know.

When America has a war or problems with an Asian country, the xenophobia and racism against Asian Americans, the view of us as an alien threat, march to the forefront, as they did for Japanese Americans during World War II. Or, say, during the auto industry crisis of the 1980s and the fear that the Japanese were outcompeting American manufacturing.

But when there's no focus on Asian countries in the news, Asian Americans are generally the least visible or considered people of color. We don't face the degree of racial animus that confronts African Americans; we don't figure in American history in the ways African and Native Americans do; we don't have the numbers of Latino Americans; our immigrants aren't seen as a crucial voting bloc or as an increasing threat to the white idea of America.

Indeed, many non-Asian Americans, if not most, don't think about us at all. As a result, when I enter a room of non-Asians, I don't have any certainty about how my racial identity will be read or received. I may be read negatively, but then I might not be read at all. I may be in danger or stereotyped—or I may merely be ignored or unseen, invisible.

There are times when I bring up the subject of my race or my identity to white people I'm just meeting and they don't know what the hell I'm talking about. Not a clue. Some of them see me through the model minority prism or as being white—or more white than Blacks or other people of color. Sometimes they think they're paying me a compliment when they say they don't think about my race. Sometimes it's that they're used to not thinking about themselves or society in racial terms or they believe racial terms only create discord. It's the luxury of being white, not having to think about your racial identity—and thus, the racial experiences of those who are not white.

And if they question me about who I am or about my profession, writing, and I bring up my parents and the internment camps or what my last book, *The Stories Whiteness Tells Itself*, was about? Unless I'm in a particularly progressive or literary setting, so often the white person will begin saying, "Oh, but isn't that like all people . . . all countries have their prejudices . . . ?"[2] Or they will try to say that there's racism in Japan or Asia too—or they will try to get me to say this.

In answering like this, they think their response is unique to them and not programmed into their white identity; they believe they are thinking for themselves, when Whiteness is actually doing the thinking for them. They will think I can't see through the ideology of Whiteness or their psychological defensiveness. They can't conceive that I have encountered white culture and whites like them all my life and I know exactly how they think—indeed, how could I not, since, when I was growing up I so wanted to be considered white. And yet my white interlocutors may have never even considered how Asian Americans think about race, even while they talk to me as if *they* know what *I* should be thinking and feeling.

Their implicit position is that if every other country has racism, why should they have to care about American racism, much less anything about Asian Americans? Of course, the racism that affects non-whites in America does not affect the white person, only me and other non-whites. So it's rather easy for a white person to downplay any difficulty

2 The other day I was watching some YouTube videos of James Baldwin, such as his famed debate with William Buckley at Oxford, and his argument with the white Yale philosophy professor Paul Weiss on the *Dick Cavett Show,* and I realized that, though in a slightly different form, I'm still having the same arguments with white people that Baldwin engaged in, with the white interlocutor constantly saying, "What's the big deal about race? Why are you so worked up?"

or problem I might have with racism in America.[3] In such conversations, I know the white person has no curiosity as to what I am actually thinking and feeling about them or race. This is in part because they can't conceive how different I am from them and in part because, well, they're white, and why really should they think much about people who aren't white?

And yet, in their white epistemology there is no room for doubt or questioning, no epistemic humility. According to Whiteness, their knowledge is always valid, objective, true, and official, while my knowledge—if it challenges any way they think of themselves or me—is just the opposite—invalid, subjective, false, or suspicious, and certainly unofficial and minor. They can't imagine that throughout the whole conversation I am doing my Asian American version of what Skip Gates calls "signifying"—trying to talk to white people in ways that won't upset or challenge them more than you, the person of color, want to deal with in a given social setting. For in that moment I am calculating how much I want to say that will upset them, and if I don't want any friction, they can't conceive that I'm just smiling at them to get along and go on with my day as best I can.

When a white person asserts that they don't think of me as Asian American, unlike when I was in high school, I don't take it as a compliment. Instead, I know they have no context to understand what my life experience has been, much less possess any acquaintance with Asian American history or what my parents and grandparents experienced during their World War II incarceration. I know that this white person is psychologically closed to any real discussion of race; they've already determined they have nothing to learn.

In other words, I know they have no ability to configure who I really am. Any attempt to try to explain to them who I am and how my race and ethnicity have affected my life and that of my family is doomed to failure. It's safer—and certainly far less disruptive—not to talk

3 Unless they're MAGA and believe the only racial discrimination that exists now is against white people. Obviously, if I told someone I had cancer or my leg was broken in a car accident, the white person would not respond, "Well, there's cancer everywhere" or "Car accidents occur in every country." No, it's only racism that gets dismissed as universal.

about race or my identity, and so I make a calculation. Oftentimes, then, meeting white people outside of the literary world (and sometimes within that world too), I remain in hiding. I'm disguising the fact that I'm a race man or that I even think much about race. Sometimes whites even read my calculated reticence as mysterious—an adjective not that far from the old stereotype of Asians as inscrutable, unreadable, unknowable.

Here I think of how, in her memoir *Woman Warrior,* Maxine Hong Kingston describes her grade school years. She and her Chinese American classmates were quiet and well-behaved at their public school, and this might have seemed to the whites they encountered to be a Chinese or "Oriental" trait. But then, at Maxine's weekend Chinese school the Chinese kids were boisterous, bold, and loud. Freed from the gaze of their racial others, what her mother called the white ghosts and black ghosts, the Chinese kids displayed a totally different aspect of their personalities.

In recent years, the debate and court cases surrounding college admissions and affirmative action have become a key Asian American issue. Still, I doubt that the Harvard admissions office ever considers what Maxine Hong Kingston is saying about how outsiders could not assess and understand her Chinese American classmates. She and her classmates would not reveal themselves to outsiders, outsiders whom they did not trust and who could not see them for who they were as individuals. So what does that say about the accuracy of the character evaluations of Asian American students by non-Asian teachers or guidance counselors or Harvard's alumni or admission officers?

In the Harvard admissions lawsuit, the facts are similar to those of other elite schools: Asian American applicants achieve *higher* grades and test scores than other racial groups. However, the rate of acceptance of Asian American applicants is *lower* than any other racial group. The reason for this? Asian American applicants score lower on *personality* and *character.*

Of course, as an Asian America one might wonder why this low evaluation of our character or personality or leadership skills occurs and how it relates to what so many Asian Americans find to be a "bamboo ceiling" in corporate life. Do our Asian faces/bodies matter in these evaluations of our personality? Are Asians deemed less likeable, helpful, courageous, kind, positive, and respected because of prejudices against the way we look and because of the stereotypes associated with our faces/bodies/cultures? Certainly, if Asian men are deemed the least sexually attractive on Tinder and OkCupid, where judgments are almost entirely made by appearance, wouldn't it be reasonable to think that if others find you distinctly sexually unattractive, you're not going to be perceived as likeable or kind or respected or a leader? If certain people think all Asians look alike and/or have trouble telling us apart, why would such people think any of us could be a leader or any of us could stand out? (At the Associated Writing Programs conference, I've been mistaken for the Asian American writers David Henry Hwang and Li-Young Lee, even though on each occasion they were in the same room and had just spoken from the stage.)

Think of that most common question Asian Americans face: "Where are you from? . . . No, really, where are you from?" If Asian Americans' faces/bodies are never seen as fundamentally part of America, might that also cause non-Asian Americans to question whether Asian Americans really should belong in their social group or be regarded as likeable or as leader material? Moreover, if you've never seen or rarely seen an Asian American face on television or in the movies, and almost never as a leader or a romantic partner, might that also affect your evaluation of the personality within Asian faces/bodies? "How can they be likable or personable? Where are the Asian American stars? Celebrities? Political leaders? Sex symbols? Rock and roll stars? I've never seen one on television, so can they really exist?"

All these assumptions don't have to be held consciously by the evaluator; they can be there subconsciously, in implicit rather than explicit bias.

Evaluation takes place in the eyes of the beholder. In issues like the Harvard admissions case, these questions arise: Who is judging whether Asian Americans and their cultural values can be part of America? What makes those values emphasized in an Asian cultural family inferior to those emphasized in an upper-class WASP family? Who decides which is more valuable? Useful or kind? Attractive and winning? After all, Asian cultural values work in Asian societies. Why couldn't such values or qualities be regarded as assets rather than negatives in American society?

Yes, many of us grow up with a more family- and group-based Asian cultural psychology; yes, we may at times seem quieter or less likely to "toot our own horn," and thus we may find that our cultural roots place us at odds with certain individualistic, ego-driven imperatives of the mainstream white culture.[4] Yes, because of our cultural values we may write college entrance essays that are less eccentric or centered on our unique selves or less linearly narrative.[5]

But there's also a different, contrasting way of viewing such values. What if being bicultural and melding and mixing Asian and American

4 Here, for example, is what J. D. Hokoyama, former president of Leadership Education for Asian Pacifics (LEAP), said in his presentation to 1,500 Asian American employees of Microsoft: "So let's say I go to meetings with you and I notice you never say anything. And I ask myself, 'Hmm, I wonder why you're not saying anything. Maybe it's because you don't know what we're talking about. That would be a good reason for not saying anything. Or maybe it's because you're not even interested in the subject matter. Or maybe you think the conversation is beneath you.' So here I'm thinking, because you never say anything at meetings, that you're either dumb, you don't care, or you're arrogant. When maybe it's because you were taught when you were growing up that when the boss is talking, what are you supposed to be doing? Listening." After going through LEAP's training, Sach Takayasu, who works in the marketing department of IBM and who herself hit the Bamboo Ceiling, observed: "The more we got into it, as we moved away from the obvious things to the deeper, more fundamental values, I began to see that my upbringing had been very Asian after all. My parents would say, 'Don't create problems. Don't trouble other people.' How Asian is that? It helped to explain why I don't reach out to other people for help."

5 The Chinese American novelist Gish Jen has written two books, *Tiger Writing* and *The Girl at the Baggage Claim*, which explore the differences between the Western self and the Eastern self and how those differences lead to very different ways of telling tales. One of Jen's examples comes from her own family. When her father presented her with his autobiography, the narrative contained little of the specific events of her father's life; it lacked any descriptions of his consciousness or the idiosyncratic aspects of her father's personality or psychology. Nor did it contain dramatic events in her father's life—the material that one might associate with your standard contemporary tell-all, bare-all type of memoir. Instead, the bulk of the eighty pages was focused on his family, his village, the region from which he came, and Chinese history; he detailed the context around him, because to his mind that was far more important to understanding his life. That context *was* his story.

cultural values make us inherently creative in ways most whites don't appreciate? After all, we're creating new types of Americans, new versions and takes on the American story. Creativity doesn't come from sameness; it comes from difference. This is one reason why the literature of Asian American writers is so significant to us Asian Americans—the writers can see us as individuals, with complex and particular stories to tell. (Yet as many publishers make clear, it's often hard to find a mass audience for Asian American writers.) Could it be that the more group-oriented Asian American students are better able to work in a group and more sensitive to the needs of others?

Again, who gets to judge our character or personality? What if the group/family-oriented Asian American parents were judging the character of the supposedly more individualistic upper-middle-class or upper-class white applicants to Harvard? Wouldn't the Asian American parents find the white students less sensitive to the needs of their family or less inclined to pay attention to the feelings and needs of others in a group? Wouldn't these Asian American parents tend to regard these white students as selfish or arrogant or immodest, as deluded in their emphasis on their own independent achievement, as disrespectful to their parents? Such white students could be said to be relatively ignorant or disregarding of the benefits they have received from their white families or from being a member of a group that has dominated American society since its inception, in part through grossly unjust means.[6]

Oh, but that would be ethnocentric, wouldn't it? That would be reverse racism.

So white/Western ethnocentrism is okay if it's used to evaluate Harvard's Asian American applicants, but Asian cultural values can't possibly be considered when evaluating Harvard's white applicants or Asian American applicants?

But, hey, as Ann Coulter informed Vivek Ramaswamy, a 2024 Republican Presidential candidate, that's just the way things are in America; as she told him on her podcast: "I agreed with many, many

6 To quote Vice President Kamala Harris's Indian mother, "You think you just fell out of a coconut tree?"

things you said . . . when you were running for president, but I still would not have voted for you because you're an Indian. . . . There is a core national identity that is the identity of the WASP. And that doesn't mean we can't take anyone else in—a Sri Lankan or a Japanese or an Indian. But the core around which the nation's values are formed is the WASP."

So much for judging by the content of your character rather than the color of your skin. So much for the value of diversity. Or the fundamental contributions to America's culture and values from African, Native, and Latino Americans.

As for my community, whenever I hear that Asians don't have leadership qualities, I want to reply, "Then who's running Asia?"

It seems ridiculous to point out that Asian countries have no trouble finding leaders who are Asian. Character evaluation not only depends on who's doing the evaluation but in what circumstances and in what context someone is being judged. Certainly, my own character has shifted depending on how I identified myself and with whom I was interacting.

Back when I was in a white suburban high school, I wanted to be white and thought of myself as just like a white guy. In terms of my character, I had an arrogant streak then that I no longer possess. I was more of a braggart, louder, at times even obnoxious, certainly more extroverted (perhaps a little similar to the personality Ramaswamy evinces). At a dance sophomore year, I pretended to be a Southern preacher, chastising sinners to the amusement of a small crowd. I boasted I'd hit .750 in Pony League. (I didn't, but hey, I'd hit .500 in Little League.) I was the first jock to dress like a hippie and won best dressed. I ran for every student office, from homeroom representative to class president, but never won a single election. That I wasn't leadership material was not a thought I had back then because there weren't even enough Asians for that stereotype to take hold—and yet I see now that these cumulated defeats did change me.

In college, I was neither as loud nor obnoxious, and I stopped running for anything. Indeed, I thought of myself as a loner, an alienated romantic, and became more introverted—sort of emo before there was emo (picture me alone in my dorm room at night listening in the dark to Laura Nyro or Leonard Cohen). I still possessed a certain arrogance, which irked my freshman basketball coach; I couldn't disguise that I thought him a poor coach with little sense of strategy, or as I said to a teammate, "Our coach is an idiot." In class, I wouldn't sit in the back of the room, as Asian American students are often accused of doing, but in the front row, and I'd often be the first to raise my hand. When it came time for tests, I thought to myself, *I'm going to get an A because I've studied twice as much as anyone in this class.* I didn't think of myself as a racial minority; I didn't think very consciously—or tried not to think consciously—that the white people around me might regard me as different from them; nor did I much consider how my fellow Black students might regard me, though even back then I sensed they regarded me as different from the white students, as not representative of white exclusion or prejudice.

But after I finally admitted in my late twenties that I was not white and that I was a Japanese and Asian American, I began to be more conscious of the othering of the white gaze. I understood more clearly that I might be viewed through the lens of racial stereotypes and exclusions, that whites might regard me as foreign or strange or less than. I began to understand how racial prejudice had led to the imprisonment of my parents and 120,000 Japanese Americans during WWII. I realized that whites might have an entirely different take on me from the ways I regarded myself. They might be prejudiced or hostile, might regard me as a strange other. At the same time, as this was the Midwest with fewer Asian Americans, perhaps they didn't think of us at all; we weren't important or worth noticing. Why would they even give a shit about who we are or what happens to us—and this meant, my earlier arrogance or sense of my significance could not be sustained in the same way as when I delusionally thought I was white.

Although I bridled against this othering, it made me in certain ways more cautious, more wary in white spaces, and sometimes quieter, less inclined to call attention to myself. I understood the need to read the room for signs of exclusion or hostility before I would even begin to speak or expose myself. This reading of the room became more and more precision oriented and conscious, as I came to understand that my views on race could elicit dismay, disapproval, or backlash from whites—that my safety depended on the accuracy of my reading the whites around me.

At the same time, in literary or political appearances and on visits to colleges and arts organizations, I became more outspoken, more willing to challenge the dominant culture and its representatives. I was clearly angry, though in a less openly emotional way than many activists, perhaps a result of my family's Japanese cultural norms or something in my own temperament. Instead, I used my smarts and intellectual training to expose and combat the practices of Whiteness, and in the space of public debate I wouldn't back down, wouldn't try to get along simply to get along. And yes, some whites took that for arrogance (i.e., being uppity).

And yet, in Asian American spaces, which I was joining with other Asian Americans to create locally, I began to feel safer and more supported. Initially I was the only Asian American writer in town to have published a book and won grants, and so I realized that I could and should take up leadership roles, which suddenly seemed to open up to me in ways they hadn't in high school. Because there were expectations that I would act as a leader, I didn't need to thrust myself forward with quite the same vehemence as I did in high school. Instead, it was more important for me to help others in my community speak up and find their voice, to mentor and encourage younger artists and community members. If one of us succeeded, it was better for us all, and I lost some of the competitive or jealous streak I had when younger. I felt myself in service to my community and in that way more humbled. Though some would probably still label me as arrogant, I don't think that's the judgment of me that runs through my community. I am, though, thought of as someone who's not afraid of pissing off white people. And I recognize that my being a race man is often read differently in white spaces than in BIPOC spaces.

I'm a Sansei, a third-generation Asian American. My Nisei parents, not me, were the children of immigrants. So my relationship to Asian and Japanese culture is at a greater remove. Indeed, when I was younger, I wore my ignorance of Japanese and Japanese culture as a badge; I thought it made me an American.

I don't feel that way now. Now I regret not having learned Japanese or about Japanese culture.

At the same time, though, I do realize that any evidence of my speaking Japanese or knowing Japanese culture makes me not an American in the eyes of white Americans and, indeed, for many people of color. Instead, any sign of my association with Japanese culture becomes further evidence that I'm not from here. I know, in many ways, I will never be regarded as from here; my face tells a different story. Nothing I do can stop the narrative of my face and all that comes with it.

But I try, I try. Consciously, unconsciously. On the golf course I'll start talking about the Vikings quarterbacks, what kind of season Kirk Cousins is going to have after his rehab, how we might have done so much better last year if we hadn't had to rely on the back benchers, Nick Mullens and Josh Dobbs. I'll add something like, "When we first got Dobbs from the Cardinals, I thought he might be a keeper, he was far more mobile than Cousins, and I loved his story of being nicknamed the 'Passtronaut.' (Dobbs majored in aerospace engineering and even interned at NASA.) "But I guess there was a reason he's been on seven teams and never stuck." I say all this because if I can demonstrate that I know the intricate details of the Viking quarterbacks, I might prove I really do know something about American culture, that I'm not a recent immigrant. And that, supposedly, will prove I'm an okay guy, a guy, as they say, you could have a beer with.

As I'm doing this, I don't consciously question the logic behind my actions. That is, why would my status be worse if I were a recent immigrant? Is that devaluation in the heads of the white people I meet? Or is it in my head? Or both?

In my defense, part of me just wants to convey who I am, who exactly I am. Because I actually like football and do know about the Vikings quarterbacks and their long history of failure (sigh). Because I'm a third-generation American. Because I played football in high school and always played quarterback in gym class and in park and intramural leagues in high school and college. Because I've told my boys, since they were little, "There's only one sports rule in this family: You can never ever count on the Vikings! They will always break your hearts."

But of course there's more to it than that. I want to be seen without the scrim of stereotypes and prejudices that keep white Americans and even other Americans of color from seeing who I am, seeing my particularity, my individual history. Indeed, that's why I've written and published two memoirs, one novel, four books of poetry, two books of literary criticism, four plays, dozens of essays, and a PBS documentary.

The novelist Amy Tan has frequently asserted she is an American writer, *not* a Chinese American or Asian American writer. Is this because she believes the appellations *Chinese American* or *Asian American* somehow lessens her achievement or bars her from serious literary consideration? Or is it because the terms *Chinese American* or *Asian American* are of no use in understanding either who she is or her writing?

The second assertion makes no sense to me. As to the first, Tan's refusal smacks of an aversion to being regarded as a minority, of secondary status—and of course I understand that. But contrary to some Asian Americans, I feel one advantage of being Asian American is my perspective: I know my concerns, my community, my life will never be considered central or essential to telling the American story. I can't assume my importance; I can't assume that what I say or write automatically matters. Indeed, there has been for me a comfort—well, not comfort—but perhaps a sense of defiance and clarity in saying to myself, *You will never be fully accepted as an American: you will always be regarded as tangential.*

Like other people of color, my relationship to language is also connected to the stereotypes and prejudices around me. When I was younger, my mother often complained that I talked like a jock; she cited the way I sprinkled the phrase "you know" over and over in my speech. For me as a teenager, talking like a jock was a way of throwing off the role of foreigner, the immigrant, someone who wasn't born here and didn't belong. And yet now that I no longer speak like a jock, I also know that resorting to the talk of a jock is a way to put white people I meet at ease. At times, what I'm trying to make safe is not just my body, but also my intelligence and the way it is associated with my body and the stereotypes it invokes. Indeed, I feel that way about sections of this book.

For in certain situations, I know the more articulate and educated I appear—that is, if I actually let loose at full throttle my intellect and learning—the more I run the risk of being perceived as a threat because of my Asian-looking face and body. Even when I have taught at a university or an MFA program, I've had to pick and choose when and where I let my intelligence and learning show and to what degree. Because in certain situations where a white writer or intellectual would be met with respect and admiration for their intellect and learning, my intellect and learning can in an instant become perceived as uppity, arrogant, showing off. And if that happens, the foreignness that is my face, my body can then be turned into that of the outsider, the inscrutable threat, the one who wants to take something from white America.

Just as, whenever America's relationship to countries in Asia takes a turn for the worse, Asian Americans can feel the shadow of that worsening falling inevitably upon us.

Much of this first essay derives from years of observation and analysis of the place of Asian Americans in America. But my observations and analysis did not come without a cost. Back in 1992, when I was forty and *Miss Saigon* came out, that musical became not only a significant event in Asian American political and cultural history; it taught me a valuable lesson—claiming my racial and ethnic identity would come with a price, a price I had to decide if I was willing to pay.

Part of that price was to lose every white artist friend I had.

The cause? The following article on race I published in 1992 in *Mother Jones.*

Raising a Multicultural Daughter in a Multicultural World

> Each night, in our apartment in St. Paul, before we go to bed, I lay my head on Susie's stomach and feel the kicks of our daughter. Only one pound, she kicks with a sound that has come from nothing, from everything in our past, from my Japanese gene to the genes of my wife, English and Austria-Hungarian Jew. Susie remarks that although our daughter lives in her belly, she will look more like me than like her mother, but that, of course, is a matter of viewpoint, a product of cultural sight. Our daughter has made me feel much older than I was in Japan, much more tied to my grandparents, my parents, and to the future. This split I have felt between America and Japan, this fusion of two histories, will reside in her, in a different, more visible way.
>
> —David Mura, *Turning Japanese: Memoirs of a Sansei*

On the day our daughter was born, as my wife and I waited for her cesarean, we talked about names. Standing at the window, I looked out and said spontaneously, "Samantha, the day you were born was a gray and blustery day." We decided on Samantha Lyn, after my sisters, Susan Lynn and Lynda. I felt to give her a Japanese name might mark her as too different, especially since we live in St. Paul where Asian Americans are a small minority. I had insisted that her last name be hyphenated, Sencer-Mura. My wife had argued that such a name was unwieldy. "What happens when Samantha Sencer-Mura marries Bob Rodriguez-Stein?" she asked. "That's her generation's problem," I laughed.

I sometimes wish now we'd given her a Japanese middle name, as my wife had wanted. Perhaps it's because I sense that the world she's inheriting won't be dominated by the melting pot model, that multiculturalism is not a project but a reality, that in the next century there will no longer be a white majority in this country. Or perhaps I simply feel guilty about giving in to the dominant culture once again.

I am working on a poem about my daughter, about trying to take in her presence, her life, about trying to link her with my sense of the past—my father and mother, the internment camps, my grandparents. I picture myself serving her sukiyaki, a dish I shunned as a child, and her shouting for more rice, brandishing her *hashi* (a word for chopsticks that I never used as a child, and only began to use after my trip to Japan). As I describe her running through the garden, scattering petals, squashing tomatoes, I suddenly think of how someone someday will call her a "gook," that I know this with more certainty than I know she'll find happiness in love.

Later, I talk to my wife about possibly moving out to the West Coast or Hawaii, to a place where there would be more Asian Americans. Samantha would find there more children like her (in Hawaii, more than half the children are *hapa*; she'd be the norm not the minority). I speak of the need to spend more time living in an Asian American community. My writing comes out of that community, is addressed to that community. I can't tell its stories, though, if I'm not a part of it. As I talk about moving one evening, my wife starts to feel uneasy. "I'm afraid you'll cross this bridge and take Sam with you, and leave me here," she says.

"But I've lived all my life on your side of the bridge. At most social gatherings, I'm constantly the only person of color in the room. What's wrong with living a while on my side of the bridge? What keeps you from crossing?"

Susie, a pediatric oncologist, works with families of all colors. Still, having a hybrid daughter is already changing her experience. Often, when she's in the grocery with Sam, someone will come up to her and say, "Oh, she's such a beautiful little girl. Where did you get her?" This has happened so often, Susie swears she's going to teach Sam to say, "Fuck you, my genes came all the way over on the Mayflower, thank you."

These incidents mark one of the first times Susie has experienced something negative over race that I have not. When I'm with Sam, no one asks me where she came from. They assume I'm her father. For Susie, the encounters are a challenge to her position as Samantha's biological mother, a negation of an arduous pregnancy and the physical work of birth and motherhood. For me, it stirs an old wound. The people who mistake Sam for an adopted child can't picture a white woman married to an Asian man.

Six ways of viewing racial identity:

Identity is a social and historical construction.

Identity is formed by political and economic and cultural exigencies. Our racial categories were created at certain periods in history for certain purposes.

Identity is a fiction. Because our racial identities were created by certain people in a certain society, they are arbitrary and certainly do not respond to clear biological markers. Blacks in Africa were never black until whites came. Asians in Asia do not assume they share a common identity.

Identity is a choice. At one time, I denied I was Asian American or a person of color. People can refuse to be identified by the racial categories others would press upon them. Or they can acknowledge that these identities are arbitrary and fictional but still have an effect upon them and society. Immigrants can choose whether they identify with their country of origin or with their place as hyphenated Americans.

Identity may appear unitary but is always fragmentary. Each racial group contains multiple differences—in class, in terms of sexual orientation or preference, in region, in genetic makeup, in immigration history, etc.

Identity is choosing to acknowledge or not acknowledge political and economic and cultural exigencies. Many whites deny that their being white provides them with any advantages or that people of color suffer disadvantages. They do not acknowledge the historical bases of America's racial categorizations and their harmful history. Conservative people of color may make similar arguments in reverse.

When I address the question of raising my daughter, I address the question of her identity, which means I address the question of my identity and her mother's, and our parents, and so on. But this multiplication of the self takes place along many lines. Who knows where it stops? At my grandparents? At the woman in the grocery store? At you, the imagined reader of this piece?

In the matrix of race and color in our society, there is the binary opposition of black and white. And then there are the various Others, determined by race or culture or gender or sexual preference—Native Americans, Hispanic Americans, Asian Americans, Japanese Americans, woman, man, heterosexual, homosexual. None of these definitions stands alone; they form an intricate, maze-like weave that accounts for both our history and our present.

As part of this multiracial complexity, I wrote my memoir *Turning Japanese* to explore the cultural amnesia of Japanese Americans, particularly those of the third generation like myself who speak little or no Japanese. When I give readings, people often ask if I'm going to raise Samantha with a greater awareness of Japanese culture than I received as a child. The obvious answer is yes. I talk of how I'd like our family to spend another extended period in Japan, so Samantha can pick up the language. I also acknowledge that the prospects of teaching her about Japanese culture feel to me rather daunting. Given my lack of contact with that culture growing up and the overwhelming presence of the dominant culture, I feel inadequate to the task, and I have more sympathy with my Nisei parents, whom I have criticized for forgetting the past.

And yet, near the end of my stay in Japan, I decided that I was clearly not Japanese, that I was never going to be Japanese, and that I was not even going to be someone who would become an expert on Japanese culture. My identity was as a Japanese American. But what did that mean? That meant claiming the particularities of Japanese American history; it meant coming to terms with how the forces of the dominant culture had formed me; it meant realizing my identity would always be fragmentary, would always be partially occluded. Finally, it meant that the issues of race were central to me, that I see myself as a person of color.

Can I teach these things to my daughter? My Japanese American identity comes from my own experience, something I know. But I am still trying to understand that experience, and I am still struggling to find languages to talk about the issues of race. My failures are caused by more than a lack of knowledge; there's the powerful wish not to know. How, for instance, can I talk to my daughter about sexuality and race? My own experience is so filled with shame and regret, is so filled with experiences I would rather not discuss, that it seems so much easier to opt for silence. It's much simpler to pretend multiculturalism means teaching her *kanji* and how to conjugate Japanese verbs.

I know every day my daughter will be exposed to images that tell her that Asian bodies are marginalized, that the women are exotic, sensual, sexually submissive, that the men are houseboys or Chinatown punks, kung fu warriors or Japanese businessmen, robot-like and dangerous, or robot-like and comic. I know that she will face constant pressures to forget that she is part Japanese American, to assume a basically white middle-class identity. When she reaches adolescence there will be powerful messages for her to conform to an unspoken norm, to disassociate herself perhaps from the children of recent Asian immigrants. She may find herself wanting to assume a privilege and status that come from not calling attention to her identity, or from playing into the stereotype that makes Asian women seem so desirable to certain white men. And I know I will have no power over these forces.

Should I tell her of how, when I look at her mother, I know my desires for her cannot be separated from the way the culture has inculcated me with standards of white beauty? Should I tell her of my own desires of a "hallucinatory whiteness," of how such a desire fueled in my twenties a rampant promiscuity and addiction to pornography, to the "beautiful" bodies of white women? It's all too much to expect her to take it in. It should not even be written down. It should be kept hidden, unspoken. These forces should not exist.

One day last year, I was talking with two white friends about the landmark controversy over the Broadway production of *Miss Saigon*. Like many Asian Americans, I agreed with the protest by Actor's Equity and Asian Americans in New York against the producer's casting. I felt disturbed that again a white actor, the British Jonathan Pryce, was playing a Eurasian, and that no Asian American actor had been given a chance to audition for that role. Beyond that, I was upset by the *Madama Butterfly* plot of *Miss Saigon*, where an Asian woman pines for her white male lover—who, by implication, is always more desirable than the Asian men around her.

Both my friends—Paula, a painter, and Mark, a writer—consider themselves liberals; Mark had been active in the antiwar movement during the sixties. He was part of my wedding and, at the time, perhaps my closest male friend. But neither of them agreed with me about *Miss Saigon.* They argued that art represented the freedom of the imagination, was trying to get inside other people's skin. "Isn't colorblind casting what we're striving for?" they asked.

"Why is it everyone gets so upset when a white actor may be denied a role?" I asked. "What about every time an Asian American actor tries out for a part that says 'lawyer' or 'doctor' and is turned down?"

"But reverse discrimination isn't the answer," they replied.

I don't recall exactly what happened after this. I think the argument trailed off into some safer topic as such arguments often do. I didn't want to press the issue, and I don't think I knew how upset I was about their inability to understand my point of view. But afterward, I felt angrier and angrier and, at the same time, more despairing. For me the fact that Warner Oland played Charlie Chan and Keye Luke the bumbling number-one son was humiliating, just as the buck-toothed thick-spectacled Mickey Rooney in *Breakfast at Tiffany's* made me flinch with discomfort and embarrassment each time I saw it. These examples of yellowface did not show me that art was a democracy of the imagination, quite the opposite. But for Paula and Mark, my sense of shame was secondary to their belief in "freedom" in the arts.

When I talked to my wife about my anger and despair, she felt uncomfortable. These were her friends, too. She said I'd argued before with them about the role of politics in art. Mark had always looked ruefully at his political involvement in the sixties, the times he felt he had gone overboard with his zealous self-righteousness. "He's threatened by you, and your increasing political involvement," my wife said. She felt I should take our disagreement as just another incident in a long friendly dialogue.

But when I talked with Alexs Pate, a black friend who's a writer, he replied, "Yeah, I was surprised too at the reaction of some of my white artists friends to *Miss Saigon.* It really told me where they were. It marked a dividing line. And I just backed away from certain people."

For a while, I avoided talking about my feelings with Paula and Mark. I did, though, accuse my wife of wanting to protect them and so argued with her. My wife urged me to talk to them, to work it out. "You're trying to get me to have sympathy with how difficult this is for them or for you, how this creates tensions between you and them," I said. "But I have to have this conversation about *Miss Saigon* with every white friend I have. Each of you only has to have it with me." My wife argued that I was taking my anger out on her—which, in part, I was.

Finally, in a series of telephone calls, I told Paula and Mark I not only felt that their views were wrong about *Miss Saigon* but that they were racially based. In these emotionally charged conversations, I don't think I used the word *racist,* but I know they both objected to my lumping them together with other whites. Paula said I was stereotyping them, that she wasn't like other whites. She told me of her friendships with a few blacks when she lived back East, of the history of her mother's involvement in supporting civil rights. "It's not like I don't know what discrimination is," she said. "Women get discriminated against, so do artists." Her tone moved back and forth between self-righteousness and resentment to distress and tears about losing our friendship.

Mark talked about his shame of being a WASP. "Do you know that I don't have a single male friend who is a WASP?" he said. I decided not to point out that within the context of color, the difference between a WASP male and, say, an Irish Catholic isn't much of a difference. I also didn't remark that he had no friends of color other than myself. I suppose I felt such remarks would hurt him too much. I didn't feel it was safe to say them since it might provoke more negative reactions, and it would be impossible to get him to see how I and other people of color might view his position. (We people of color are constantly weighing how much of our truths we should express or expose to the whites around us.)

A few months later, I had a few calmer talks with Mark, but they always ended with this distance between us. I felt I needed some acknowledgment from him that when we began talking about race, I knew more about it than he did, that our arguing about race was not the same as our arguing about, say, free verse versus formal verse. That my experience gave me insights he didn't have.

"Of course, that's true," he said. "I know you've had different experiences." But for him, we had to meet on the subject on an equal basis, where his views were considered at the start as just as valid as mine. Otherwise, he felt he was compromising himself, giving away his soul. He likened it to the way he gave away his self in his alcoholic family, where he denied his own feelings. He would be making himself a victim again.

At a certain point, I suggested we do some sessions with a white therapist whom I had gone to and who was counseling Mark. "No," said Mark. "I can't do that now. I need him on my side."

I can still see us sitting there on my front steps, on a warm early spring day. I looked at this man with whom I've shared my writing and my most intimate secrets, with whom I've shared the process of undergoing therapy and recovery, and I realized we were now no longer intimates. I felt that I had embarked on a journey discovering myself as a person of color, discovering the rage and pain that had formed my Japanese American identity, and that he would deny me this journey. He saw me as someone who would make him a victim, whose feelings on race were charged with arrogance and self-righteousness. And yet, on some level, I know he saw that my journey had been good for me. And I felt I was asking him to come on that journey with me.

Inevitably, I wonder if my daughter will understand my perspective as a person of color. Will she identify with my white friends, fearful and suspicious of my anger and frustration, seeing it as alien to her experience? Or will she be working from some viewpoint I can't quite conceive, some line that marks her as both a person of color and white and neither all at the same time, some new being whose experiences I will have to listen to and learn from? How will I prepare her for that new identity?

And after all this, will it be fair or accurate or helpful for me to tell her, "Unless the world is radically different, on some level, you will still have to choose—are you a person of color or not?"

It took me many months to figure out what had gone down with Paula and Mark. Almost invariably, when I talked about it with a friend of color, whether Asian American or African American or Hispanic American, I came away feeling better, with more understanding and self-assurance. For instance, when my black friend Alexs and I talked about how whites desperately want to claim that they are victimized too, we came up with the term the *victim limbo.*

When a white person is charged with racism or engages in a conversation about racism, the first thing they often do, as Paula did with me, is the victim limbo: "I'm a woman, I know what prejudice is, I've experienced it." "I'm Jewish/working class/Italian in a WASP neighborhood/etc. I know what prejudice is, I've experienced it." If they are white, WASP, and male, like Mark, they are still able to do the victim limbo: "Yeah, I'm a white male. I know what that means—overly rational, uptight, oppressive, power hungry, racist"—a statement that implies, oh yes, they call all white males these things, but I'm not any of them, so I too am being unfairly labeled and judged.

The purpose of this limbo is to show the person of color that he or she doesn't really experience anything the white person hasn't experienced, that the person of color's social/ economic/political/cultural position is actually not very different from the white person's. Therefore, the white person doesn't have to feel guilty, doesn't have to acknowledge the system of racism in a direct way, since the white person is a victim too. But Alexs and I both knew that the position of a person of color and that of a white person in American society are not the same. The victim limbo—which is offered by many as a token of solidarity: "I'm just the same as you"—is really a way of depoliticizing the racial question; it ignores the differences in power in this country that result from the system of race.

"Whites don't want to give up their privilege and psychic comforts," said Alexs. "That's really why they're so angry. You see it in the young skinheads. They know they're coming into a different world. They have to choose whether they're going to give up power or fight for it. That's why liberals are so uneasy now. We're forcing them to choose."

When racism is discussed, white liberals may feel a gulf open up between themselves and their friends of color. But the gulf that seems to open up was always there. And the person of color has always been aware of it in a deeper, more conscious way than the white person. Indeed, the system of racism has helped blind the white person to that gulf. What he or she is objecting to is a new knowledge of reality, is the revelation of something the white person has always subconsciously known. Their claim that they feel left out keeps them from seeing the ways that their friends of color have always been left out of the white world.

None of this, though, assuages the pain and bitterness I feel over losing white friendships over race or the distance I have seen open up between me and white friends as I've become more and more conscious of race. Nor does it help me explain to my daughter why we no longer see Paula or Mark when she asks about them or mentions their names. The compensation for these changes I've been going through, for shedding my white-identified consciousness, has been the numerous friendships that I've begun to have with people of color. My daughter will grow up in a household where the people who visit will be from a wider spectrum than those Japanese Americans and whites who visited my parents' house in the suburbs of Chicago.

Not that teaching her about her Asian American self is any easier. Recently, my wife searched all over Japantown in San Francisco and the International District in Seattle looking for an Asian baby doll. Store after store turned up nothing. Then she walked into a generic toy store in St. Paul and found one. We've named her Kei-chan, *chan* being the affectionate suffix added to Japanese children's names. But when we call our daughter Sami-chan, she immediately becomes indignant, "I'm not a chan, Daddy, I'm Sammy."

My wife has also been more conscious than I am about telling Sam that she's Japanese. Last week we took Sam to the circus, and as the Chinese acrobats were stacking themselves like Legos in a human pyramid, Sam remarked, "They're Japanese." Susie explained to Sam they were Chinese, not Japanese. A few days later, after playing with blond Shannon, the girl from next door, Sam said, "She's not Japanese, mom. We're Japanese." "No," said Susie, "Daddy's Japanese, and you're part Japanese, but I'm not Japanese." Sam refused to believe this. "No, you're Japanese." After a few minutes, Susie finally sorted out the confusion. Sam thought being Japanese meant you had dark hair.

For many liberal whites, what seems most important in any discussion of race is the need for hope, the need to find some link of solidarity with people of color. They do not see how much their hope serves as a tool of denial, since they tend to view the history of race in this country as one of a steady progression rather than progression and retrenchment; they tend to underestimate how much such retrenchments have made claims of progress more prominent in name than in deed and accomplishment.[1] They have a difficult time understanding how their claims of solidarity not only ignore real differences but also blot out the reality of people of color that whites don't see or don't want to see. How can we move forward, they ask, with all this rage you seem to feel? How can you stereotype me or group me in this category of whiteness?

I tell them they are still unwilling to examine what being white has meant to their existence. They think their rage at being classified as a white person is the same rage that people of color feel when they are stereotyped. It is not. When whites, whether liberal or conservative, feel anger about race, it almost always means they sense some attempt to lessen their power and comfort.

In the end, whites must exchange a hope based on naivete and ignorance for one based on knowledge. For this naive hope denies connections, complexities. It is the drug of amnesia. It says there is no thread from one moment to the next, no cause and effect. It denies consequence. Responsibility. Moreover, it denies the racial realities of American society, the deep racial disparities in any area of our society, from education to the justice system to economics to politics—or how such disparities are caused by a deeper and more pervasive system of white supremacy that most whites will not let themselves see or acknowledge, much less confront their own place and role in that system.

1 I am struck here by how this sentence presages certain key portions of my last book, *The Stories Whiteness Tells Itself: Racial Myths and Our American Narratives*, especially the chapter on Reconstruction and the period following the Civil War. Also see Douglas A. Blackmon's *Slavery by Another Name: The Re-Enslavement of Black Americans from the Civil War to World War II*, which details the ways the South tried to reestablish slavery and new forms of oppression and restriction of the rights of blacks; Khalil Gibran Muhammad's *The Condemnation of Blackness: Race, Crime, and the Making of Modern Urban America* and the pseudoscientific studies of supposed black criminality, which spawned an ideology of anti-blackness, an ideology that continues to shape the justice system to this day and is instrumental to ways white America still contextualizes race in urban environments—or look simply at the continued presence of segregated school systems throughout the United States.

For my wife, this journey has been a difficult yet fruitful one. The arguments we have over race mirror our other arguments—after all, the same two personalities are involved—and, at the same time, exist in an impersonal realm where I am a person of color and she is white. "I realize that in a way I've been passing too," she said a few months ago. "There's this comfort I've got to give up, this ease." At her clinic, she challenges the mainly white children's books in the waiting room or a colleague's unconscious assumptions about Hmong families. More and more, she finds herself at gatherings where she, as a white person, is in the minority.

Breaking through denial, seeing how much needs to be changed, does not have to blunt the capacity for hope. For both of us, our daughter is proof of that capacity. And if I know someday someone will call her "gook," I know today she's a happy child. The love her mother and I share, the love we bear for her, cannot spare her from pain over race, and yet it can make her stronger. Samantha will go further than us, she will know more. She will be like nothing I can imagine, as I am nothing like my parents imagined. Today, my daughter told me she will grow up and work with her mother at the hospital. I'll be a grandpa and stay home and write poems and be with her children. Neither race nor ethnicity enter into her vision of the future. And yet, they are already there, with our hopes, gathering shape.

Post-note: Rereading this essay I'm struck by my fears that my daughter would identify more as white and distance herself from her Japanese American identity. I don't think those fears were unreasonable; many hapa *Asian Americans don't readily identify with any formulation of Asian American identity. Growing up, her younger brothers identified more strongly as Asian and with people of color, in part because of their multiracial sports teams and interest in hip-hop. Even though Samantha looks the most Asian, she did tend to argue that I made too much of racial issues; she was constantly trying to demonstrate she had a mind of her own.*

But Sam grew up in an increasingly diverse Minneapolis and went to a high school that was 20 percent Native American (Dakhóta, Ojibwe), 20 percent Black and East African (Somali, Ethiopian, Eritrean), 20 percent Latino, 10 percent Asian (Hmong, Vietnamese, Tibetan) and 30 percent white. She then went to Occidental College where she majored in Critical

Studies in Social Justice and even took a class from the daughter of famed Asian American author Frank Chin. After college, she worked as an educator at a heavily Latino junior high in Oakland (many of the students' families spoke Mam, a Guatemalan indigenous language, and Sam spent a summer in Guatemala to improve her Spanish). After obtaining an MA in Educational Leadership from Harvard, she returned to Minneapolis. She headed 826 Minneapolis, an organization started by Dave Eggers that teaches creative writing and tutors K-12 students from marginalized communities, including the heavily Somali neighborhood where the organization is housed (my middle son Nikko recently married a Somali American woman).

Three years ago, Sam successfully ran for the Minnesota House of Representatives from the multiracial South Minneapolis that's part of Ilhan Omar's district and includes Sam's high school. Sam's now in her second term and is one of ten legislators in the Minnesota Asian Pacific Caucus and a member of the People of Color and Indigenous Caucus. In public appearances, Sam introduces herself as the first Japanese American to serve in the Minnesota legislature and she explains why she sponsored the state's ethnic studies bill: "When my dad was growing up, he didn't learn about the internment camps in school. I wasn't able to learn about the internment camps in school. I want my son Tadashi to be able to learn about Japanese American history in his school." Recently, celebrating Women's History Month, Sam posted, "I follow in the footsteps of powerful Asian American women leaders such as Yuri Kochiyama and Grace Lee Boggs, who lifted up the unique struggles of Asian American women and connected our experiences to other marginalized groups."

Sam's two children are named Tadashi and Yuna Sencermura-Witzig—hyphenated names for the new America.

Letter to a (Former) White Friend

Dear _____:

In your letter, you talk about your need for safety. I cannot of course say what you need to feel safe. I do want to talk about my need to feel safe. I realize what I say here may not use the term *safety* in the way you would.

First, with the possible exception of Susie, there is not one white person I know with whom I feel I can talk honestly about my feelings on race and feel safe. This does not mean I do not talk to people about that issue. Indeed, just about all I seem to do now is talk about it, in one way or another. Much of the time I speak in front of mainly white or all-white audiences about this subject. I do not feel safe, but I do it because I believe certain things need to be said. From time to time, in meetings, in talks, I get in arguments with people about this subject. I do not feel safe, but I say what I need to say, not because I think I will necessarily cause the person I'm arguing with to rethink their position, but because there are other people in the audience I know I might reach. Or else I continue the conversation because I know that the person I'm arguing with can help make changes that will benefit the people I am supporting, which can change the systems that work against diversity. So I will sit at a board meeting and work with people who are concerned about how white people are being left out or silenced by the organization whenever the subject of diversity or race comes up. I stay there because I represent a community, and if my voice is not there my community loses.

I also speak out because I know that many people of color are afraid to speak out on these issues. They do not feel safe. I feel I am trying to confirm their feelings and their perceptions about their lives, to give them the courage to speak up. When I challenge whites about race, other people of color see that they too can do the same thing.

All this takes a toll on me; it is not easy; I would rather not have to do it. But I do. It is worth the effort.

When I write an article on Japan bashing in the *New York Times*, I do not feel safe. I know I am opening myself to a public I have no control of. And when I write articles like the one in *Mother Jones*, I also do not feel safe. Indeed, I was told that the article angered certain white people on the staff there. As you probably know, that article has resulted in the end of several of my friendships with white artists that we know. But I also know that a lot of people of color have told me they felt reaffirmed by that article (one said she was Xeroxing it and sending it to the white people she knew). I feel the same thing when I read the writings of James Baldwin or Frantz Fanon or bell hooks. So it is worthwhile for me to undergo not feeling safe.

However, I have found that when I argue with white people about this subject in my private life, it is as draining or even more draining than when I do it in public. And, usually, I feel less safe. For one thing, because I am afraid of hurting people's feelings or upsetting the social decorum of the moment, I am apt to hold back my feelings and words, even as I speak out. It leaves me feeling schizophrenic and drained, and when I look back, little is usually accomplished. In public, it's often much easier for me to simply disagree outright with people, to be myself. To give full throttle to my arguments and position.

As a result of all this, I've come to feel that when I talk with people about race in private, I want to do it with people who support me. If there's criticism, I want to hear it from someone I feel safe with. Invariably, such people are people of color. It's not that I don't necessarily want to hear the other side. Indeed, I hear it all the time when I speak in public. But I don't want to deal with it in my private life. There I want to rest, to feel safe. In addition, it seems that doing things this way conserves my energies for the times I need to speak out in public.

In your letter, you talk about caring for M., about how I did not mention he was in prison to protest the Vietnam War, and you question whether or not I'm willing to recognize the power I'm granted as a male. You note how you have talked to the people involved with or "embroiled in the break." (I assume that all of these people are white, since M. had no other friends of color here than me.) You write about how "you are not averse to experts," implying that I am setting myself up as both expert and tour guide. You talk about "feeling invisible" in my article in *Mother Jones*, about the silences in the article, about how you feel silenced by the article.

Nothing in your letter makes me feel safe about the prospect of talking to you about my article. Nothing there acknowledges the position of power white people occupy when the subject of race comes up. Nothing there acknowledges the invisibility of people of color still in this society. Nothing there acknowledges the forces in this society that are there to silence me and others like me or people of color in general. My acknowledging my power as a male, which I do, does not address or change the power of whites or the invisibility and erasures of people of color. Perhaps you assumed all this, I don't know. But to me the fact that you do not mention it tells me something. And it's hard, looking at what you've said and haven't said, for me to see how a "dialogue" would be of benefit to me. If you want me to know that I haven't given a three-dimensional portrait of M., I accept that. But frankly, I don't see that as the purpose of the article. There are three-dimensional portraits of white people throughout this culture, twenty-four hours a day. People can fill in the blanks. To me, the point of the article was that he did not respect who I was and he held racist beliefs and was not willing to change those beliefs. You could point out all sorts of wonderful qualities about him that I might agree with. But for me that lack of respect and that racism outweighed everything else. Perhaps, for you they do not. Or perhaps you do not think his views were racist. If that is the case, then we disagree. And you can write your own article. And M. can write his own article. I hardly feel that white people in this society who disagree with me on race lack opportunities to voice or enact their views.

You write in your letter that you want your friends to understand your need for safety, and what you mean by that term. You imply that if people cannot understand this need, you may not be able to be friends with them.

I too want that.

Sincerely,

David

Secret Colors

I

In the early eighties, after a failed stint in graduate school, I became part of the Twin Cities literary scene. At that time, many of my friends who were artists had gone into therapy and begun dealing with the problems of addiction and abusive family systems. Feminist critiques of the patriarchy, of pornography, of sexual roles figured prominently in our discussions. These friends supported me through my questioning of my family, the ways I had learned to deal with sexuality, my own unexamined rage and depression. They helped me climb out of a deep cavern of shame, which seemed to echo the world of my childhood. We discussed addictions in our families, the craziness or inscrutability or remoteness or abuses or addictions of our parents. We supported each other in creating a "family of choice" to replace our "biological family."

At the same time, I was learning what it was to be a poet, a writer, in this country. This role included not just discussions on the "deep images" of surrealism or the relevance of meter and rhyme or the feminist poetics of Adrienne Rich. There was also a community we felt we were all building, a new way of supporting writers through arts organizations like The Loft in the Twin Cities. There were questions of whether we wanted to teach at a university or not. Though even as we questioned the "academic poet," many of us saw such jobs as enviable positions, the just reward for success as a writer.

There was also a lifestyle, which seemed to seek an existence of quiet solitude and work. Whether with summers in a cabin at the North Shore of Lake Superior or within everyday life in the city, one tried to arrange one's life and its surrounding objects so that they were infused with a sense of beauty and poetry—not an ostentatious, opulent, upper-class style, but a lyrical bohemianism that probably dated back to some notion of Paris in the Twenties. (Not that this lifestyle was always affordable to each of us, only that it shaped our desires.)

One summer, everyone I knew seemed to be reading James Salter's *Light Years*, a book that I reread several times because of Salter's exquisite prose and its depiction of a cultivated lifestyle; the book is set in the late fifties and early sixties and it anticipates many of the trappings of Yuppiedom without the crassness of that term or the backdrop of the Reagan eighties:

> November evening, immemorial, clear. Smoked brook trout, mutton, an endive salad, a Margaux open on the sideboard. The dinner was served beneath a print of Chagall, the mermaid over the bay of Nice. The signature was probably false, but as Peter had said before, what difference did it make, it was as good as Chagall's own, perhaps even better, with just the right degree of carelessness.

For me, the book invoked certain assumptions about the ideal writer's life—Hemingway in Paris or later incarnations, William Styron, James Jones, Irwin Shaw. It marked a way of living where one thought of how to gather beauty around oneself, where the violations of the outside world did not enter. (In such worlds race, of course, is checked at the door, and this was probably part of its unconscious appeal to me.)

What is obvious to me now is that my friends, the community I saw myself a part of, the artists and writers I admired, the lifestyle I aspired to, were all white. And yet, even if at times I was aware of myself as a single Asian American in one of the whitest cities in this country, on another level I hardly ever thought of the issues of race. I rarely thought about how my life or my friends or my writer heroes related to the people of color or artists of color in this country. When an anthology of Minnesota writers came out and there were no Black or Hispanic or Native American writers in the anthology, I did not really think of myself as a token person of color.[1] Instead, I felt my presence

1 Rereading this, I find it ironic that in 2022, with African American writer Carolyn Holbrook, I coedited an anthology of Minnesota BIPOC writers, *We Are Meant to Rise: Voices for Justice from Minneapolis to the World.* Many of the essays focused on the murder of George Floyd and the local political protests that spread throughout the country.

in the anthology meant I was one of the top poets in the state. One of the editors was a close friend, and when someone wrote to complain of the lack of writers of color, I told my friend I supported his decisions. I believed he wasn't a racist; I knew how hard he had struggled over the editing process; I knew he had chosen to exclude his own work. I also felt there just weren't any other really good poets of color in the state. Look at the demographics, I thought. And the poems I had seen by a few of the Black writers, well, they were just flat. They lacked technique.

You see, I believed I was a good liberal. I believed my white friends were good liberals. We were for equality. We were also for literature of quality. If I went to a party of writers and I was the only person of color in the room, well, that didn't say anything about me or my white friends.

A few years passed. On a warm spring day in the early nineties, I went walking with a white friend through the streets of St. Paul. This friend was a fellow poet, someone who had read a poem at my wedding. We had worked together in the Writers in the Schools program. We were close in age and, in many ways, close in politics, literary interests, sensibility. We had shared our intimate experiences with therapy, with rummaging through the closets of our dysfunctional family systems. We both grew up in middle-class white suburbs. She was blond and big boned, her ethnic group Scandinavian like many Minnesotans, and I a Japanese American from the Chicago area, but till now that difference had never surfaced as a tension in our friendship.

Recently, though, I had begun more and more to question my sense of my own identity, prompted in part by reading Black authors and other writers of color. And so my white friend and I were arguing about race. At one point, she complained that although I seemed to be publishing articles and poems concerning race, her poems on the subject weren't getting published.

"I'd like there to be a dialogue," she said, "but it seems that my voice doesn't count."

As our conversation progressed, I remarked to her that if I want to apply for a job, most often the person in charge of the hiring would be white. Whites rarely have the experience of applying for a job to a person of color.

"Yeah, well, I know how that feels," she replied. "I'm a white, middle-class woman and I can't get a teaching job anywhere."

At the same time she was making these remarks, my friend insisted on her good intentions: "I'm trying to deal with race as best as I can. I teach writers of color, I teach your works, I go hear writers of color read."

She protested that she really didn't disagree with me about the basic issues, that she too wanted to live in a society without racism and was working to make this happen. In my conversation with my friend, I did not point out to her that her focus on herself as an individual did not give an accurate picture of her or my reality. To her, the fact that I was being published and she was not meant there was not a balanced dialogue in the literary world about the issues of race. She was the one being discriminated against.[2]

Yet in reality my friend only had to turn on the television news or open a paper to see her views about race affirmed. Even if she was not being published, white writers who thought like her were, and still are, being published everywhere. To people of color, it's obvious that the views of whites dominate our cultural discourse about race, and that the people who control the media and other institutions of culture are white. Yet to my white friend, it seemed it was she as a white person who was being marginalized, not people of color.[3]

Later, I talked to my wife, who is white, about this conversation. My wife and I had been having our own conversations about race and were about to reenter couples' counseling to sort some things out. At times she seemed to understand the way I felt, and at times she worried she was agreeing with me simply to give in. But there was a trust there, a commitment and a sense of movement that I did not feel with my white woman friend. (Recently, a Black friend remarked that white women are often more open to seeing the issues of race than white men, but the difficulty for white women in truly addressing racism

2 Just as the MAGA crowd now complains that whites are more discriminated against than Blacks.

3 This was not a member of the so-called forgotten white working class who was proclaiming she was discriminated against as a white person; this was a liberal middle-class highly educated white artist.

often stemmed from their loyalty to white men, particularly their husbands or lovers; this wasn't the case for my wife.)

My wife, at this point in time, was not quite willing to let go of her white friends over issues of race. She offered that perhaps my friend was trying as best as she could.

"I thought that at first," I replied, "that's why I didn't challenge her as much as I might have."

But later, I thought, *No, it's not about trying.* My white friend *chose* to believe certain things about the world. She chose to look at the world in a certain way, and she chose not to change. She chose to look at herself as the victim of racial politics. She chose not to examine what her resentment and envy might mean; she chose not to see the ways her views continued to support the racial status quo.

I can still recall vividly that walk with my friend, her querulous tone, her confusion about why I had already broken off a friendship with another mutual white friend. Like many white liberals, she kept wanting to believe it was just differences in personalities, professional jealousies perhaps. She wanted to believe that she and I did not really view things that differently, that we were on the same side. Yet even as she spoke, she seemed more and more distant from me. I felt she had been talking to herself or to someone else other than me, some vision she still clung to of who I was. I sensed she'd reached a line and was not going to cross it. But I had crossed, and there was no going back for me. She did not want to move, and she could not quite admit I was moving.

And yet, in another sense, a gulf had opened up that had always been there. Only before I hadn't wanted to admit its existence. In a sense I felt as if I had become a stranger, perhaps even to myself. Confronted with this stranger, she could not see me. The new part of me, or the long-buried part of me I'd finally claimed, remained beyond her view. Because if she truly saw it, she would have to change.

In looking back on this friendship, I am making all this perhaps clearer to me than it was at the time, granting myself a lucidity that comes only in retrospect. I know I also felt guilty, as if I had done something wrong, as if I had somehow betrayed her or become suddenly this judgmental monster. My shifting sense of self scared me, as well as her. And, on a certain level, I was right to be scared.

I had a couple other subsequent conversations or arguments with this white woman friend, but each ended in a kind of stalemate, a place not much different from our first disagreements on race. I think this sense of stasis led us both to feel it better to let the friendship go, without really formally marking an end. We just drifted apart, into other spheres. These days I don't see her at the literary gatherings I go to, mostly cabarets or spoken word readings with a young multiracial crowd. It's sometimes surprising to me how we never seem to run into each other. And sometimes it's not.

In writing this I cannot help but add that today, despite voicing complaints about her employment prospects, my ex-friend has a teaching position in a local MFA program. I believe my views on race and my identity have had something to do with my job prospects in the town in which I live (and indeed elsewhere). I'm considered by many to be difficult and overly conscious of race, to be too up front with my views and too angry. I've become the proverbial rageful man of color.

At the same time I know I was not always this way. At one time I had many white friends. And virtually no friends of color.

II

A couple of years later, I'm standing outside on the sidewalk in January. It's Minneapolis and well below freezing—five degrees. Snow whirls past, blown by an icy blast of arctic air. I'm arguing with my Black friend, Alexs Pate, a writer. We're standing outside the house of a producer from the local public television, with whom we've been discussing a film of the performance piece Alexs and I are creating. But right now, the whole performance piece seems in jeopardy, falling apart like a jigsaw puzzle lifted up and now crumbling; the issues that have been brewing beneath the surface as we've worked together for a couple of months are now cracking up what's held us together. Our voices are strained, not so much shouting but exasperated, on edge.

Alexs is about my age, a poet and a fiction writer. He's someone I've known a few years as a member of the local literary scene, and in the past couple of years, I've become closer to him. Alexs grew up in the Black inner city of North Philly. I grew up in a white Jewish suburb in Chicago. While I registered as a C.O. in college during the Vietnam War, he entered the Navy. He has worked in a public relations firm and in corporate America, and only in recent years has he given himself over to his longtime desire to become a writer. His literary heroes are Langston Hughes, James Baldwin, Toni Morrison, John A. Williams, the first three whom I read only after I was drummed out of English graduate school and the last of which I have not yet read. His poetic background comes out of the Black Arts Movement and figures like Amiri Baraka, the Last Poets, Haki Madhubuti, Ishmael Reed. My early literary heroes were Robert Lowell, John Berryman, Randall Jarrell, white Ivy League–educated males.

But it's not our literary forebears we're arguing about. It's our performance and our own individual working methods. I don't recall exactly what sparks our argument. Perhaps it's trying to set a time for our next rehearsal or some pages of writing I've given Alexs or pages he hasn't written. But one topic leads to another and it's all spilling out: Alexs is angry because he feels I'm always trying to control things. I'll decide to write on a topic before telling him, he says. Or if I do tell him, I'll come to our meetings with ten pages written even before he feels we've had a chance to discuss things. When we come to a rehearsal space, I arrive first and take the best chair, the best music stand; I stake out my area of the backstage and the stage even before he's there or has had a chance to settle down. I put the whole script on my computer, I do revisions and do not always consult him first. I print out the scripts on too small a type, one I prefer.

Part of me is puzzled at why Alexs is so angry. I'm always there on time, I'm always waiting for him. Sometimes I wait so long I wonder if he's going to show up at all. I write what I'm supposed to write and have to wait to see if he's going to write anything in response. I've done all the paperwork for our grants, I've written them and had to badger him for things like his bio. I don't notice whether I'm taking the best chair or music stand. I just arrive before him and take what I see. I have to put my stuff down somewhere, I have to sit somewhere on the stage. The script has to be on someone's computer, and why isn't he grateful I'm at least doing the work to type and arrange his stuff? I'm always waiting for him, for his writing, always in the position of urging him that we've got to get going.

Alexs's tone is louder, angrier than mine. Mine is exasperated, frustrated. I can't argue with what he's charging me with doing, just his interpretation of it. In other situations, I myself am often the late one, so how can I be angry at something I expect others to forgive in me? At the same time, I try to tell myself I've seen him angrier, such as the time he blasted back at a white stage tech. I'm on safer ground than the white tech. Still, it's not like I'm Black. Even though I learned through therapy the value of honest arguments, I'm worried where this might lead. There's the risk that the whole project may blow apart, that he'll just decide the differences between us are just too difficult. Or even worse—that those differences are due to something racist in me.

This is hardly the vision we started this piece with. For about a year we'd been talking about doing a performance piece together; then the Rodney King decision went down and the L.A. insurrection erupted. In terms of Asians, all you saw on television were images of Korean store owners and local Blacks in conflict, shooting at each other, or one side defending their stores and the other looting them. Alexs and I believed that if we simply just sat on the stage, as friends, and conversed, that would be a revolutionary image. Where else would people see an African American man and an Asian American man working together?

So why were we fighting now? Was it personality? Was it race? What was going on between us?

Therapy and conversations with my wife had taught me it's best to get down to the basics of your fears and feelings. At a certain point, I threw up my hands and said to Alexs, "I just want to know that you care about me."

He looked at me, surprise in his face, and said, "Of course I care about you. I wouldn't be doing this show if I didn't. I wouldn't be out here in this damn cold talking with you like this!"

Some part of me wanted to say, "But you don't show it." But I knew it was enough to take him at his word. Still, I also felt scared. I felt Alexs had a more forceful manner than me, was more willing to argue and engage in conflict. Like Rodney King, part of me kept wanting to say, "Can't we all just get along?" But Rodney King's plea implied that we should simply stop talking about the difficult things that pulled us apart; it was a general message meant for a city. Alexs and I weren't a city of strangers, we were friends already. Part of me sensed we had now moved things to another level, that I should follow where our words were leading us. Our mutual admissions of affection, though each in his own style, had changed the atmosphere between us. Perhaps I needed those admissions to be stated out loud in a way Alexs didn't.

I don't remember who took the next leap. I think Alexs said something about his feeling like I was acting like a stereotypical Asian. He implied I was like the theater version of the Asian nerd—always on time, always prepared, always doing more than anybody else. It made him feel uneasy. He just didn't work like that.

If a white friend had said something like this, I might have been angry or at least reacted more guardedly. But I placed Alexs's remarks in the context of what I knew about his own battles with stereotypes; I knew he hadn't said this as an insult. It was an admission, a revelation of what had been really going on inside him.

When I first thought about what he said, though, I didn't quite realize all these implications; I simply felt them. So I told him I worked like that not because I was trying to outdo him, but because that was simply the way I worked.

"Yeah," he said, "but I don't work that way. I just think about things in my head."

I said I worried about getting things done on time. Then I paused. Suddenly I realized something, something I don't think I would have reached if Alexs hadn't admitted the way the stereotypes of Asians had entered into his thinking.

"Besides," I said, "I feel like I'm always behind."

"That's the way I feel," Alexs replied. I sensed he was referring to the number of pages each of us had written.

"But I feel I'm always behind because I feel you know more about race than I do," I said. "I'm just catching up. I've been going around for years thinking that I was white. You've been dealing with this stuff and thinking about it a lot longer than I have. I feel like I've got to run as fast as I can to catch up, and even if I do, I'll never catch up."

We went on like this a while longer, through the conception of the piece, through the writing of the grants, the doling out of the script. Gradually it dawned on me: in certain ways, I told Alexs, each of us thought of the other in stereotypical terms—the nerd Asian, the loafing Black.

Just as important, each of us thought the other held more power and feared the other was taking control and feared they were being left behind. We both thought we were dealing from positions of weakness.

But now, each of us had come to see our differences were just that—differences. And they were actually what made us such a formidable team—if we could work together, if we could trust each other, if we could see the value in the way the other was working, if we could accept the other.

Neither of us had more power. Or—we both did.

Later I realized: Alexs and I could never have become such good friends, could never have had this argument, if I had not had arguments with white friends, if I had not broken off certain white friendships, if I had not shown myself willing to let certain white friendships go down over my beliefs about race. He knew about my argument with my white female writer friend about things like job prospects and race, and he knew that those arguments had been reenacted in various ways with other white artist friends, generally with the same results—the end of the friendship. Indeed, at one point, he had even met with three of my white women friends that he knew to try to explain to them my new racial positions. If he hadn't seen me go through all that, if he hadn't seen that I was willing to pay the price, he would never have trusted me enough to have that argument in the snow with me; he would never have been that open and vulnerable; he would never have believed I was someone who would, as he put it, "have his back."

III

During the late eighties, I found myself sitting on more and more multiracial panels and readings for audiences of color, and I was becoming friends with more artists of color. I began to see how what appeared to threaten white artists and audiences in my writing seemed to affirm and energize artists and audiences of color. As I began to speak about white shame over the issue of race or how racism is based on a system of unequal distribution of power, I was sometimes faced with incomprehension or even anger on the part of white audience members. I would be speaking at, say, a small liberal arts college with 3 percent Black students, one Filipino faculty member, and no Black faculty, and people would tell me, *There was no racism in their town or campus.* (Eventually, at such remarks I would say, "Don't you think if this was the one place in America with no racism, people of color would be lining up to come live here?")

At the same time, Blacks in the audience would come up afterwards and embrace me or shake my hand, thank me for what I said, and speak somewhat bitterly of white denial. It seemed I was being presented with a choice about whom I would speak to, about where I was moving along the color line.

At a certain point, I wrote an article for *Mother Jones* on my breakup with a white male friend, a breakup that started with the *Miss Saigon* controversy. We had argued about the casting of a white actor in the role of a Eurasian and about the Orientalist stereotypes in the plot of the musical. This led to more general arguments on race. One crucial sticking point was that he could not accept my insistence that I knew more about race than he did, that we didn't start there on equal grounds.

This breakup was a landmark event for me. I knew my white friend loved me, I knew it pained him to end the relationship. But I felt that he would rather have given up the friendship than his beliefs about race; these beliefs involved not just *Miss Saigon* but the way he viewed his place and my place in the world.

As this breakup occurred, many of my white artist friends—most were his friends too—were puzzled by it; they wanted to read it in light of personality or character differences. These friends were scared by my increasing anger about race and felt uneasy with talking to me about the subject. And yet, unlike a couple of nonartist white friends, these artist friends seemed unable or unwilling to avoid the subject or let it go. I soon found myself in arguments with other mutual white friends, like the argument with the white woman poet I described earlier. Gradually, as with this white woman poet, I found myself spending less and less time with these white friends.

Later, when my article was published in *Mother Jones*, many mutual friends were outraged at what they took for a breach of privacy (though I didn't use any actual names); they saw my article as an act of betrayal and a mean-spirited attack. I received letters asking me if I'd become "a racial separatist" or if I couldn't have white friends any longer. There was speculation I was going to leave my white wife. One friend wrote she wasn't looking for a "guru" on race. Another quoted Wendell Berry who said the reward for destroying community was power. I pointed out that Berry was referring to huge agricultural corporations displacing family farms and not one Japanese American writer arguing about race in a community of white writers. When my name came up as a suggested hire at a local university, my article was cited as a negative against me; so was my appearance: "He dresses too well to be a minority." I found myself eliminated from an editorial board I'd been on, and somehow was never asked to write for the publication again.[4] When my friend the writer Garrett Hongo was at a literary conference in another Midwestern state, a white Minnesotan writer whom I didn't know spoke of me as a dangerous and unscrupulous person because of my article. "They're talking about you, disparaging you," Garrett said. "You should be aware of that."

A change in consciousness is hard to map with precision. I can't recall exactly when I began to feel more comfortable with a group of Black artists than a group of white artists. But as many of my friendships with white friends began to unravel, I found that the person who could best explain my own process and feelings, who was the most supportive of my efforts to see myself as a person of color, who seemed to intuitively understand the anger and rage I was feeling was my Black writer friend Alexs Pate.

In a way, in my own naivete and racism, I was somewhat shocked by this. Alexs was someone I was just becoming close to, yet he understood what I was going through during these breakups with white friends better than my white wife did. Moreover, his understanding of race was so far superior to mine or any of my white friends, and I began to realize, with a certain feeling of shame, that I had underestimated him and his artistry. Soon I realized that Alexs was in many ways much more qualified to help me through what I'd been experiencing than

4 My being jettisoned from the review came despite the fact that C. K. Williams said he and his editor felt my review of his book was the most incisive they had seen, and I'd heard something similar from Frank Bidart about my review of his work. But after I was let go from the review, I rarely wrote reviews again. I just didn't have it in me to keep trying to carve a spot for myself in a space where I would constantly be fighting the guardians of Whiteness. My experience of discouragement mirrors that of many BIPOC writers. Ironically, it was the editor of the review who brandished my article in *Mother Jones* to my circle of white friends, sounding the alarm like a supremacist Paul Revere—"The gooks are coming!" (This is a tad unfair, but, hey, I like the joke.)

any white therapist. I then realized that he was smarter than I thought he was.

And then it hit me: the reason I hadn't seen all this was my own racism.

I thought, *If I held that much racism inside and I was another person of color, the strains of racism in our society went far deeper than I thought.*

Obviously, Alexs and I could not have reached another level of intimacy if I hadn't gone through these realizations, if I hadn't come to terms with my own racism. Nor would he have trusted me enough to open himself to me and to try and help me.

At a certain point Alexs told me that in confronting racism I needed to establish a base at which I thought my being and integrity were being threatened. There are conditions under which it's better to die than to continue living. But if you are not suffering these conditions, you need to negotiate your way through the difficulties that confront you; you need to rest; you need to know when it's time to fight and when to walk away.

He spoke of a Black friend in the Navy who had been sprayed with a hose by a white petty officer. The friend lost his temper and smashed the officer in the head with a wrench.

"I went to visit him in the brig," said Alexs, "and when I asked why he didn't think about the consequences, he said, 'That's something you can do—maybe it's because you have the abilities to do something with yourself. You see a future, but whatever the reason, it's something I can't do. I couldn't hold back.' That whole incident taught me something about survival."

Alexs recalled how a Writers-in-the-Schools arts administrator had recently handed him a schedule for teaching as a writer in a high school. The administrator had constructed a schedule where Alexs was never in the classroom alone; there was always another white writer with him. All the other writers, who were white, had solo classroom appearances. Upon reading the schedule, Alexs chewed out the administrator and left the room, because if he had stayed in the room, there was no telling what he might have done.

The perception of the behavior of Black men in this country is that they're constantly angry. Uncontrollable. Irrational. Indeed, I used to regard Alexs, from a distance, as being a bristly character, someone with a chip on his shoulder. But as we became more intimate, I began to glimpse the enormous amount of anger and insults Alexs had to negotiate through his life, day by day; I learned the history of the racism he had had to fight against in his life, how difficult it had been for him to survive, to not explode in anger or implode in self-destruction. How, for instance, when he was in eighth grade the principal wanted to send him to a vo-tech school, and only his mother coming in and protesting got Alexs sent to an almost all-white mainly Jewish school across the city. At the first assembly, the principal of the new school said, "This would be a great school except for the lousy 3 percent." Alexs looked around—3 percent of the students were Black. Such insults didn't stop in the Navy or in the corporate world or in his life as an artist. And so I realized with what grace and equanimity, with what quiet resolve he went about his life. Alexs, his actions, made sense to me now; I saw a rationality and justification for aspects of his behavior that I didn't understand before.

On a broader level I began to see how much I had been taught not to look at African Americans as individuals, how little my experience or the culture had equipped me to understand their place and history in America, how little I knew of the ways Black people think about themselves or whites. Instead, I was taught to dehumanize them, and this dehumanization had played itself out not only in my conceptualization of race but in my perception of artistic, intellectual, and spiritual matters as well.

In other words, my reevaluation of Alexs's abilities and character paralleled a process I'd been undergoing in terms of aesthetic standards and the traditional canon: I'd come to understand how little of my literary training or my immersion in mainstream culture had prepared me to take an interest in the art of African Americans, much less to understand and evaluate that art or the lives and community it came out of. Similarly, I'd begun to understand more and more how our evaluations of morality in a historical context needed to be filtered through the lens of race. Figures like Malcolm X or the Black Panthers suddenly took on, in retrospect, a more complicated and human form in my mind, and again I realized how deeply I had been influenced by a white vision of what was right and what was wrong. Gradually, I began to reevaluate my own understanding of our country's history.

These days there are things Alexs and I share that have little or nothing to do with race—we're both sports fanatics, for instance. We can go on elaborately about the benefits of the latest Timberwolves trade or their prospects for the upcoming playoffs. We'll talk about what's bothering us in our careers or intimate relationships in a way that's probably more open and fluent with feelings than most men. (As I mentioned above, he's one of the most psychologically astute people I've met.) I'll talk to him about my dealings with my adolescent daughter; he'll talk to me about the breakup of a relationship or the start of a new one—each of us assuring and challenging the other, probing with questions only best friends can ask. If either of us gets down, the other is the first person we'll call.

We're roughly the same age and at the same stage of our careers. We can strategize about our writing or careers or criticize each other's work in a way someone older or younger could not. We both work in multiple genres—poetry, essays, drama, fiction. We're both naturally night owls; we cherish our solitary hours. We're probably both a little too unwilling to ask for anyone's help, to seek a mentor. We don't like to be beholden. If someone thinks that means we have chips on shoulders, so be it. And those chips on our shoulders—we're both facing a literary world where the gatekeepers are almost entirely white and don't want to hear about race or our racial anger. In contrast, I feel safe to express with Alexs an anger about racial matters openly, and I know he feels the same with me.

IV

A few years ago, a Japanese American I know was teaching a multicultural literature course. When the course got to the writings of Asian Americans like Janice Mirikitani and Frank Chin, many whites in the class became upset at the anger of the Asian American authors. The Japanese American teacher replied, "We've been reading people like Amiri Baraka and Nikki Giovanni, and you weren't as upset by their anger." As the class continued to talk, the students revealed that they didn't expect Asian Americans to be angry; after all, they've been treated so well.

For many years, I lived an unconscious life that constantly tried to repress anything in my experience related to race; the white friends I had then were comfortable with that repression. When I started to break down that repression, I had to look not only at my identity but also at their identity, at the ways they were comfortable with that repression and what that told me about the way they saw me, about what they meant when they said they loved me. (After all, Scarlett loved Mammy, and where did that get Mammy?)

With other whites with whom I am still friends, I now recognize a zone of intimacy I do not cross, certain feelings I choose not to talk about. I avoid bringing up my racial anger in ways that I would naturally do with friends of color. Nor do I feel that if some particularly ugly or difficult issue or incident came up I could count on these white friends to back me up. Like many Asian Americans who subscribe to the model minority myth, I believed that if I worked hard and produced work with quality, all would be fine, I would be accepted as an equal.[5] But my experiences with arts organizations, judging panels, writing programs, and universities—most English departments look no different from Marge Schott's Cincinnati Reds front office—have shown me this is not so.

Still, my wife and Alexs have told me that what I have yet to do is write about what I loved in the friends I have lost; what I miss from those circles or art or pleasures I no longer feel can engage me; what has hurt so much in this transition I am still making. But to me, it feels too difficult and bewildering to do this; some part of me doesn't see the point of it. I think about the white friends I have lost often, though not so constantly as before. They appear to me in dreams as awkward, sometimes invasive, presences. Occasionally, I see them when I'm out in public, and we smile politely. Some part of me still wants their approval, wants their love. The ache of distance does not go away.

The other day I saw a former white friend in a local bookstore and smiled hello. He came up and shook my hand. It was an awkward yet open gesture, which I did not know how to take. We said nothing more. He was having lunch with another former friend. I did not sense any acrimony in him, though I felt some, along with a renewed sense of pain. Though I had no concrete proof of this, I felt that what had

5 Even today, I am constantly chagrined with how on an emotional level something inside me still wants to believe this.

happened between us had had many more repercussions for me than for him.

There is a great bitterness in me. And anger. Jealousy perhaps—of their continued sense of community and the advantages, professional and personal, that community provides my former white friends. None of what I've written here means they aren't good, caring people who have given to others. Part of me feels that the reason they are no longer in my life is a mystery, a bad dream. But more deeply, I know this severance was necessary. That I have still more difficult choices ahead.

As for Alexs and me, we continue to work and perform together. We call each other up late at night and talk, go out for dinners at a local Italian restaurant where we hash over reviews of our books, our individual writing projects, criticize each other's work, and plan new co-productions. Occasionally we go to a Timberwolves game or go golfing together, an image that amuses our mutual friends: two middle-aged men of color, one Asian with a pony tail, one Black with dreads, playing what Alexs—and myself—have called the White Man's game.[6]

Both of us spend time meeting and mentoring young writers of color, attending a spoken word scene where Asian Americans and African Americans mix and perform together before mixed-race audiences, audiences Alexs and I did not experience when younger. A few weeks ago, in a tribute series arranged by younger writers of color, I was honored by both local Black and Asian American writers for my work in the community, my writing, and my teaching. Alexs spoke about some of the trials I've gone through, and he tried to set a historical context for the younger writers. I felt both protected and loved.

I never see my former white writer friends at the literary events I go to; their scene is older, still as white, and more suburban than urban. What all this means for the state of race in America I don't know.

Alexs always tells me our time is coming, our audience is coming. I try to believe him. We're older now, calmer, perhaps more focused on our own particular work. We don't do hip-hop or rap or even

6 But of course, this was written before Tiger, that Afro-Asian American superstar.

participate regularly in the spoken word scene. We're the elders, though Alexs sometimes bridles and wants to shun this role: "I refuse to be put out to pasture like that. When they start calling you an elder, that just means the younger writers are saying, 'Hey, old man, why don't you shuffle off the stage?'"

Still, he's the one who carries reading glasses that I borrow to read the menu in the dimly lit upscale Italian restaurant where we usually meet. When I hand his glasses back, he always chides me about my vanity: "You ought to get your own glasses." I counter that at least I'm honest to people about my age. He laughs and tells me his age is no one else's damn business. Then I ask him what he's going to order.

More often than not, we share an appetizer, usually calamari. When the waiter comes up, I know Alexs is going to explain he's lactose intolerant, he wants this pasta or pizza or other dish but without cheese. Alexs knows I'm going to order some big hunk of meat, and that later, when we're handed the dessert menus, I'll ask for his reading glasses once again.

This essay was published in the anthology Some of My Best Friends: Writings on Interracial Relationships, *almost ten years after my breakup with white writer and artist friends over* Miss Saigon *and my* Mother Jones *article.*

Slowly, This

In 1993, the African American novelist Alexs Pate and I were shooting a small film, *Slowly This,* in Manhattan for the PBS Series *Alive TV.* We were working with the visual artist and director Arthur Jaffa, who was the cinematographer for Julie Dash's groundbreaking *Daughters of the Dust* and Spike Lee's *Crooklyn.* We were still working out the script with A.J., and we were basing it in part on a performance piece Alexs and I had done in the Twin Cities, *Secret Colors.*

That piece centered on the 1991 beating of Rodney King by the police and the subsequent violence that occurred in L.A. after two officers, Stacey Koon and Laurence Powell, were acquitted of assault and use of excessive force. Koon and Powell and other officers had surrounded King outside his car after King had been stopped for speeding, and they repeatedly beat him with their police batons as he knelt on the pavement.

Ordinarily, the King beating would have been just another unknown incident where police were never charged with unnecessary violence or violating protocol. The beating took place in 1991, well before the omnipresence of cell phone videos. But it so happened that a white man with a video camera had peered out his window and saw the police gathered around King; this white man videotaped the police beating King with nightsticks for a minute and a half, even though King was on the ground on his knees. Normally, it would have been the word of King against the police officers and no charges would have been filed. It was the chance video that raised this case to citywide and national attention.

But beside the issue of police brutality and racism against Blacks, there was another reason Alexs and I created the show. One of the key strains of that subsequent violence in L.A. involved Korean store owners and the African Americans of their neighborhood. Shots of the so-called L.A. riots or insurrection on the national news almost always included clips of Korean store owners standing in front of their stores with guns pointed at potential African and Latino American looters. Previous to these events, Alexs and I had long been talking about doing a collaboration; after the L.A. events, we thought we could offer ways of aligning the struggles of African Americans and Asian Americans in terms people had not considered.

As part of our piece, we included material on Soon Ja Du, a Korean store owner who had gotten into an argument with a Black teenaged customer, Latasha Harlins. In a store video played at Du's trial, Harlins is standing in the back of the store and she places a carton of orange juice in her backpack. As Harlins approaches the counter, Du seems to charge Harlins with trying to shoplift the orange juice. Du and Harlins argue; they grapple with each other and then they each grab at a chair Du has raised above the counter, perhaps to use as a weapon. Harlins throws change down on the counter. As she turns and walks away, Du takes out a gun and shoots Harlins.

Du received a sentence of probation and served no jail time for killing Harlins. This decision occurred in the time period before the Rodney King decision, and it was part of the African American community's reaction to the King trial of two policemen charged with undue force and then acquitted.[1]

Ironically, Du's light sentence mirrors the case of two white out-of-work Detroit auto workers, Ronald Ebens and Michael Nitz, who,

1 A Black writer friend gave me this account of the resentment toward the Korean store owners: "Listen, say I went to Korea and opened a shop. Let's say they let me do that, which I have some doubts about. Of course, I'd learn the language. I'd learn the customs. I wouldn't sit there and play the ugly American and expect my Korean customers to act the way I did. Because that's just not cool, that's just not cool. And where did you learn about Blacks in Korea? From American movies, right? And all you saw were crooks and rapists and dope fiends. You didn't see any Blacks like me, teaching in a university, did you? And I bet now that you're here, you and your father have white friends, don't you? But does your father have a single Black friend? And yet, he's there in our neighborhood making a living off of us. And he won't even make friends with us. I don't care if he's scared, I don't care if it's hard for him. He's making a living in our neighborhood. He's got to look at us as more than customers or robbers. He's got to make an effort."

angered by the influx of Japanese autos, beat Vincent Chin to death with baseball bats in 1982. That Chin was American and of Chinese ethnicity and not Japanese did not matter to them. Ebens and Nitz served no jail time but were given three years' probation and a $3,000 fine. Explaining this sentence, Judge Charles Kaufman proclaimed that Ebens and Nitz "weren't the kind of men you send to jail. . . . You don't make the punishment fit the crime; you make the punishment fit the criminal." So much for equal justice. So much for equal value for the life of each citizen.

In retrospect, I see now that our piece failed to present adequately the experience of the Korean L.A. community and that failure falls on me. As Professor Elaine Kim points out in the documentary she coproduced, *Sa-I-Gu,* the same clip of Korean store owners wielding guns was used over and over, as if that clip was all that was needed to characterize the response of the Korean community to the events in L.A. Kim maintains that the use of this clip implied that all the Korean store owners cared about was their property and that they were not concerned about human life or the community around them.

During the L.A. riots, the police moved to protect the lives and property in the more wealthy, white sections of L.A., but did little to protect the lives and property of the Korean community. At the same time, the Korean community was harmed by a violence and conflict that arose out of racism against Blacks, particularly in the justice system. The Korean community did not originate this racism or the workings of the justice system, but they suffered far greater damages than the white inhabitants of L.A., who were protected by this system. And yet the views of the Korean community and what that community suffered were markedly absent from the news, as it was in our piece. In that, I was as guilty as the news media in absenting the narratives of the Korean community.[2]

In New York City, as we prepared to film, A.J. was moving us away slightly from the more politically focused issues of Alexs's and my

2 After the riots, there began to be more dialogues between the Korean American and African American communities in L.A.

performance piece. Instead, he was conceiving the film as a sort of interracial version of *My Dinner with Andre,* where Alexs and I would talk about our friendship and our lives as men of color in a Manhattan restaurant. In the movie, the restaurant where we entered would be filled at first with white patrons, then with Black patrons, including friends of A.J., such as essayist bell hooks and filmmaker Isaac Julien, and then with Asian American patrons, including the Filipino American writer Jessica Hagedorn. The conversation between Alexs and I was centered more on our friendship and lives as men of color than on the events in L.A. related to the Rodney King beating.

One of the things that got put into the film was an incident that occurred the first day after Alexs and I had arrived in New York. We were waiting outside our hotel, trying to flag a cab on an east-west side street. No cabs came down the street for a few minutes, and I suggested we walk up to Broadway to hail a cab. Alexs turned to me: "Okay, maybe because I'm with you, we can get a cab. But I'm a Black man with dreads. I stand here in front of the hotel because then the cab driver will think I stayed at the hotel overnight and so he can pick me up. But otherwise, because I'm a Black man with dreads, no cab driver will stop for me. That's why I stand here."

Immediately, when Alexs said this, my mind went back to a night we spent together a few weeks earlier. Alex and I were in a Twin Cities bar with a Black theater director, a Black television script writer, a Black actor, and a Black visual artist. At one point in the evening the five Black men started in on a talk about being arrested DWB—Driving While Black.

I don't think the five Black men would have launched into the conversation in the same way if a white man were at the table, and I think the other four might have hesitated a bit if they hadn't known that Alexs and I were good friends and that my political awareness of Black issues was in part vouched for by our friendship and our working together on our performance. So as they proceeded, I had the sense of being granted a privileged glimpse into their sense of being Black men in America as they each discussed the times they had been arrested driving while Black.

The first thing that struck me was that they treated their DWB arrests as something absolutely expected, almost a rite of passage; it was not a trauma they could escape; it was their fate as Black men in America. The second thing was that although they were clearly angered by their arrests, much of their talk was laced with humor, with a sense of irony and a slight self-mocking of their own personal reactions to being arrested—as if they knew their personal feelings were nothing to the justice system that had ensnared them—and the inevitability of the ensnarement; as if they recognized that their being successful Black male middle-class artists did not prevent them from sharing the same fate as working-class Black males. They might tell themselves they were successful and there was certainly a truth in that, a truth they had worked hard to earn, but they were still Black men in America and no different from their brethren. Their success and hard work and even their lives could be taken away in an instant for no justifiable reason. That was a truth they ignored at their peril, and their joking was in part to remind themselves of that fact.

My guess is their humor about DWB was not something these Black male artists would have so revealed had a white person been at the table, particularly a white man. Even if the white man did not counter with his belief that America is not as racist as their experiences belied, these Black men would have worried that the white man would not have sensed the pain and anger behind the humor or the seriousness with which each day they had to face the potential threat of ill-treatment, injustice, or even death in interactions with the police. I think they would have feared, as Dave Chappelle has, that the white listener would not be laughing at their jokes for the same reason that they as Black men were laughing. In contrast, my status as an Asian American didn't necessarily mean that I would completely understand the grounding of their humor, or the ironies and self-ironies it contained, but they also didn't see me as someone who had ties to the powers of white privilege, who created the systemic racism they had to endure.

But what I was most struck with in dealing with Alexs's fears about getting a cab or the fears he and these other Black artists felt in dealing with the police was that in superficial ways I was just like these four Black men who all had college degrees, awards for their art, and were living middle-class artistic lives. We were all men of color. But clearly, I didn't share their fears. As an Asian American I could get a cab in New

York City and so never had to think of why my friend Alexs would only hail a cab in front of a hotel. Certainly, I didn't look at being arrested while driving as an Asian as an inevitable fate or even something I had to worry about. It was not a reality I shared with these Black colleagues; it was not a reality I thought of daily. It was my privilege as a middle-class Asian American not to have to think about these things.

And that was why I had to learn and think about these things. I could not live just inside the bubble of my own concerns or those of Asian Americans. I had these friends and colleagues, these fellow community members who were facing injustices I did not have to face. I had a responsibility to be aware of this and to educate myself as much as possible in what I did not learn growing up, in what I had not experienced because I was Asian American and not African American. Contrary to the ways I had been educated in the ideology of Whiteness, I had to investigate and learn about race in America in a deeper and more thoughtful and active way.

And the more I found out, the angrier I got.[3]

It was around this time that I adopted a rule, a position of epistemic humility, which I had already begun to adopt with women: whenever a person of color said something regarding race that I didn't understand or agree with, I did not argue with them. Instead, I asked them more questions. I assumed that the problem might be my ignorance

3 In 2016, the dangers of Driving While Black came for Philando Castile, who was murdered by a policeman about three miles from my home, on a road I travel frequently. As I began to write about his murder, it became clear to me that to understand what happened to him and why it happened, I had to investigate our racial history in a deeper way, and I began a series of essays that became my most recent book, *The Stories Whiteness Tells Itself: Racial Myths and Our American Narratives.* I had handed in what I thought would be the complete manuscript to my editor when George Floyd was murdered, also a few miles from my home. I then joined with Black writer Carolyn Holbrook to edit an anthology of Minnesota BIPOC writers, *We Are Meant to Rise: Voices for Justice from Minneapolis to the World.* Many of the essays in that book focused on Floyd's murder and the demonstrations that ensued, including an essay by my daughter Samantha. The title of that anthology comes from a phrase in Alexs Pate's essay on the demonstrations.

or my lack of a proper framework to understand them.[4] My friendship with Alexs taught me that. At a certain point in our friendship, Alexs acknowledged to me that our relationship had helped him realize that retiring some of his anger was better for him and the people close to him. My anger allowed him to give some of it to me or to let some of his go, because there were now two people fighting on the same issue.

And so, near the end of our film, Alexs says to me, "You developed anger [about racial issues]. You didn't have that anger before. And the development of your anger led me to feel I could let go of some of mine. I didn't have to carry it all the time, because you were carrying it. And in some ways, you can fight in ways I can't. They don't always see you coming. You're like a southpaw. You're swinging from a new direction."[5]

4 Neither the patriarchy nor Whiteness encourage epistemic humility—the ability to say "I don't know"—since both the patriarchy and Whiteness are supposedly all-knowing and infallible.

5 In the years since, Alexs and I have worked together in various ways, from doing readings and panels together to my working as a trainer and director of training for his Innocent Classroom, a program designed to help K-12 teachers improve their relationships with BIPOC students. He married a Korean adoptee and scholar, SooJin Pate (they've since divorced), and their daughter Sxela Pate, like my children, is of mixed heritage, Korean and African American.

The Asian American Renaissance

> How could I tell my parents that I loved reading Jane Austen and the Romantics? That I had discovered Asian American literature, which had saved me because it showed me that a writer could look like me, and that I could look like a writer? How could I say that as a writer, while I was still an other to many, even to myself, I could also find a voice in literature to assert my self?
>
> –Viet Thanh Nguyen, *To Save and to Destroy: Writing as an Other*

By 1992, I'd published one book of poetry, *After We Lost Our Way*, which won the National Poetry Contest, and a memoir, *Turning Japanese*, which had appeared with three other books on the cover of the *New York Times*. Jay McInerney, author of the coke-fueled yuppie best-seller *Bright Lights, Big City*, wrote the review, and not because he knew anything about Asian Americans but because he'd lived for a while in Japan. In fact, the *Times* editor, who liked my book, asked McInerney to reconsider his review because the editor felt it was a bit too negative. McInerney belonged to a literary world I sensed I'd never belong to, the cool young white writers, the *Paris Review* crowd. But after that review, *Turning Japanese* was widely reviewed and praised in publications all across the country; it seemed my career was launched.

In retrospect, I see now that a deep change occurred in me when I started doing readings on the West Coast and in Hawaii and began to meet other Asian American artists. In L.A., someone told me this Japanese American playwright, Philip Kan Gotanda, was doing a reading of his play *Fish Head Soup* at the Mark Taper Two. And so I met Philip and the Japanese American actor Lane Nishikawa, who'd done a performance piece on his JA identity—*"Saturday Night, J-Town, Positive Ions in the Air!"*[1] After the reading I pondered why I'd never thought of writing a play, and I realized I'd never seen Asian American actors on stage in an Asian American play. I had to see that possibility before I could imagine doing so myself. Now I knew there were Asian American actors I could write for, who needed such plays. This eventually led to my writing plays and performance pieces, including the one I created with the novelist Alexs Pate on the Rodney King decision and an adaptation of the poet Li-Young Lee's memoir, *The Wing Seed.*

In San Francisco, late one night in a bar near J-Town, I conversed with the actors Marc Hayashi and Kelvin Han Yee. In the middle of our conversation, another Asian American actor, Greg Watanabe, breezed in and said he'd just been wowed by Margaret Cho's set down the block at a comedy club. I'd seen Marc as a cab driver in Wayne Wang's first film, *Chan Is Missing,* which had inspired Spike Lee. (If this Asian American cat can do a feature film for $70,000, Spike thought, so can I.) It was Marc, a tall, handsome, mustached JA, who told me, "Every culture needs its eunuchs and we're it. Asian American men are the eunuchs of America."

A few years later Marc would play an Okinawan thug in *Karate Kid Part II*—he had that type of body and presence—but eventually he retreated from acting in part because of the lack of opportunities. But it was also because he came to feel that playing white characters in plays like *Death of a Salesman* in regional theaters made him confused and a bit crazy. When he told me this, I replied, "If playing white on stage made you feel crazy, think how crazy I was when I wanted to think I was white in real life." Marc talked to me about his younger days, running with other wild rebellious JA's, sometimes armed with guns, like a Sansei street gang: "Man, we ran the city. No one, no one fucked with us! There was this one kid, he should have gone on to become an engineer or dentist or something like that, he went absolutely nuts." As a nice JA boy from the white suburbs, I could barely imagine that. It wasn't just the violence or guns Marc was referencing, but the bravado

1 Later Lane would go on to make a film, *Only the Brave,* about the famed 442nd JA regiment.

and braggadocio that seemed part of his persona—no quiet JA modesty for him.

Marc said that in San Francisco he grew up with whites who may not have liked Asians but understood they were part of the city, a force to be reckoned with. He described how, when he first went out East and was walking in New York, he'd be striding in a direct line with a white guy and Marc wouldn't veer and they'd bump up against each other because the white guy consciously or unconsciously thought this Asian dude would be the one to move aside to let the white guy pass. That never happened to Marc in Frisco; the white guys there knew they couldn't count on him to step aside. Yes, I thought, all the unconscious rules and assumptions of Whiteness. But also I thought: I'm like that too; when I see a white guy walking straight in my line, I don't move aside. I'm not going to defer to him (which I suppose makes me kin to Dostoyevsky's Underground Man).

Kelvin was a bit rougher in looks than Marc, wider, squarer in shape and sporting a crew cut; even more than Marc, he carried himself like a kid from the streets, which was what he was when he wandered as a teenager into an Asian American Theater Company rehearsal. And yet even though he grew up more working class than Marc, Kelvin seemed less troubled and more concentrated on his craft. In my eyes, Kelvin eventually became a Chinese American Larry Fishburne, a not quite typically handsome actor, slightly pockmarked and rough-hewn like Fishburne, but with great and diverse chops—a cat who can play Shakespeare but also a cop or a Koreatown gang boss or more recently, in *May December*, a Korean immigrant father.

In his first film, Kelvin played the son in *A Great Wall,* where a Chinese American father hits the glass ceiling as an engineer, quits his job, and goes back to Beijing to visit relatives. At the start of the film, Kelvin first appears in his bedroom lying in bed with his white girlfriend under a poster of the great 49ers quarterback Joe Montana. I thought of Kelvin as the first Asian American actor I'd seen playing a character that was like the Asian Americans of our generation. I told him that he projected a sense of athleticism playing in a Ping-Pong tournament in the film, and even more striking, he carried himself with a sexual presence. I asked if there were other Asian American actors with such a presence, and he replied something like, "You can't represent what's not there in the culture yet."

Later I met the poet-activist Janice Mirikitani, who had done readings with Thulani Davis, Jessica Hagedorn, and Ntozake Shange—the seeding ground for the latter's *For Colored Girls. . . .* Janice was beginning to write on sexual abuse in the Japanese American community, a topic that had yet to be broached. With her Black pastor husband, Cecil Williams, she had served the indigent and homeless of the Tenderloin district through their Glide Memorial Church, and she was one of the first Asian American activists that I met. I also connected with Brenda Wong Aoki, the Japanese-Chinese American actress and performance artist and her husband, the jazz bassist Mark Izu, the sax player Francis Wong, and the Chinese American pianist Jon Jang. (Eventually Jon, Kelvin, and I would do a performance piece on Asian American men.) Brenda would soon create and later bring to the Twin Cities her one-woman performance piece narrating how in high school she started dating a member of a Samoan gang, a move that launched her into a very different life story from the one charted out by her family or the model minority myth.

At one point, I traveled to Hawaii to give readings, including one in Hilo where I read to an all–Japanese American audience, many of them older. Facing them, I realized I didn't have to give historical explanations or footnotes for my poems. Instead, it was like reading to my aunts and uncles. I felt my poems landing with a resonance and acceptance I'd never experienced before, as if I were an honorary member of their community. Indeed, in the Q&A afterwards, the audience felt even more familial and embracing.

And there on the Big Island where he'd spent his first six years and where his family had lived for four generations, I met the Japanese American poet and memoirist Garrett Hongo. As anyone who encounters Garrett knows, he can be intimidating: he's got first-rate literary and intellectual chops, but he carries himself like an inner-city kid of color, like the ex–nose guard he is, and he moves through the world as someone who won't be taken by surprise, who will throw the first punch if he senses a fight is coming—literary, political, or physical. Unlike me who grew up in a white suburb of Chicago, Garrett grew up in Gardena and multiracial L.A., and he went to a high school with Blacks, Chicanos, whites, and Japanese Americans. (Gardena sports the highest concentration of JAs on the mainland.) In his teen years, he'd formed a singing group with fellow African American students; he'd gone to Chicano dances with his Portuguese American girlfriend; he'd also been beaten up by a gang of Sansei for dating outside his race. In terms of Garrett's later becoming a writer, the African American novelist Ishmael Reed and the critic Stanley Crouch, both later MacArthur Genius fellows, became Garrett's mentors when he was a sophomore in high school.

Just before the school year ended, a fellow Black student said to Garrett, "Hongo, you're interested in poetry, right? There's this poet Ishmael Reed who's doing a summer poetry class in Watts." So that summer Garrett took the hour-long bus ride to Watts, and although the workshop was obviously meant for young Blacks from the neighborhood, Reed welcomed Garrett in. Then one day Reed announced, "Tomorrow we're going to see a play by a Caribbean brother," and he brought Garrett and the workshop to Derek Walcott's *Dream on Monkey Mountain* at a Taper Forum matinee. Afterwards, lying on a bench outside the Taper, trying to take in what he'd just witnessed, Garrett felt stunned by the connections he'd sensed between Walcott's island creole and the island pidgin Garrett had grown up with, the possibility that his pidgin and ethnic culture could be part of literature.

One day Garrett walked into a café where Stanley Crouch was holding court on jazz, literature, and politics; when Garrett crept closer, Crouch, like Reed, waved him into the circle. I've often thought about Garrett's walking through that threshold into a group of older Black men—a move some of his fellow Sansei wouldn't think of making—and, conversely, of Crouch beckoning him in and thus coming to shape Garrett's own multiethnic, multiracial artistic journey. (Crouch would later mentor Garrett at Pomona College.) Both the novelist/poet Reed and the critic Crouch brought a combustive combative style to their artistic and political joustings (*Writin' Is Fightin'* is one of Reed's titles), and Garrett picked up on this. Later, in grad school Garrett learned a quieter literary approach through the great Black poet Robert Hayden. But many in the academy still don't know what to do with Garrett's mix of the high literary and intellectual with the street juking style of Reed and Crouch and Garrett's own urban argot and Hawaiian patois.

In a way, when Garrett and I first met at a sushi dinner before my reading, I myself felt a little off balance and didn't quite know what to make of him—or, rather, I worried about what he made of me. For one thing, in addition to having traveled to Japan and taken graduate courses in Japanese, he seemed much more knowledgeable of Japanese American culture and history, and this knowledge included both the mainland and Hawai'ian communities. When he was younger, he'd started an Asian American theater company in Seattle, the Asian Exclusion Act, and he had worked with—and then literally fought with—the flame-throwing Chinese American playwright Frank Chin, whose *The Chickencoop Chinaman* was the first Asian American play produced in New York.[2] Garrett had met older Japanese American ac-

2 At the beginning of what could be termed contemporary Asian American literary history, Chin launched a blistering attack on the work of Maxine Hong Kingston, decrying her *Woman Warrior* as fake, kowtowing to the expectations of the white literary world; he charged that she was ignorant of Chinese culture and its traditions. Chin, I believe, was absolutely wrong about Kingston on a literary level—for reasons that have been hashed over by many others—and she was also the superior writer, so there are ways he's been written out of that literary history and relegated to a relatively obscure spot in the Asian American pantheon, especially given how prominent his clash with Kingston was when I first became aware that an actual Asian American literary scene existed. Early on I realized that the feminist critique of Chin's position was fairly obvious. And yet I learned from Chin a great deal about the Japanese American draft resisters—the No-No Boys—in World War II, and I never would have written my novel about the son of a No-No Boy if I hadn't met Chin.

Still, until today I never quite realized that whether one agreed with Chin's literary and political arguments or not, his anger and his rage were palpable to us all; he did not hold back. I once watched him say to a class at the Catholic St. Thomas University in St. Paul, "A Chinese Christian is like a Jewish Nazi." When I was growing up and when I came of age as a literary writer, Asian Americans were not supposed to be angry, and in certain ways it's still like that. But Chin's rage, the freedom he felt to display his rage? I believe that even if one vehemently disagreed with his literary take and cultural analysis, his rage had an effect on almost all of us Asian American writers. It gave us an emotional freedom that many still don't acknowledge partly came from him. (Kingston's complex literary legacy also helped us all, but not much with expressions of anger.) Now my friend Garrett, given how he grew up and who he is, always possessed an angry streak, but Chin also served for a brief period as Garrett's mentor, and the fact that Garrett and Chin would have come to blows at a rehearsal in Seattle if someone hadn't held Garrett back was significant, I believe, to Garrett. It was part

tors like Pat Morita (*The Karate Kid* films), Pat Suzuki (*Flower Drum Song*), Jack Soo (*Flower Drum Song, Valentine's Day*), and Mako, who'd won an Academy Award for his role as a Chinese ship engineer working for Steve McQueen's character in *The Sand Pebbles.* Morita had even hired Garrett to write for his comedy show, mainly staffed by older Jewish writers, but after a short while Morita fired Garrett saying, "You ain't funny, kid. Go write your poetry."

But despite his often truculent stance and superior knowledge of JAs, Garrett somehow took to me, the suburban JA kid. Perhaps this was because he liked my poetry—or perhaps because he was charmed by my wife, Susie, and our young daughter. (Susie told me that when she walked into a local shop in Hilo, she got the *haole* tourist stink eye until the woman behind the counter saw Samantha, her *hapa* daughter.) When he said I brought an intellectual weight to my work and I demurred, he chastised me, saying I was being "disingenuous" (and he has often chastised me since, sometimes calling me a *katonk,* the sound of a hollow coconut, which is what the old-school Hawai'ian Japanese, including members of the 442nd regiment, called the mainland Japanese).

Later, from Garrett's description of me in his memoir, *Volcano,* I learned he was struck by my dressing in a pastel shirt and white silk pants and sportscoat, and he describes me as a dandy (I was dressed for the reading in Hilo). In contrast to categorizing the poet Li-Young Lee as air, Garrett places me as water—not directly resistant, not directly pushing back but slowly seeping in, enduring, not letting up. (Perhaps, I like to think, he was thinking of Bruce Lee's phrase, "Be water, my friend.") Years later, Garrett would tell me how the way I dressed unsettled older white writers like Gary Snyder. (My upscale outfits gave Snyder the "creeps.")[3]

of the way Garrett liberated himself as a writer. And though I was and still am much too much the polite suburban JA boy to physically fight anyone, I see now that Chin's rage gave me permission to find my own racial anger and willingness to fight. In him, I saw an Asian American writer who was not afraid of pissing off either white people or Asians, something I would go on to do in my own ways with my writing.

3 This was not how I was received by older Asian American writers or by the older Black poets Lucille Clifton, Gwendolyn Brooks, and Ishmael Reed, who greeted me as if I were part of their poetic family.

My friendship with Garrett has lasted until the present; it's a friendship that has helped me survive as a writer and made me feel there was another Japanese American writer who understood the literary, historical, political, and cultural antecedents of my work, who acknowledged the complexity of my sources and inspiration and what I am trying to achieve. I think I've done the same for him. Our conversations can range from Langland's *Piers Plowman* or Augustine's *Confessions* to Basho or Mishima to Fredric Jameson or Edward Said or Fanon to Donald Hall or Carolyn Kizer to Wakako Yamauchi or Frank Chin to the 442nd or the No-No Boys to Baldwin or Stanley Crouch to Walcott or Brodsky or Neruda to Milton or Wordsworth to Ai or Ishiguro, Robin Coste Lewis or Viet Thanh Nguyen—and neither of us has to hold back our references, our literary and intellectual chops, our views on race or Asian American issues. In each other's presence, we stop being a racialized Other in America but Asian American writers of the same generation, who share a common literary, historical, and cultural past.

Today, reading what I've written here I realize these were my first meetings with Asian Americans who had decided they weren't going to be good Asian American boys and girls; they weren't going to grow up to be doctors or dentists or corporate types or take over the family business; they weren't going to be traditional stay-at-home wives or mothers. We were all in our own ways mutants: we didn't fit into the neat slots laid out for us either by white society or by our own. To quote from the Elton John biopic *Rocketman,* we had to kill the people we were supposed to be—according to our families, according to our communities, according to the stereotypes—in order to become whom we wanted to be. Of course, the same is true of artists from other communities, but we were the first generation of Asian Americans to really contemplate careers in every art form, who possessed the economic and political freedom to do so.

When I began this essay, I was going to focus on the sociopolitical lens of my experience, the Asian American group historical lens. But I feel now that the mystery was what was happening *inside me* as I began to encounter these other Asian American artists, how *I* was being transformed through these contacts. Unlike those West Coast or Hawaiian Asian American artists who'd experienced belonging to a group, I was moving from thinking of myself as an isoloto, a singular entity with no companions or similar beings, to instead contextualizing myself within a group.

Counter to Jay Caspian Kang's characterization of Asian Americans as the "loneliest Americans," suddenly I wasn't alone anymore. And yet, that did not take away my individuality, my uniqueness, but made me see it in a different light—and that began to open possibilities in me as a person and an artist that I had not detected or imagined before. I could see these new possibilities because others like me were exploring them in their own unique ways and I could learn from them; I could expand the limits of my imagination and empathy, of possibility—both for other Asian Americans and for myself. And in my interactions with these artists, such as Garrett with his Hawaiian background and his father in the 442nd regiment, or later, Wakako Yamauchi and her plays and short stories about Nisei life before the war, or Frank Chin with his research and activism on the Nisei draft resistors, the No-No Boys, I began to learn portions of my own community's history, a history my parents had never talked to me about. Indeed, I would never have written my novel *Famous Suicides of the Japanese Empire,* about the son of a No-No Boy, if I hadn't met Frank, who gave me lectures and source material on the No-No Boys as well as on JA history in general, such as the assimilationist bent of the head of the Japanese American Citizens League (JACL) during World War II, Mike Masaoka. On reading my memoir *Where the Body Meets Memory,* rather than disapproving like my mother, the Nisei Wakako praised my work and observed that her generation's silence surrounding the camps had obviously harmed our Sansei generation, kept us from having a historical context to understand what our parents had experienced and thus who they came to be. If my Nisei mother disapproved of my writing for outsiders about our family, here was a Nisei woman author who understood and—just as important—approved of my work.

But back then, in so many ways, how I was being transformed by these contacts was something I wasn't completely conscious of. No, I felt them, more than understood their significance. It is only now, years later, that I can see that these new shiftings within my consciousness made possible the artist I've become, the one who is writing this book. In my travels, these encounters with other Asian American artists seemed wayward, by chance. Decades later, they've taken on an air of inevitability—destiny, fate.

I am writing here from a sense of history, history and consciousness, of a period in Asian American culture that few have recorded, and perhaps few will ever pay attention to. And yet that matters to me so much less than the fact that I have lived through this history and am part of it. And no one can take that away.

But let me return now to that period in the early 1990s. I came back to the Twin Cities from these exchanges with West Coast Asian American artists and I was fired up. I realized that I was part of a new generation, sired in part by those slightly older like Frank Chin, Maxine Hong Kingston, and Randall Duk Kim (a brilliant Shakespearean actor whom I first saw as Hamlet but is sadly best known as the Keymaker in *The Matrix*). But our generation was more numerous and various and in many fields. Having grown up in a white Chi-town suburb and then coming of age as an artist in the Twin Cities of Mary Tyler Moore and all-white Lake Wobegon, I suddenly realized there were others like me. I had artistic brothers and sisters, and the work we were doing was unprecedented.

Indeed, during that period the *LA Times* published an article by Edward Iwata on the rise of new Asian American writers, including myself and Garrett: "Hot Properties: More Asian American Writers Suddenly Are Winning Mainstream Literary Acclaim." Something was happening. And I wanted to create the same sense of promise and possibility in the Twin Cities, where the refugee populations from Southeast Asia—Vietnamese, Hmong, Laotian—were just coming of age along with the largest number of Korean adoptees in America. (Minnesota's state motto is Land of Ten Thousand Lakes, but in the Asian American community it's the Land of Ten Thousand Korean adoptees.).

As refugees, the Southeast Asians settled in mixed-race, working-class communities and experienced a racism and police harassment I hadn't experienced in my middle-class Jewish suburb. My friend the Vietnamese American poet Bao Phi vividly recalls walking to Powderhorn Park at age eight and suddenly being bombarded by a variety of racial insults, starting with "gook." The Korean adoptees had grown up in white, often conservative religious families; they had been told by their parents not to think about race, that they were just like the white members of their families. But as they grew older and came of age, many adoptees discovered they were not white, as I did too, and they began to feel inside them an intense anger at the racism they experienced and the denial of that racism by their parents. And yet despite the racism both groups faced, many Southeast Asian refugees and Korean adoptees had not been exposed to the concept of Asian America, to a political and historical context for the racial issues they'd been grappling with. Around that time, I even received a note from a Korean adoptee and student at the Minneapolis College of Art and Design, who was questioning her identity and asked if I could mentor her in that struggle. She later came to work at the Asian American Renaissance, an organization I helped found.

In 1992, in Minneapolis, I met the Chinese American community activist Valerie Lee. I described to her the trips I'd been making to the West Coast and how I'd met a number of Asian American artists—not just writers, but theater artists, filmmakers, jazz musicians. I wanted others in the Midwest to see these artists. We talked about presenting an Asian American arts conference in the Twin Cities. Valerie had recently attended an Asian American film conference at the University of Wisconsin, and she felt the same way. We met a couple of times for lunch or dinner to discuss Asian American art and artists and what could be done to bring those artists here. Then a mysterious thing occurred. Almost like spontaneous combustion, local Asian Americans began to ask us when we were going to present this conference, even though we had made no public announcement of what we'd been discussing. Valerie and I began to work together, she on the community side, I on the artistic. We started a series of Asian food potlucks where we discussed how to make the conference happen. We invited local Asian American artists and community leaders from various organizations like the Japanese American Citizens League, the Filipino American Women's Network, and the Asian American student center at the University of Minnesota.

One lesson: if you want to organize Asian Americans, call for an Asian food potluck.

In one of our early grants, here's how I stated our mission:

> The Asian American Renaissance believes the arts are crucial to the building of the Asian American community. The arts help us to ask vital

> questions about who we are, what we have in common and how we differ, to investigate the complexities and paradoxes of Asian American identity. Such questions are not merely academic; only by knowing who we are can the Asian American community begin to formulate and achieve our social, economic, or political needs. Moreover, only by working together can we achieve the power necessary to meet those needs. We have found the arts are perhaps the most useful tool for bringing Asian American groups together, for initiating a spirit of cooperation and mutual assistance across ethnic boundary lines.
>
> There is today a shift in the arts world from an emphasis on product-oriented art to an emphasis on process and social change. We at AAR are not only interested in individual works of art but also in transforming the systems within and outside the art world.

After several months of discussion and planning—Valerie wanted to create as broad a community network as possible—I started writing grants; this and a lot of volunteer labor—a community—helped us produce an Asian American arts conference. The conference presented theatrical performers like solo artist Brenda Wong Aoki and multimedia performance artist Walter Lew, jazz musicians like Mark Izu and Francis Wong, filmmakers like Janice Tanaka and Renee Tajima-Peña.

I remember a breakfast at my house during the conference with the poets Garrett Hongo, Li-Young Lee, and Marilyn Chin. Marilyn pointed out how, back in Asia, she and Li-Young would be at odds with Garrett and me because they were Chinese and we Japanese. She would also be at odds with Li-Young because she was from a line of peasants and had grown up above a Chinese restaurant and Li-Young's family was from the upper class.[4] But in America, all four of us Asian

4 Li-Young Lee's maternal great-grandfather was Yuan Shikai, the warlord who took over China from the Last Emperor and became the first official president of the Republic of China; later he had himself declared emperor. In the film *The Last Emperor*, the adolescent emperor Puyi and a eunuch are standing atop the wall of the Imperial Palace and they look down and see a limousine leaving through the gates. The eunuch points to the car and tells the young former emperor that the man in that car now rules China. That man is Li-Young's great-grandfather. Li-Young's father was a

Americans could learn from and support each other, could establish friendships and a sense of community.

Later, at a dinner party at the end of the conference, on my front porch two theater artists, Korean immigrant Dong-Il Lee and Japanese Canadian Rick Shiomi, began to talk about creating a local Asian American theater company. Their discussion eventually led to the founding of Theater Mu, the second-largest Asian American theater company in America. (The fact that Theater Mu is located in the Twin Cities runs counter to expectations of where the centers of Asian American art reside.)

I have so many memories of that conference, from the wonderful performances by storyteller Brenda Wong Aoki—a two-fer, Chinese and Japanese American—to the jazz concert by her husband, Mark Izu, and Francis Wong to Walter Lew's performance piece, which mined the Korean tradition of the *pyonsa,* the oral narrator of silent films, and then presented clips from Korean films, American horror films, and cartoon superheroes.[5]

Garrett, Li-Young, and Marilyn gave a magnificent reading and after there was a Q&A. When I asked for questions, a white guy raised his hand and I called on him. Later Garrett chastised me for this. "But he raised his hand first," I said weakly. Garrett snapped, "Then you wait

physician to Mao but eventually had to flee China, at first to Indonesia. Once the Lee family came to America, though, they faced the hostility that many Asian immigrants faced and were not well off economically, despite the class backgrounds of his parents. A few years after the AAR conference, I adapted Lee's memoir *The Winged Seed* into a play for the Minnesota-based Pangea World Theater. I ended up playing Li-Young's father, and I was pleased when Li-Young said, "David, you were scary as my father."

5 I also remember some younger Asian American artists complaining because we were asking them to help set up chairs; I thought, "If you don't want to set up chairs or put out spring water and punch, then join the corporate world. This is the nonprofit arts world and this is what we do—we set up chairs and put out the refreshments." But being the polite JA that I am, I didn't say this; nor did I tell them that others in the community had been working long hours to put on the conference, from arranging for the space to contacting artists and setting up their housing to writing grants. In the time since, I've noticed that in our BIPOC communities there sometimes exists a moat between those who like to criticize and complain and those who are willing to do the work to make things happen.

till some Buddhahead raises his hand!" After this, I always noticed that in any Q&A, the first person to raise their hand, even in a mainly BIPOC audience, is always a white guy. (But, hey, let's not talk about white privilege.) I can't recall the exact question this white guy asked—it was something questioning the idea of an Asian American anthology—but the question irked Garrett and it provoked him into this brilliant summation of Asian America and Asian American arts:

> We are postcolonials. Because of history, we are Americans. By race we are Asians. That is a complicated identity, not only racially, but historically. Yeats may be considered the greatest poet in English in the twentieth century, but the Irish say that he is a great Irish poet and Yeats thought of himself as an Irishman. His poetry . . . comes from a different way of speaking the language, the imagery, the mythology, the cultural values, the politics, wishing for an Irish-free state. He even became a senator. He was Irish. But does that *lessen* his poetry because he was Irish? Does it diminish the fact that he is a great poet? Does it diminish me to be an Asian American Poet? No! That might be the problem of the critic, but that is not my problem. I am happy to be called or not. People constantly tell me, "Garrett, I'm so happy you didn't go that ethnic route, you became a poet in your own right." People with Pulitzer Prizes would say this to me at cocktail parties. "You are just a poet." Or other people say, "You know, Garrett, you really inspired me a long time. Nobody has been up there like you from the beginning with Asian American writing and words." So what is going on here? What's going on here is that society impinges its values on the individual constantly and reinterprets what interaction you have on its own terms.[6]

6 In college I had studied Yeats in a course named Major British Poets. It wasn't until I read Said's *Culture and Imperialism* and his essay on Yeats that I fully understood that Yeats's poetry should be contextualized by the Irish resistance to British colonization; despite Yeats's inherent conservatism, his work needed to be understood against a historical background that suddenly seemed so obvious to me later, and yet not at all back in college. Again, this was not part of the way poetry was taught later in my white-dominated MFA program. In the early 1990s, guided in part by Said, I taught a course on Third World Postcolonial Literature in English, which included Derek Walcott, Jamaica Kincaid, V. S. Naipaul, Ama Ata Aidoo, Bessie Head, Salmon Rushdie, J. M. Coetzee, and Nadine Gordimer, where the themes of colonialism, race, and politics all

After that conference, our group of potluck Asian Americans voted to start a community-based arts organization, the Asian American Renaissance (which of course echoed the Harlem Renaissance). Valerie became the executive director, I the volunteer artistic director and grant writer. We put on readings, a regular cabaret, exhibitions, classes in writing and the visual arts, a literary journal, music and dance concerts, festivals, even dragon boat races. We hosted talks by the legal activist scholar Evelyn Hu-Duhart and by the famed Japanese American activist Yuri Kochiyama, who was friends with Malcolm X and cradled his head after he was shot at the Audubon Ballroom. Both argued for the need for interracial coalition building for Asian Americans. We found that if we presented a Hmong beat dance group or a Filipino theater group, the majority of the audience would be from that ethnicity, so we held a dance concert with many ethnic dance troupes—Indian, Hmong, Filipino, Cambodian, Chinese, Vietnamese, Japanese—and brought those audiences together. After the concert, dancers from the different groups began exchanges and worked together.

All this was how the Twin Cities began to become perhaps the most unlikely of centers for Asian American arts. In our first annual report, I talked about how video artist Mark Tang remarked, "It's important for us to tell others how we see ourselves":

> For me, a particular highlight of the year was the premier of *Rough Cuts/Smart Talk,* the documentary made by Mark Tang of the first Asian American Renaissance conference. Although I had been present at the conference and the talks shown on the tape, I wasn't prepared for the effect of seeing a group of Asian American artists on a big screen talking articulately and passionately about topics ranging from Asian American aesthetics to the L.A. riots. I realized I had never seen anything like this

helped me contextualize and understand their work, even with the two white South Africans. I realized that if I put, say, John Updike or Ann Beattie or Jay McInerney in this group, they would seem as if they came from another universe. But if I put Toni Morrison or Leslie Marmon Silko into the group, they would fit. This led me to write an essay asking: when we talk about universal literary values, whose universe are we talking about?

> before. It was as if I had turned on the *MacNeil/Lehrer Report* to find a whole program controlled and presented by Asian Americans.

Before AAR, most people seemed to think I was one of about five Asian American artists in the Twin Cities. But within a couple of years we published a directory with about eighty artists and a few dozen Asian American arts and cultural organizations. In any field, a frequent reply by white institutions to the lack of representation of people of color is, “We looked but couldn’t find anyone.” Our success in gathering, chronicling, and publicizing Asian American artists and culture belied such excuses.

A synergy began to take place. When *Miss Saigon* made its first appearance in the Twin Cities, AAR helped organize demonstrations and a cabaret specifically meant as an answer to the lies of that musical. Having lost white friends over arguments about the musical and race, I now found myself part of an Asian American community that also deemed *Miss Saigon* objectionable. During the intermission of the cabaret, members of the audience got up and testified about their experiences at the demonstration, and the division between the cabaret performers and the audience seemed to fall away. Whether of Hmong, Vietnamese, Filipino, Japanese, or Chinese ethnicities, whether recent immigrants, refugees, or third-generation Asian Americans like me, the artists and the audience members were testifying to their experiences not just of the demonstration but to the various instances of racism they had personally encountered and their anger at a culture that still refused to recognize us or see us accurately, without the ridiculous stereotypes produced by Western culture. In the process, we were all building a sense of community, of belonging to something greater than ourselves.

Little did we know then that, like a vampire, the dreaded *Miss Saigon* would come back to the Twin Cities not once, but two more times. Our fight against that musical had just begun.

PART II

Armed with Language

> We, the members of the FPC, are not afraid to go to war—we are not afraid to risk our lives for our country. We would gladly sacrifice our lives to protect and uphold the principles and ideals of our country as set forth in the Constitution and the Bill of Rights, for on its inviolability depends the freedom, liberty, justice, and protection of all people including Japanese Americans and all other minority groups. But, have we been given such freedom, such liberty, such justice, such protection? No!! Without any hearings, without due process of law as guaranteed by the Constitution and Bill of Rights, without any charges filed against us, without any evidence of wrong doing on our part, one hundred and ten thousand innocent people were kicked out of their homes, literally uprooted from where they have lived for the greater part of their life, and herded like dangerous criminals into concentration camps with barbed wire fence and military police guarding, AND THEN, WITHOUT RECTIFICATION OF THE INJUSTICES COMMITTED AGAINST US AND WITHOUT RESTORATION OF OUR RIGHTS AS GUARANTEED BY THE CONSTITUTION WE ARE ORDERED TO JOIN THE ARMY THRU *DISCRIMINATORY PROCEDURES* INTO A *SEGREGATED* COMBAT UNIT! Is that the American Way? *No!*
>
> —The Heart Mountain Fair Play Committee, World War II

Interned at the Heart Mountain concentration camp, the second-generation Japanese Americans—Nisei—of the Fair Play Committee openly criticized and resisted the imprisonment of their community during World War II. In contrast, a sizeable majority of the 120,000 mainland Japanese Americans went along with Roosevelt's Executive Order 9066. In part this majority believed their cooperation would prove their patriotism. Most believed there was nothing that could be done (*sho ga nai*—it can't be helped); they were a small racial minority, no one was coming to their defense or protesting what was happening to them. Years of Yellow Peril journalism and politics had set the stage for anti-Jap hatred and their removal from the West Coast.

Early on, all adults in the camps, men and women, were given a loyalty oath. Responses differed on two key questions:

> Question #27: Are you willing to serve in the armed forces of the United States on combat duty when ordered?
>
> Question #28: Will you swear unqualified allegiance to the United States and faithfully defend the United States from any or all attack by foreign or domestic forces, and forswear any form of allegiance or obedience to the Japanese emperor, or any other foreign government, power or organization?

Fervently patriotic, eager to prove her loyalty to America, my Aunt Ruth was among those who believed the Japanese Americans should cooperate with the government. She went around her internment camp asking people to sign "Yes-Yes." When she came upon my grandfather, he spat in the dirt, "When they let me out of here, then I'll sign that oath." Later he realized if he didn't sign "Yes-Yes" he would be separated from his family and deported, so he signed "Yes-Yes"—this despite the fact that he was not allowed legally to become a citizen. Years later, my aunt would tell me she felt bad that she didn't understand her father's perspective.

Members of the Fair Play Committee signed both questions in the negative and became known as No-No Boys. They protested that they were U.S. citizens and that their Constitutional rights had been taken away without a trial or writ of habeas corpus. They would be happy to join the armed forces as citizens, with all the rights of citizens, but they would not participate willingly in giving away their rights. Some even objected to the language of Question 28: they never felt any allegiance to Japan; so why should they foreswear allegiance to that country? They were loyal U.S. citizens.

After the war, Nisei John Okada, who served in the Air Force in the Pacific, wrote the classic novel *No-No Boy* about one of these men. I myself have written a novel about a son of a No-No Boy, *Famous Suicides of the Japanese Empire,* a Sansei who must deal with his No-No father as the father falls into a depression after the war and eventually commits suicide.

As a boy growing up in Chicago, no one told me anything about the No-No Boys. That silence was not unusual in our community. For one thing the No-No Boys were considered black sheep by many of the community. The "heroes" were those young men who answered the call to join the armed services. Why talk about the protesters who had stained the community? But more generally, the second-generation Nisei grown-ups seldom talked at all about their experiences in the concentration camps during World War II. At family gatherings, when a Japanese name came up, someone might ask, "What camp were they in?" But no one explained to us what the adults were referring to. I had a friend who thought the adults meant summer camps, until she found out in high school that her parents had been imprisoned in World War II.

In certain ways, then, rather than focusing on President Roosevelt's Executive Order 9066, I was more aware of the fact that my Uncle Elbert had served in the 442nd Regimental Combat Team in Europe and received a Purple Heart from a wound he suffered somewhere in Germany. My Uncle Lou had also served in the Army and I knew that my Uncle Tad had spent some time at Fort Snelling in Minnesota. But I didn't know then that Lou had also been in the 442nd while Tad had been in the Military Intelligence Service and served in the occupation of Japan. Years later I learned that my Uncle Byron and Byron's brother, Ike, had also served in the MIS.

Despite all these ex-military in my family, none of them told me anything about their service during World War II. And yet as I boy I carried the knowledge of their service as a badge of my Americanness, long before I understood how their Americanness had been challenged and repudiated during World War II by their imprisonment.

What knowledge I had of their military service came not from them but from the 1950s black-and-white film *Go for Broke!* about the 442nd regiment. The movie starred Van Johnson as their white commander, since Japanese Americans were not allowed to serve as officers. The film covered some of the heroic accomplishments of the racially segregated Japanese American 442nd, including their rescue of the famed

Lost Battalion of Texans, who had been trapped behind German lines. Several attempts were made to rescue the Texans, but only the 442nd finally accomplished the task. After that battle, Major General John Dahlquist, whom many Nisei soldiers believed viewed them as "cannon fodder," ordered the regiment to assemble; seeing the small number of men in formation, he told Lieutenant Colonel Virgil Miller, "You disobeyed my orders. I told you to have the whole regiment." Miller replied, "General, this *is* the regiment. The rest are either dead or in the hospital."

Years later, I interviewed a member of the 442nd, Eji N., and he explained that their unit possessed the sort of cohesion that comes only in highly trained and specifically chosen units. If your unit is crossing a field or going up a hill in battle and the soldiers around you are being shot or hit by mortars and cannon fire, at a certain percentage of losses almost all troops begin to retreat. But according to Eji, the men in the 442nd were different:

> One thing you could be sure of: when you moved, others moved with you. You could rely on them. There was a sense of protection, trust. The first day going across the field back in Bruyeres I sensed that . . . we were Japanese culturally. There was a shared group cultural ideal. The old country sense of *giri* (obligation) and *gaman* (hard work). You get this sort of thing in elite corps. The Marines had it. They're trained for it. I don't think most of the ordinary white soldiers had it. We had it for cultural reasons.

Part of the fortitude and group cohesion of this Nisei unit came from their mutual cultural bonds, from the Japanese emphasis on the group over the individual. At the same time, especially for many of the mainland Japanese Americans, their commitment came from their sense that they had something to prove: their serving heroically demonstrated how wrong the camps were, that their patriotism was beyond question.

The 442nd was the most decorated unit in Europe and, indeed, in all of American military history. Generals fought to command the Japanese American troops because they accomplished what other units could not, such as rescuing the Lost Battalion. As for the Texans, at first they were surprised or flummoxed by the Japanese faces wearing American uniforms who were coming up the hill to rescue them: *I thought we were fighting the Japanese.* But afterwards they sang the praises of the Buddhaheads who had saved them.

As a nine-year-old boy, watching the film *Go for Broke!* on our television in our Broadway apartment in Chicago, I took immense pride in the accomplishments of the 442nd. But I never imagined that I too would end up helping to make a film about Japanese American soldiers.

These past few months, along with Twin Cities Public Television producer Katie O'Rourke, I've been working on a documentary, *Armed with Language,* about the second-generation Japanese American—Nisei—soldiers who studied the Japanese language at Camp Savage and Fort Snelling, Minnesota, during World War II. At the beginning of the war the Army and its Military Intelligence Service knew there were white Americans who spoke Italian and German, and these speakers could be used in the war effort. But there were almost no white Americans who spoke Japanese. As the military historian James C. McNaughton says in our documentary, the military "damn needed" Japanese speakers. They had to recruit these Japanese speakers from Hawaii and from the camps where the government had imprisoned the Japanese American community. In other words, the Army had no other choice but to ask for Japanese-speaking volunteers from the prisons where the government had segregated 120,000, ripping them from their homes and imprisoning them behind barbed wire fences and beneath rifle towers with the guns pointed inwards.

These MIS Nisei soldiers—including fifty-one women—ended up working as linguists throughout the Pacific theater; they translated captured Japanese documents and messages, interrogated prisoners, guided American forces on the battlefield. General Douglas MacArthur's assistant chief of staff for intelligence, General Charles Willoughby, estimated that the MIS Nisei linguists *shortened the war in the Pacific by two years and saved a million American lives.* Among their accomplishments, the MIS Nisei were responsible for capturing and translating a message that led to the downing of the plane of Admiral Isoroku Yamamoto, the architect of the Pearl Harbor attack.

Ironically, the cultural background of the Nisei, the very thing that made other Americans fear and hate them, is what became one of the greatest assets for America in the war against Japan. While the Germans used a complicated code to encrypt their messages, the Japanese believed their language was too difficult for foreigners, especially white Westerners, and generally left their communications uncoded. In doing so, they did not consider the population of Japanese Americans. In regards to the work of the MIS Nisei, General MacArthur remarked that no army in history went to battle knowing more about their enemy. The value of such knowledge is what Sun Tzu refers to when he writes in *The Art of War*, "It is said that if you know your enemies and know yourself, you will not be imperiled in a hundred battles."

After the war was over, the MIS Nisei were crucial in the pacification and democratization of Japan and in making Japan a valued ally. The Japanese population expected the occupation by the American forces to be brutal and filled with violence (not unlike how Japan occupied other countries in Asia). But then the Japanese were confronted by Nisei who spoke their language and told them not to be fearful, that the U.S. forces were there to help Japan rebuild. As retired Colonel Bud Nakasone relates in our documentary, the Japanese said America must be a great country if these Japanese Americans were serving as part of their forces.[1] (Of course, this is not a greatness the current Trump administration would ever recognize, much less celebrate.)

Over and over this past year, I've been listening to interviews with these MIS Nisei soldiers, interviews made when they were in their seventies or eighties. Some were from Hawaii, some were from the mainland; with the latter, they and their families were interned in concentration camps through desolate areas of the West, Southwest, and Arkansas. Many were *kibei*, that is, educated in Japan, some for a year or two, some for longer, and thus they were often more culturally Japanese than their fellow Nisei who had never lived in Japan.

These men are from my parents' generation, the children of immigrants, and what I find hard to capture here is the tenor and timbre of the ways they talk about their experiences. The soldiers from Hawaii

1 Carrying on his father's service, Bud's son, four-star general Paul Nakasone, has served on the Joint Chiefs of Staff as head of U.S. Cyber Command.

are a bit flashier, more outspoken, though not all of them; they come from a place where as Asians they're in the majority.[2] But for the most part, all these Nisei soldiers display a sense of humility and a certain guardedness, a quietness that hides as much as it reveals—and reveals only if you're perceptive, only if you can detect the nuances beneath their looks and words and tone, depths they don't expose even when talking about exploits of great danger on the battlefield or various instances of racial prejudice. Almost only in passing do they speak of their lack of promotion while less linguistically skilled white soldiers were made officers; or the ways their own troops would eye them with suspicion both in America and when they first arrived in the Pacific; or the dangers they faced from both American soldiers and Japanese soldiers on the battlefield; or the knowledge that their parents and brothers and sisters were imprisoned behind barbed wire fences. These men were deeply patriotic, but not in any chest-pounding way, not in a trumpeting nationalism; theirs was not a patriotism that they wore as a badge of great distinction and fanfare or a challenge to others, and certainly not as a testament to their masculinity. In some cases, it's almost a mumbled avowal: "I wanted to show that I'm, uh, you know, just as American as any, anybody. And this was one way to prove it," says Sergeant Bill Doi.

One of the more well-known MIS Nisei, Roy Matsumoto, fought with the famed Merrill's Marauders in Burma, the group of guerilla fighters who worked behind Japanese lines in the deep jungles. This unit faced enormous dangers with casualties of 90 percent. In his interview, Matsumoto relates a series of battlefield feats of great courage but in a manner that is quiet and matter of fact. One incident in particular stands out: trapped in the Burmese jungle, Matsumoto's unit

2 Indeed, Japanese Americans were so fundamental to the economy and running of Hawaii, while some of the leaders of the community were imprisoned, they weren't imprisoned en masse as on the mainland. One might think if the internment of those of Japanese descent was a military necessity for the West Coast of the United States, it would be even more of an imperative for Hawaii, where the Japanese attacked. But of course, the cause of the internment of Japanese Americans on the mainland was never actually military necessity, as the government, Congress, and President Ronald Reagan acknowledged in the 1988 official apology to the Japanese American community.

is surrounded by a superior Japanese force; they are running out of ammunition, water, and supplies. There seemed no way of escaping. Matsumoto crawls in the jungle to get behind the Japanese lines, and hidden in the underbrush he hears the Japanese commanding officer plan an attack from a certain direction. He crawls back and directs his unit's machine guns toward the point of attack. If you're surrounded, you have to place guns in every direction, but if you know where the attack is coming from, that's a tremendous advantage. When dawn comes, the first Japanese attack is mowed down by the American unit's machine guns. But the second wave stops. So Matsumoto crawls back again behind the enemy lines, and using the tone and linguistic register of an officer, he tricks the Japanese and orders them to attack. At this point, his account is suddenly laced with a surprisingly animated and dramatic energy as he spouts the Japanese phrases he used to imitate an officer in the Imperial Army and order the Japanese troops to charge into the ambush. But then his tone falls away into the quiet of his normal, almost parsimonious and muted conversational voice, and there's no sense of bravado, no notice of his courage or his cunning, but instead a modest disavowal: "They say I saved the unit. But . . . I wasn't so special, I just did what any of us would do, what any of us soldiers were doing." Roy's smaller stature, too, even compared to the other Nisei, belies the hugeness of his battlefield accomplishments, which decades after in the 1990s led to his being awarded a belated Bronze Star medal.

In the interviews, I'll see something flicker across the face of one of these men, a feeling, an unspoken thought, and it's there and not there. Their emotions, their inner life are not, as they sometimes say in acting, highly indicated, and I have to strain to see it. The drama in their faces is not meant for the stage or stage acting; it's not visible to the balcony or even to the front row. And perhaps it can't even quite be captured on film.

But these men are familiar to me: they're like my uncles or family friends. When one of them says that the camps in a way ended up breaking the isolation of the Japanese American community, I recognize an echo from my father, who's said something similar about the camps. And yet in his interview this same Nisei soldier talks about becoming an activist in the sixties, protesting the Vietnam war, and how he looks back now at the internment camps and thinks, *Why didn't we protest more? Why didn't we see how wrong they were?* But rather than with a pronounced bitterness or volumed anger, he says this more as an aside. It's not rhetorical the way he's saying it, it's not blatantly political; it's internal, regretful, rueful, slipped through in passing. *But you know, that's in hindsight. You did what you did.*

I don't know exactly where I'm going with all this. But it has to do with the quiet tones of their Nisei speech, a tone I myself have sometimes been so critical of and that, as a Sansei, I've perceived as passivity. And yet, as I've gotten older, I've realized that a part of me has inherited, almost unconsciously, something of these verbal practices and the cultural values that underlie it. I suppose my concern here in part has to do with the ways Asian Americans are seen as silent and inscrutable and not leadership material. It has to do with monolithic ideas of what masculinity can or might be.

It also has to do with the stereotypical ways we view political protest or activism, with the ways racial prejudice and hate crimes and the anger and outrage they provoke aren't the whole story. Blazing headlines, however needed, can flatten our communities, can make us more faceless, less individual, and in the case of Asian Americans, turn us into another version of "All Asians look alike." I'm also trying to say that's it sometimes too easy to impose my politics or my voice on a different generation, as sometimes younger activists will try to do and as I myself have sometimes misguidedly done at times to the Nisei: "Why didn't you protest? . . . How can you say the camps broke the isolation of the community as if they were a good thing? . . . Why should you have to prove your patriotism? You were already citizens."

I suppose one reason for this is that I myself am now one of the old. During the period around Covid, there was a 150 percent rise in anti-Asian hate crimes. Reading about these attacks, I had this rueful realization: if I experienced a hate crime, the headline would read, "Elderly Asian Man Attacked." Yes, I'm sixty-eight, most people would consider me an old dude, but certainly the term *elderly* does not refer to any way I think or feel about myself.

What the story of these MIS Nisei illustrates is a basic principle of American democracy: our diversity is our strength. Of course,

Trumpkin and his minions, with their racism, xenophobia, and anti-immigrant stances, don't believe or understand this. But when I speak about this film in public at my readings, I always say to audiences:

> If these MIS Nisei shortened the war in the Pacific by two years and saved a million American lives, that means there are anti-Asian, anti-immigrant white Americans who are alive today because these Japanese American soldiers helped save their white fathers and grandfathers. And yet these Nisei were children of immigrants and part of a community the government imprisoned during World War II. These MIS Nisei and their 442nd brothers demonstrated a patriotism and love of country that America still doesn't recognize.

But what I don't say out loud is this: "And I doubt America ever will."

The Internment of Desire

In eighth grade, on a gray rainy day in November, I discovered my sexuality.

It's late afternoon. I am lying in bed. My room, on the second floor of our bilevel, is dark. My mother has gone to the store. I cross the hall to my parents' room. There's a dresser in Swedish modern, two mirrors at each end; a night stand on both sides of the bed. Everything is neat, uncluttered.

I slide open my parents' closet. The hangers all face one way, as do the shoes, lined up precisely in a row. There's a gold quilted garment bag. I slip my hands inside—I don't know how I knew it was there, though my therapist, years later, remarked that news travels unconsciously, silently, in families—I pull it out. A *Playboy.* June 1964.

Quickly, I open to the foldout. I have seen *Playboy*s before, in my friend Terry Steinberg's basement and in the locker room once at school. Each time I felt fascinated, drawn to them, at the same time feeling their forbidden nature, the sense of trespassing on something I couldn't name. But this is the first time I have seen one alone. The woman inside, Donna, is a blonde, a UCLA coed; her breasts seem enormous, the areolae as large as my fist. Though only eighteen she seems frightfully older. Overwhelming, imposing in her beauty.

I sit down on my parents' bed. My penis is hard. I keep staring. I pull down my pants and look at my penis, fascinated by how big it is. I look at the glossy picture. How she leans on the edge of a red folding screen, over which a red blanket is draped, so that her body seems to be emerging from the act of undressing. She doesn't stare at the camera: it's me she's staring at. The curves of her breasts, the dark brown of her nipples, float off the page, both attached to her body and detached, constituting a vision, a realm of their own. I make a game of pulling my foreskin tighter, trying to make my penis grow bigger. It too seems somehow detached, to take on a force of its own.

I look at the blue vein on the back of the shaft, the way it rises, can be seen through the skin. I feel this pleasure coursing through my body, a trembling I cannot control. A wave washes over me, another, a rending of my body from my consciousness, my consciousness from my surroundings, this instant from the continuum of time.

The moment I ejaculate I'm startled, overwhelmed, staring at what shoots out of me, seeing, sensing that this is what explains the morning sheets, wet, sticky, cold. At the same time, I feel I've done something wrong, something that should be kept secret; I know somehow I'm trespassing. But whatever frightened or guilty feelings arise, there also arises an urge to feel this pleasure again, to look at the pictures again, to experience this explosion inside. I bend down and wipe up the milk-white pool on the floor. I repeat the ritual. My secret life has begun.

My discovery of sexuality was, I suppose, no different from that of many American adolescents. But the fervor with which I subsequently went back to this discovery, the endless, compulsive repetition of that act marked me as different, though at the time I had no way of knowing this. I simply put the magazine back in my parents' closet and again and again waited for a chance to steal back, to take another look. In between, I contented myself with the darkness under my covers, each morning when I woke up, each night when I went to bed. Two, four, six times a day. In a way my father's *Playboy* was like a stash of alcohol an adolescent alcoholic has discovered, only I didn't need that stash. All I needed was to be alone, behind a closed door.

Only now does it occur to me to think of how my father perceived these *Playboy*s, why he bought them or what my mother thought. Did he too masturbate over them? Did my mother object to them and, if she did, did she voice this objection? How did he reconcile these pictures with his increasing participation during those years in our Episcopalian church?

All of these seem the expected questions an American son might ask in such a situation. But there is an added element here. My father was a Japanese-American in a generation where Japanese-Americans almost always married inside their race (and of course, the era's miscegenation laws forbade interracial marriages).

I remember reading a journal my father kept when he was twenty-four and living in Chicago, working at a country club. In the clubhouse kitchen one night, he and a few other Nisei boys are talking about women. The line that sticks out in my memory went like this, "Mas has gone out with white girls, and he says it wasn't that bad." I'm surprised at this remark that dating white girls wasn't significantly different, and at the same time I wonder if he could have expressed what those differences were. His awareness of the color line was not the same as mine. From adolescence on, I felt that my inability to attract girls had something to do with my race. Yet I was only attracted to white girls: that was all there was in my high school.

I try to imagine my father staring at the foldout of Miss June, the UCLA coed, try to imagine what the connections are through which he yokes his sexuality to hers. He is sitting on the toilet, in a washroom of blue walls and blue tile and blue porcelain. I can see him there, a magazine on his lap, but when I try to imagine him staring at that image, I feel distressed, that unbearable ache when we see the pain of a parent in a moment of vulnerability, yearning, shame. He puts down the magazine. She, the girl, the woman, is too far away. Beyond his world. Perhaps this explains why, in a few years, I find no more of these magazines in his closet; in a way, they are like my mother's longings for higher culture, for the Mahler and Beethoven records she bought as part of the Columbia record club.

It's me, not my father, who keeps the images from *Playboy* in my briefcase, my closet, in my head. The images there, the beautiful white bodies, are not too far away for me to dream of, though they seem beyond my touching. By coming back to them again and again, perhaps I am completing a path of desire that my father started, driving further into the psyche of America, piercing beyond his sense of sexual possibility. In this pursuit, I will experience frustrations and denials he never approached, though, for a brief period these images, these *Playboys*, were part of his life too.

M. Butterfly

I

The most famous play by an Asian American is probably *M. Butterfly*. The play is David Henry Hwang's take on the case of a French diplomat, Bernard Boursicot, who was stationed in China and for several years conducted an affair with a Chinese actress. In the play, during the course of this affair, Hwang's protagonist, René Gallimard, reveals diplomatic secrets to a Chinese actress, Song Liling, including information about U.S. plans and intentions in Vietnam. Eventually, Gallimard is brought to trial for passing on these secrets to his lover. At the trial, the Chinese actress is revealed not only to be a spy—but also a Chinese man.

In his introduction to the play, Hwang says that he tried to envision what sort of man this Gallimard might be—that is, how Gallimard's preconceptions about the Chinese and other Asians, particularly in regards to women, might have played a role in his being deceived by a Chinese man pretending to be a Chinese woman. Hwang pictures Gallimard as obsessed with the Puccini opera *Madama Butterfly*, where a Japanese woman falls in love with a caddish American sailor who gets her pregnant and abandons her. Gallimard thinks of the opera as a heartbreaking romance, a depiction of the Asian woman as soft and beautiful, feminine and submissive, as pining away for her superiorly masculine white man, so much so that at the end of the opera she commits suicide when she believes he will never return to her. But when Gallimard presents his opinions about the opera to the Chinese actress (who is actually a gay male), her response is quite different:

SONG: Consider it this way: what would you say if a blonde homecoming queen fell in love with a short Japanese businessman? He treats her cruelly, then goes home for three years, during which time she prays to his picture and turns down marriage from a young Kennedy. Then, when she learns he has remarried, she kills herself. Now, I believe you would consider this girl to be a deranged idiot, correct? But because it's an Oriental who kills herself for a Westerner—ah! you find it beautiful.

The scorn and logic of Song's reply never penetrate Gallimard's psyche or its ideological underpinnings. Gallimard's Orientalism is far too powerful a force to be denied. The endurance of that trope can be seen in countless Western works—in a line running from Puccini through *South Pacific* and *The World of Suzie Wong* to *Full Metal Jacket* and *Miss Saigon* to contemporary porn.

At the end of the play, Gallimard faces his eventual comeuppance and is exposed for giving state secrets to Song. To the French public and press, the diplomat is regarded as a ridiculous fool, reviled and laughed at. Song his/herself taunts Gallimard for his blindness, his ability to be duped. And yet despite all this, Gallimard remains unchanged; he clings to his belief in the trope of the "Oriental" woman as the height of femininity—submissive, self-sacrificing, sensual, mysterious:

GALLIMARD: I have a vision. Of the Orient. That, deep within its almond eyes, there are still women. Women willing to sacrifice themselves for the love of a man. Even a man whose love is completely without worth. . . . The love of a Butterfly can withstand many things—unfaithfulness, loss, even abandonment. But how can it face the one sin that implies all others? The devastating knowledge that, underneath it all, the object of her love was nothing more, nothing less than . . . a man.

M. Butterfly can certainly be read as a story of a man who is so in denial of his own homosexual feelings that he refuses to believe his lover is a man even after the whole world around him accepts this truth. But of course, such a reading must still be considered through the lens of racial stereotypes, which move from concrete practice to its ideological underpinnings: in the experience of Western soldiers, the Asian bar girl or prostitute submitting herself to the white male Westerner became a familiar practice and trope. But this trope then connected with the ideological underpinnings of colonialism. Thus the inherent superiority of the white male West and the heterosexual white male as a lover of the Asian female is set in contrast to the weaker and less masculine—i.e., feminine—Asian male. In this ideological binary, the East is seen as submissive, inferior, and feminine and, thus, naturally suited to bow to the powerful, superior, masculine West.

Ironically, though created by and for a white heterosexual masculine West colonizing the Orient, these same tropes have also been adopted by white gay males. Gay white men who are attracted to Asian men are called *rice queens*. In relationships between gay white men and Asian/Asian American men, historically, the most frequent pairing is an older white gay male with a younger Asian/Asian American male. In gay porn, up until a few recent exceptions, Asian/Asian American males were always bottoms to white males—the white male is seen as the dominant and masculine partner and the Asian/Asian American male is the submissive and feminine partner. Obviously, in gay Asia there are male tops as well as bottoms. But in America, the former would seem not to exist. Relying on this white Western reading of Asian gay sexuality, there's an old gay joke that Hwang cites in his introduction to *M. Butterfly*: *What do you call two Asian men together? Lesbians.*

To repeat, in traditional colonial discourse, Asia must be the feminine submissive to the more masculine dominant West. Believing such a paradigm, certain heterosexual white men—and today certain Black men—come to prefer Asian/Asian American women to white women or Black women. Why? Well, for many of these men, white and Black women are not submissive or feminine enough (the two terms for these men are equivalent, synonymous). Within such a paradigm, the Asian/Asian American gay male plays the submissive feminine to the dominant masculine, often older (and richer) gay white male. This is how the gay world reduplicates both the racism and sexual paradigms of the straight white male world.

But flip all this and start with the alternative to this paradigm: the Asian/Asian American male is male—who in actuality can be dominant or submissive, a top or a bottom. Clearly, then, the possibility of the supposedly femme-appearing Asian/Asian American male being considered masculine or dominant is a threat to the traditional white heteronormative paradigm. Even in the gay world, that would upset the white patriarchy's notion of what a "real" man looks like—and how a "real" man acts.

Such a way of looking at Asian American sexuality brings up several questions. On a broader level, what if the Asian/Asian American male is seen as countering the equation of masculinity with dominance? Why does femme appearance equate with submission? And why couldn't the female be dominant or at least not submissive? And of course, femme in whose eyes?

Suppose the white woman or Black woman no longer wanted to be placed in their eternally assigned position as submissive females. Might they not find themselves seeking a masculinity that did not insist on dominance for the male and submissiveness for the female? Might they begin to suspect that they are less likely to find such qualities in white or Black heterosexual males who are concerned about their dominance and a monolithic heterosexuality (if for different historical reasons)? And might they also begin to question the white patriarchal notions of what a "real" man—or woman—looks like?

To put it another way, if heterosexual white or Black women begin to find Asian/Asian American males attractive, that would actually be the most threatening to traditional notions of the All-American heterosexual white male. And perhaps also to African American heterosexual males—despite the tradition that runs through Little Richard to Michael Jackson to Prince to Lil Nas X. The response of conservative commentators to the popularity of K-pop stars like BTS, with their legions of American female fans of all races, is symptomatic of this insecurity. No wonder such a possibility—the Asian/Asian American male as attractive or even more attractive—must be ridiculed, excluded from even the possibilities of thought.[1]

1 I wrote this essay several years before I became aware of the general phenomenon of K-pop and the popularity of male groups like BTS, which display a masculinity that is quite different from the traditional macho heterosexual American male. There are now white and Black American women who travel to Korea looking to find Korean boyfriends.

II

Back in college, when I was young and slim, my girlfriend dressed me in drag one day. I can't recall why we did this; perhaps we were just bored. I had long hair to my shoulders at the time, and she and her girlfriend put makeup on me, a skirt and blouse, and she went around the dorm introducing me to people as "David's cousin, Naomi." David was supposedly at the library and would join them later.

I don't know how we did this without my voice betraying me—perhaps she told people Naomi was Japanese and didn't speak much English—but a few people, including the adult residential advisers, truly believed I was my cousin, though a couple remarked on how much Naomi and I looked alike. (A couple of others weren't fooled.) My girlfriend was pleased that on the whole we pulled it off, though she also wondered if the success of my drag had as much to do with white people not being able to tell Asians apart and thinking all Asians look alike, as with my softer feminine-looking face (to this day, I can't even grow a decent mustache, much less a beard)—or at least feminine looking to white American eyes.[2]

About fifteen years later, I saw Hwang's *M. Butterfly* on Broadway. I vividly recall the penultimate scene where, as Song, BD Wong stripped to a lean muscled torso, his sex visible to all in the audience. I think even back then I knew Wong was gay in real life. I recall a slight gasp from the audience even though some knew what the play was leading to—that Song was not a woman but a man.

Afterward, I made my way down from the balcony, through the

2 In the early 1990s, as part of the Asian American Renaissance cabaret series, the gay playwright and performance artist Ken Choy and I would emcee in drag, in one skit playing Charlie's Angels. (Yes, I was Lucy Liu before there was a Lucy Liu.) One evening, after I left home to teach a class, my four-year-old daughter remarked to my wife, "I just hope he doesn't confuse the students." After questioning Samantha, my wife discovered that my daughter was referring to my dressing in drag. Samantha then asked, "When Daddy dresses up as a woman, does he become a woman?" When Ken was moving from L.A. to Minneapolis, he asked the gay performance artist Tim Miller if he knew of any gay Asians there, and Miller replied, "The only one I know is this guy David Mura." Miller had seen a short film of my performance pieces, including a monologue delivered as I was dressing up in drag and talking about being a rice queen's bottom.

crowd, which was a typical Broadway audience—mostly middle-aged, middle- and upper-class whites. As the lone Asian/Asian American male among them, I felt vividly self-conscious. I still had long hair down to my shoulders back then, which I sometimes wore in a ponytail. But I didn't put up my hair in a ponytail that day. From experience with gas stations attendants ("Can I help you, ma'am?"), I knew that at first glance my appearance was sometimes read as feminine. (Also, I was younger and slimmer back then.) I wondered if the other patrons at the theater saw me as feminine or saw me in light of the play they'd just seen. I knew that some would read me first as Asian and not Asian American. What type of Asian/Asian American I might be was probably not a question they would have asked. Certainly, none of them would have thought I was a writer. None of them would have known I was a poet or that I'd written a long poem in my first book about the Italian gay Marxist film director Pier Paolo Pasolini, or that I had been deeply influenced by Yukio Mishima's *Confessions of a Mask*, a work of autofiction about a Japanese adolescent's discovery of his gay desires.[3] None of the white audience would have asked themselves whether I was Chinese American or Korean American or Japanese American, and few would have even been aware of what those different ethnic designations might signify in terms of my cultural background, the history of immigration in my family, or when we came to America, or the ways I might fit into the racial history of America.

No, I was simply an Asian-looking face, long haired and slightly feminine looking (at least to their eyes) and young, someone whom they were passing by after they had seen a play about an Asian feminine-looking man who fooled a Frenchman into thinking that he, the Asian man, was a woman. Most likely they would not have thought much about the juxtaposition of my presence and the play they had just seen—or at least not in the way I was processing it in my mind as I passed through the theater lobby, conscious of my difference,

3 Though I identify as cis, the directness of Mishima's depiction of his protagonist's sexuality and his shame about his body's desires as well as the frankness of the writing helped me to explore my own sexuality in my writings. The writings of Dennis Cooper also had the same effect on my writing—man, if this can go *there*, I need to go further with my own.

conscious of the meanings written on my face and body, and the contrast between those meanings and what was going on inside me.

Besides discomfort and self-consciousness, I know I felt inside some sense of triumph—triumph because of the success and brilliance of the play and because of the way it deconstructed the stereotypes of Asian masculinity and femininity, tropes whose roots go back to the ideologies of colonialism. I felt a sense that somehow my own reality, my own vision of the world had somehow been affirmed; certainly, as I witnessed the humiliation of the French diplomat Gallimard a thrust of schadenfreude flowed through me. He, the white man, was the object of laughter, the one who was tricked, the one who ultimately was put in the subordinate position. Song, the Asian man/woman, had played on the white man's illusions and delusions, the very construction of his desire, and this occurred because Song understood this desire arose out of racist and sexist tropes and a hopelessly ill-informed and self-inflating view of the interactions between the East and the West—the white man and the "yellow" woman.

Maybe I am fooling these audience members right now, I thought. Maybe they think I might be a woman. Maybe they read me as feminine, as submissive, as docile, as quiet, as insignificant. Certainly, I knew I was, in their eyes, insignificant; I knew that a play where an Asian American male was at the center would never attract their attention. Gallimard, the Frenchman, the white man, was played by the star John Lithgow, and Lithgow was the stellar attraction; in fact, that was one of the reasons the play was on Broadway—it told the story through Gallimard's eyes, not through Song's.

But the play was written by an Asian American man who knew what he was doing when he placed Gallimard at the center: the hetero/homosexual French man would serve better for the (mainly white) American audience to identify with—as opposed to the homosexual/trans Asian man/woman. As an Asian American male writer, Hwang understood consciously—in a way his white audience did not—how power is established and practiced through the tropes of race, gender, and orientation.

And so I believed I "got" the play at a deeper level than those white faces around me, white faces whom I saw and had learned how to read, white faces who if they read my face at all, did not know what they were seeing. And because they did not know what they were seeing, in the end I could not know ultimately, despite all the stereotypes that the play had examined and deconstructed, how they saw me, who they thought I was, how they might place me in their world (if they did even see and place me). In that interchange, for me, it was not me who was inscrutable. No, the inscrutability they saw in me—if that was the way they perceived me—was of their own creation; it involved whatever my identity might be in their eyes, whatever context they placed me within, whatever sense—if they saw me at all—they made of my face, my body, my Asian racial appearance, my Asian maleness. It was a question I could not quite answer.

It is a question I am still trying to answer. Here. Now.

Asian American Masculinity

Performing or Not Performing the Patriarchy

Back in the early 1990s when I argued with white artist friends over yellowface casting in *Miss Saigon,* they defended the practice—though none of them would do so publicly today. One friend argued, "Isn't that what we're striving for? Colorblind casting? Isn't art a democracy of the imagination?"

Of course, "Art is a democracy of the imagination" isn't what I thought as a boy when I saw Keye Luke playing Charlie Chan's bumbling comic number-one son to Swedish American Warner Oland's Orientalized face as the inscrutable Chinese detective. Or when I saw Paul Muni as a weird-looking Chinese peasant in *The Good Earth.* Or when I watched Mickey Rooney in *Breakfast at Tiffany's,* with his slitted eyes, jaundiced skin, buck teeth, thick glasses, and nerd haircut, screaming at Holly Golightly because she's forgotten her keys again and buzzed his apartment late at night and rudely awakened him. She placates him by promising she might let him take the photographs he's talked to her about and Mr. Yunioshi's anger meekly recedes into his prurient Oriental interest in the white girl.

Even today, when things are changing slightly for the portrayal of Asians and even Asian American men, we're never the protagonist. Take *Hawaii 5-O* or *Magnum P.I.,* both set in predominantly Asian Hawaii—and yet it's not an Asian American man who plays the lead. And of course, in interracial pairings involving Asians, the white guy with the Asian girl far outnumbers its opposite pairings in media portrayals, whether in television series, movies, or commercials.

Yeah, yeah, David, kvetch, kvetch, kvetch. Who the fuck cares about Asian American males?

How is Asian American masculinity constituted? What does it mean to be an Asian American heterosexual male?

In contemplating these questions, I have come up with two general theses on Asian American males. One, Asian American masculinity presents itself as a question and challenge to white heteronormative American masculinity; this is a challenge that white society—and indeed the rest of society—cannot entertain without completely undermining and taking apart the basic principles of sexual identity through which white mainstream society and white masculinity function. Two, Asian American masculinity, like other forms of American masculinity, cannot be understood without engaging gay masculinity, LGBTQ+ theory, and feminism, and their challenges to white heteronormative masculinity.

In the 2012 *New Yorker* article "Love on the March: Reflections on the Gay Community's Political Progress—And Its Future," Alex Ross remarks on role playing and drag as aspects of gay male identity and their relationship to "the role of women":

> Feminist critics have long detected misogynist mockery in drag acts and in gay men's howling response to melodramatic scenes that were not intended to be funny, such as Joan Crawford's verbal annihilation of her aloof, ingrate daughter in "Mildred Pierce." [Gay theorist David] Halperin, like many before him, sees a more complex identification at work. Crawford maintains a flawlessly high pitch as she gyrates between "feminine glamour" and "feminine abjection," and the typical gay male viewer may feel at home at both extremes: so many gay kids work at presenting a perfected surface to the world, and so many are hounded by the fear that some grotesque exposure will tear it down. . . .
>
> Furthermore, as the feminist theorist Judith Butler has argued, these extravagant diva turns, and more particularly, the drag acts that perpetuate them, reveal the artificiality of conventional gender roles, the "hyperbolic status of the norm itself." As Halperin puts it, "every identity is a role or an act." It's just that straight-male performance is granted instant authenticity. Super Bowl Sunday, seen from a certain angle, is a pageant as intricate and contrived as the annual invasion of the drag queens on Fire Island.

Ross argues that the traditional definitions and roles of "female" and "male" can be viewed as performative rather than constituting some internal and never-changing monolithic essence.

Seen in this light, the definition of gender becomes a hall of mirrors. A person of either sex can look like and perform the "traditional notions—that is, "perform" the aspects of behavior and appearance used traditionally to designate male or female, straight or gay. But here appearance can be deceiving; it may or may not indicate whether the person is a cis male or female, is straight or gay or trans. As Ross observes, many gay kids "work at presenting a perfected surface to the world"—that is, a heterosexual surface; they *perform* heterosexuality. At the same time, they live in fear that their "act" will be exposed.

In terms of Asian American theatrical history, it's not a leap, then, to surmise that gay Asian American actors like George Takei or James Shigeta learned early how to perform heterosexuality and would be skilled at doing so. But perhaps just as vexing a question: did they learn also to perform whiteness? Or more personally, when as an adolescent I wanted to be thought of as just like a white person, what did that mean? Was I trying to perform a whiteness that was always forbidden to me?

In the context of drag, we should note that there is a difference between a gay man portraying a heterosexual man and a gay man playing a woman. In portraying a heterosexual, the gay male attempts to erase any behaviors that "signal" gayness and to perform behaviors that "signal" heterosexuality. But the performer in this case is biologically a male. In contrast, when a gay male takes up drag and attempts to portray a woman, he can never—unless he surgically chooses to do so—remove the biological characteristics that make him a male. This may be part of the reason why drag carries with it, in our culture at least, the note of parody. (Such is not the case, for instance, in Japanese culture and theater.) To use Ross's phrase, the performance of drag can never be "granted instant authenticity."[1]

1 There is a distinction between a gay man donning drag and a trans person who undergoes surgery for a sexual change and identifies as a woman or a trans person who identifies as a woman. With the latter two, the trans person does not identify as a male and so the element of parody is not present, though that trans person might be

So how does all this relate to the straight Asian American male? Every year I watch the Super Bowl with my two sons. When the straight Asian American male performs this rite, in what ways is he like or unlike a straight white male who performs that rite? If the straight white male is "granted instant authenticity," how is the Asian American straight male to be regarded? Is he granted instant authenticity performing this straight white male rite?

I would argue no.

Imagine a beer commercial about Super Bowl Sunday. You can certainly picture a group of straight white males watching the big game. There may even be other token minorities among them. But if the commercial were only made up of Asian American males? (Such a commercial would never be made of course.) It would take on an air of parody, of pastiche. It would certainly not be granted instant authenticity. This would not be the case with a commercial made up of only straight Black American males watching the Super Bowl. In terms of straight masculinity, those Black American males would be granted instant authenticity.

In the eyes of straight white American culture, the Asian/Asian American male body is considered effeminate and nerdy, as lacking both biologically and culturally those signs that would grant the straight Asian American male instant authenticity as a straight American male, no matter how well he portrays or plays or performs that role.[2]

When I was growing up, I sensed the sexual parameters of my position in this culture. Of course, like many straight Asian American males I took up all the signs and trappings of the straight white American

viewed through the lens of parody by others. But there are trans performers—some who have undergone surgery, some who have not—whose performances are presented as parodies.

2 Recently, the perception of Asian and Asian American males has begun to shift slightly, and to a certain extent I can be accused of exaggerating the skepticism concerning our ability to be regarded as traditional hetero American males—except the statistics from dating sites where we are regarded as the least attractive or the fact that in gay porno we are always the bottom (i.e., the femme sub) certainly bolster my point.

male. At five years old, like so many white males of my generation, I had my picture taken over and over with a cowboy hat, wearing a belted holster with two six-guns around my waist, imitating the cowboy image that was so in vogue during the fifties. But when I look back at those photos, there seems to me something ridiculous about my donning this getup with my Asian face. Even at five, at some level did I sense I could never actually be a cowboy, the seeming epitome of the straight white American male?

In one of my poems, "The Colors of Desire," there's this section describing me riding with my father in a car. With my toy six-guns, I'm playing at being Paladin, the gunslinger from the fifties cowboy show *Have Gun—Will Travel.* When a Japanese Canadian friend, Rick Shiomi, read the poem, he asked, "Do you remember what happens at the beginning?" I said, "Yeah, Paladin comes walking down these stairs, wearing his six-guns, looking cool, all dressed in black." Rick said, "No, that's a bit later. At the start of the show, a pigtailed Chinese messenger runs into the hotel lobby shouting, 'Teragram. Teragram for Meesta Paradin.'"

But even after Rick said this, I couldn't remember the Chinese messenger.

So what was going on in my five- or six-year-old brain when I saw this television show that caused me to repress this memory of the Chinese messenger? Like other straight American males during that time, I wanted to be the gunslinger. The hero. The white guy. But perhaps I knew even then that people would more readily associate me with the pigtailed Chinese messenger, that society viewed me in the role of "the Chink"—named Hey Boy in the TV series. I would never be seen as the gunslinger or the hero. My race would forever keep me from occupying that social space.

As I grew older, I sensed more and more that this would be the case. I might wish to be regarded like Paladin or John Wayne, as the great straight white American male. But that would never happen. No matter how meticulously I tried to perform that role, my performance would never be granted instant authenticity. I would always be regarded as fake, a faux imitation.

Eventually, a part of me began to feel, *Why even try?*

Here is Ross on how the gay adolescence comes to sense his "difference":

> This alienation can happen in class, or in the locker room, or at a friend's house when straight porn is unveiled. However these experiences unfold, they have a lasting impact, equivalent to a trauma with no visible cause. One common response is preemptive withdrawal. The boy buries himself in some obscure aesthetic pursuit. One self-help book calls it "velvet rage."

Reading this passage, I'm struck by how my own awareness of my difference, my sense of racial otherness, did seem to come with a vengeance at adolescence.

In the first instance, one day in eighth grade I stayed at home ill and my mother went out shopping. For some reason I was rummaging in my parents' closet—did I sense something was there?—and in a garment bag I found a *Playboy.* I paged through looking for nude photos and came to the foldout, a blond UCLA coed. This was the first time I'd ever masturbated, and to this day I wonder how much the fact that this was a blond white woman affected what women I would be attracted to. Back then I didn't think about race, other than I wanted to be considered just like my white classmates.

But a few months later, at my first boy–girl party, I found myself confronting my racial difference, even as I tried to put it "back in the closet." The Thursday before the party on Saturday, after basketball practice, I was talking to my teammate Steve Fine about the game on Friday between our team, which had won the intramural basketball league, and the all-stars from the other teams. We both wanted to do well because we knew people would be talking about the game at the Saturday night party. I ended up scoring half my team's points, and in the last seconds I stole the ball and made a layup, which sealed our victory. On Saturday, I was eager to see what others would say about my performance.

But when I got to the party, no one talked about the game. The male centers of attention were two white Jewish guys who hadn't even played in the game and were considered "cool." Then the host came out with a Coke bottle and said we were going to play spin the bottle. I didn't know what that was, but then she explained. When the bottle spun to me and I scooted to the center of the circle, I kissed the girl longer than others had been doing and a cheer went up. So I did that again after I spun the bottle, and even more cheers ensued. Suddenly I was the center of attention.

But then Laura, a Jewish girl I had a crush on and who was my lab partner in science, spun the bottle and it landed on me. She ran to a corner and refused to kiss me. Everyone laughed.

Now it very well could have been that she was refusing because of the way I'd kissed the two other girls. But though I didn't have the precise language then to describe what I was feeling at her refusal, some part of me—almost entirely subconsciously—felt her refusal had something to do with my racial difference. And whether race actually had anything to do with her refusal or not, I suddenly became aware of my racial difference in a new way. Up until that party, being "in" for guys depended mostly on your athletic abilities. But given that I'd starred in the championship intramural game, that was clearly not the case now. Sexual attractiveness was the new coin of cachet. And it seemed that I was suddenly without any coins.

In both of these incidents, my incipient sexual awareness and an awareness of my racial otherness are powerfully linked: both incidents do not confirm, or bring me into, a shared response or identification with the other white males around me. Indeed, the event and my actions only seemed to highlight my difference.

Of course, in neither incident was my sense of difference as great as what a gay adolescent feels in such situations. And yet when I read Alex Ross's epiphany of gay adolescence, I find something similar to my experience, something familiar in his wording: "This alienation can happen in class, or in the locker room, or at a friend's house when straight porn is unveiled. However these experiences unfold, they have a lasting impact, equivalent to a trauma with no visible cause."

A trauma with no visible cause: as a book like Halperin's *How to Be Gay,* which focuses on gay men, makes clear, most often gay males do not grow up raised by gay parents; they are not taught a language to express their sense of difference as part of their upbringing. At first, in instances like those Ross references, the trauma may not be expressed or vocalized because the gay adolescent does not yet possess a language to express his sense of difference or to link his experience of his difference with other gays. The cause remains beyond articulation; this state of inarticulation remains until that gay adolescent eventually comes into contact with other gays and, just as important, gay culture and history—and through that culture and history, he acquires a language to express and explore his sense of his difference and, at the same time, to link his experiences with others in his group.

This is, I believe, similar to what I experienced as an Asian American adolescent: I was made painfully aware of my difference, but I could not quite voice or could not quite see its cause. I simply felt it, and thus that difference appeared suddenly, without any context or articulation, a trauma—*with no visible cause.* Because I wanted to be raceless or considered white, because I had little associations with other Asian Americans, and because I had not been exposed to Asian American literature or academic studies, I had no language to express my trauma; I had no framework to investigate its sources or historical antecedents, no way of connecting my experience of alienation with others who might be experiencing something similar.

It took me years of study, reading, and writing, as well as connecting with other Asian Americans and people of color, to find this language.

Fragments in Search of Asian American Masculinity

I

> Consider the fact that Leonard Chang wrote about a novel . . . that was rejected by big-house publishers for not being "Asian enough." As one editor told him . . . "You have to think about ways to make these characters more 'ethnic,' 'more different' . . . in the scene when [a character] looks into the mirror, you don't show how she sees her slanted eyes, or how she thinks of her Asianness."—Facebook post by Margie Andreason (chair of Don't Buy *Miss Saigon* Coalition)

*

Yup, every day I look in the mirror and say, "Hello, slanty eyes," but some days I go, "Bonjour, gook," and on special days, "Howdy, you Jap," and I play some *shamisen* or *biwa* music, wrap my kimono around my yellow torso—no bathrobes for me—

BUT

on the days I'm seeing the Emperor, I strap on my samurai sword, band my top knot, and grunt like Toshiro Mifune in *Seven Samurai*

BUT

I do this even though my family's been breathing and breeding in America more than a century

BUT

some days I look in the mirror and wonder, *Who the hell is that? How did that face get here?*

BUT

James Baldwin observed, "We can only face in others what we can face in ourselves"

BUT

in *Confessions of a Mask,* when the young boy wraps himself in his mother's kimono and scurries around the house shouting, "I'm Tenkatsu, the geisha magician!" he rams into his mother, who stares at him like a being from another planet[1]

BUT

can I really say, "I'm Tenkatsu, the geisha magician!" or even "I'm Toshiro Mifune"?

BUT

the racist ethnocentric spell check will not—on the first second third try—let me write those names

*

1 Reading *Confessions of a Mask,* I came upon the moment when the protagonist, who is gay, discovers his sexuality. I felt the emotions depicted in Mishima's semiautobiographical novel echoed my own feelings of shame concerning my body and my sexuality and gave me freedom to express my own sexual emotional geography. I'm not gay, but I responded to the feeling of the character that there was something wrong with his sexuality, his body, who he was at his core; what got to me was the intimacy and depth of the scorn he faced and the fact that that scorn corresponded to a voice inside himself.

"Here's one: How to Date a White Woman: A Practical Guide for Asian Men. Excuse me, do you like Asian men?" Steve Harvey asked rhetorically. Then in mock Asian accent, "No. Thank you."

"How to Date a Black Woman: A Practical Guide for Asian Men. Same thing."

"You like Asian men?" he asked again, and imitated a Black woman's answer: "I don't even like Chinese food, boy. It don't stay with you no time. I don't eat what I can't pronounce."

Harvey doubled over in laughter.

*

Apparently, the popularity of Korean pop groups like BTS among young white and Black women is a cultural shift Steve Harvey seems ignorant of.

On a less scientific anecdotal note: last night at a Black professional networking event, a Black woman executive spent several minutes expounding to us on her love of Korean boy bands, K drama stars, and the abs of Korean men.

(This despite one white male commentator complaining BTS looked like "Asian Ellens.")

*

On an even less scientific note: from the age of eighteen, when, at the Art Institute of Chicago, I was approached by a young Black woman, who gave me her phone number,

I have always known there were Black women who were attracted to me.

*

Still, the audience laughed at Harvey's "jokes"—apparently in agreement with his evaluation.

Which struck a note with Eddie Huang, the Taiwanese American chef of Vice and *Fresh Off the Boat* fame:

> Every Asian-American man knows what the dominant culture has to say about us. We count good, we bow well, we are technologically proficient, we're naturally subordinate, our male anatomy is the size of a thumb drive and we could never in a thousand millenniums be a threat to steal your girl. . . .
>
> The one stereotype that I still mistakenly believe at the most inopportune bedroom moments . . . is that women don't want Asian men. . . . we just don't have the ingredients. . . .
>
> I told myself that it was all a lie, but the structural emasculation of Asian men in all forms of media became a self-fulfilling prophecy that produced an actual abhorrence to Asian men in the real world.
>
> —Eddie Huang, *New York Times*

*

Eddie Huang: lawyer, world-class chef. Author of the best-selling memoir *Fresh Off the Boat* made into a hit television series. Travels the world on *Huang's World* for Vice. Clothing designer. Worked on the Innocence Project, president of the Minority Law Students Association, vice president of the Asian Pacific American Law Students Association at Cardozo School of Law.

Most likely, it was Eddie's *New York Times* opinion piece that made Steve Harvey apologize, which he clearly did not want to do.[2]

2 Dude thought he could punch down on the gooks. Turns out Harvey underestimated us Asian Americans, didn't realize Asian American guys like Eddie Huang and Viet Thanh Nguyen now have a hotline to the *New York Times.*

BUT

Eddie was hurt by Steve Harvey's insults.

BUT

Eddie can be faulted on issues of racism & misogyny

*

> Fanon's psychoanalytic mode of analysis . . . the black American experience which Huang seeks to emulate. Arguably, the black male gangsta rap persona who flaunts his bling and is sexually promiscuous with a range of women, including white women, is a grotesque parody of and reaction against wealthy, white America whose social respectability masks the dark underbelly of class domination and sexual violence against women of color. . . .
>
> So, too, with Huang's adoption of a hip hop influenced persona, and several discussions of how male Asian action stars "never get pussy" in his memoirs. . . . Huang's attitude in regards to women becomes a theme running through Huang's work, as in his constant reference to "shawties" (which, by the way, Urban Dictionary defines as a "fine ass woman" for those unfamiliar with the term, as I was) . . . his general tendency towards performed radicalism.
>
> —Brian Hioe, "*Fresh Off the Boat* and the Limits of Cultural Representation" (blog post)

*

Question: Can we critique Hioe's ignorance of Black culture?

(Can someone who has to look up "shawties" in Urban Dictionary

form a knowledgeable critique of Black culture and hip-hop?)

Question: What do Eddie Huang and Brian Hioe have in common?

Question: What's the difference between "performed radicalism" and "performed whiteness"?

*

Once, when I was in a club, a Black woman came up to me: "Well, I've tried white and Black. Let me try something new."

It's no accident that Asian men and Black women are the least swiped racial groups on Tinder and OkCupid.

*

In *Passage to India* another Aziz (so sorry Ansari)
did not read properly the perilous colonial cunnilinguistic signals—

a strange coincidence for his latter doppelgänger
meeting hunger with dinner at Le Bon Plaisir and his dictatorial choice

of wine and did he come on grossly with porn moves
as consent's the issue when nonconsent is not spoken

—didn't he know the scary sacred screed of Empire:
Don't touch the White Woman!

*

(self-

examination

of the testicles or else

disease)

*

Footnote brought up to the text:

When Harvey first apologized, I first thought, *Good for Eddie.* But even as I thought this, I was also aware of something else: it was clear that Harvey's remarks had *hurt* Eddie Huang, had penetrated a place in Huang's psyche where the stereotypes and denigration of Asian/Asian American males had taken root.

Now I certainly understand why Huang might have been hurt; indeed, I probably would have reacted similarly when I was younger. But I've worked for years and by many means to root out those stereotypes from my own psyche, to make their presence smaller and smaller in my mind. Beyond that, though Harvey's remarks angered me, they didn't hurt me. I knew he didn't know what the fuck he was talking about; he had no knowledge how women have perceived me.

So what surprised and bothered me was that here was a younger Asian American man, at least a generation if not two after me, and he was still dealing with the same shit I dealt with when I was younger. And this wasn't just any Asian American. This was Eddie Huang, a world-class chef, successful restauranteur, and a lawyer and TV star. He could place his op-ed in the *New York Times,* probably just through a call from his agent. And he's insecure about his sexuality? He's hurt by Steve Harvey's idiocy?

Boy, I thought, we've got a long way to go.

*

Reader, a caveat: no one would talk to me for this piece

not just Katie Roiphe's whisper network of white women

but anyone: after all my piece is about Asian men

and who wants to talk about them

*

Three white women in a bar:
"... buy us drinks...." cock-

tails in hand they quickly
walk away

which is how he learned early:
never buy white women drinks

if you look
like a rich gook

*

According to a friend, my dressing like a rich gook

—I was voted "Best Dressed" in high school—

gave the Beat poet Gary Snyder the "creeps"

*

Cuckservative, often shortened to ***cuck***, is a term of abuse formed as a portmanteau of the word *cuckold* and the political designation *conservative*.... The term *cuckold* has a long history as an insult implying that a specific man is weak and emasculated and may even feel pleasure at his own humiliation. The term *cuckservative* similarly implies that certain Republicans are humiliated through their actions while feeling thrilled and excited from their own degradation because of the abandonment of their own moral standards.

*

Thinking of the degree to which
I still think like a white man:

Am I afraid
Of losing America

To someone
Like Myself?

*

Question: Why do Asians have small dicks?

Answer: They're all women.

(Special thanks for this joke to Louis C.K. who obviously holds

no problem with exposing ***his*** *dick)*[3]

*

In Wesley Yang's article on pickup artists, the [anonymous Asian American]

"continues to lay out a story of Asian-American male distress

relevant to those who have packed Master Krauss's living room.

The story he tells

is one of Asian-American disadvantage in the sexual marketplace. Yes,

3 For the few who may not know: Louis C.K.'s #metoo case involved his coercing women, often female comics, to watch him masturbate or simply masturbating before them without warning—why would they think he had to ask permission for that? Ah, the privileges of the white male.

it is about attracting those women whose hair

is the color of the midday sun and eyes the color of the ocean,

and it is about having sex with them. He

won't apologize for the images of blonde women

plastered all over his website. This is what he prefers,

what he stands for, and what he is selling:

the courage to pursue what you want, the skills

to make whom you desire desire you back . . . "

*

"White guys do what they want," the Asian American pickup trainer proclaims. "Why not me?"

(Cause white guys are assholes?)

*

Reader, I lied: I never took the seminar.

I am

the seminar

*

After the Taiwanese American NBA player Jeremy Lin scored thirty-eight points over Kobe Bryant and the Lakers, the Black journalist Jason Whitlock tweeted:

"Some lucky lady in NYC is gonna feel a couple of inches of pain tonight."[4]

*

Eddie Huang had a rough twenties, bumping repeatedly against the Bamboo Ceiling. In college, editors at the Orlando *Sentinel* invited him to write about sports for the paper. But when he visited the offices, "The editor came in and goes, 'Oh, no.' And his exact words: 'You can't write with that face.'" Later, in film class at Columbia, Huang wrote a script about an Asian American hot dog vendor obsessed with his small penis. "The screenwriting teacher was like, 'I love this. You have a lot of Woody Allen in you. But do you think you could change it to Jewish characters?'"[5]

*

All I got out of the last paragraph: small dick

*

got to have a yellow woman if you're a yellow man

short (dicks?) have no reason to live

*

(*I'll have to pay Randy Newman for those lines*)

4 When Asian American journalists objected—and yes, some of us are now journalists and even sports journalists—Whitlock apologized. But he never actually acknowledged his use of a racial stereotype; instead he focused on how he listened to Richard Pryor records when younger and wanted to be a comedian and said he gave in to his "immature, sophomoric, comedic nature" (i.e., no racism here).

5 I used to joke that if a film were made of my memoir *Turning Japanese,* about the year my white wife and I spent in Japan, it would have starred Ethan Hawke and Lucy Liu.

*

Everything is about sex except
sex

which is about power
—Oscar Wilde

apocryphally
writing

a sentence for any
married couple

*

there is power in being

nobody

in knowing nobody sees

the things you see

*

"I pay attention to you because you matter, and if you ignore me, it's because I don't."

*

> The psychologist Dacher Keltner, who has studied the relationship between empathy and power, has written that while people usually gain power through traits and actions that advance the interests of others, such as empathy, collaboration, openness, fairness, and sharing; when they start to feel powerful or enjoy a position of privilege, those

> qualities begin to fade. The powerful are more likely than other people to engage in rude, selfish, and unethical behavior.

*

In certain situations, the more articulate and educated I appear
—if I actually let loose at full throttle my intellect and learning—

the more I risk being perceived a threat
in my Asian-looking face and body. I must pick

and choose when and where I let my intelligence and learning
show and to what degree . . . for they can, in an instant, be

perceived as uppity, arrogant, showing off. And if that happens,
the foreignness that is my face, my body, can be turned

to that of the outsider, the inscrutable threat, the one
who wants to take something from white America

*

The article's title: "Should We Fear A.I.?"

Oh great, fear of Asian Intelligence.

*

> I'm 43 now. I've been a performance poet since I was 16 or 17. In my early years, I was told by many people, some of them well meaning, that there was no "market" for Asian American men writing about Asian American men. If I wanted to get published or be successful, I would need to find a way to write about or towards anyone except people like me.—from my friend Bao Phi's Facebook page

*

Whether onscreen or in the popular imagination,

the Asian woman tends to fall into one of several predictable archetypes:

the evil temptress, obliging mistress, loyal servant,

fanatical tiger mom, ruthless overachiever. One of the pleasures

of the Winter Olympics in Pyeongchang: creating a new

stereotype:

Chloe Kim, the teenaged gold medal snowboarder from Southern California;

Mirai Nagasu, the first American female Olympic skater to execute a triple axel,

her teammate Maia Shibutani, who in the ice dance competition with brother, Alex,

helped capture the team bronze medal. Half

Team U.S.A.'s figure skaters are Asian American: How

the hell did this happen? asks the Trump voter. And how

did Kim Jong Un's sister, that North Korean dragon lady, get so close to our beloved Ivanka? (Oh white knight Jared, wherefore art thou?)

*

"Do you know Chloe Kim?"

"Do you know Kim Jong Un?"

"Do you know Mai and Alex Shibutani?"

—Not exactly but they're my cousin's kids.

"Well, I rest my case. Y'all know each other."

*

"Asians are the loneliest Americans," Jay Caspian Kang wrote in a *New York Times Magazine* story about a death and the search for identity in an Asian American college fraternity. There is no solidarity, in Kang's opinion, just a "cartoonish and blurry" sense of racial belonging. "Asian pride is a laughable concept to most Americans . . . . A common past can be accessed only through dusty, dug-up things: the murder of Vincent Chin, *Korematsu v. United States*, the Bataan Death March and the illusion that we are going through all these things together."

*

Even to another Asian American male we're a joke
(Caspian was writing about a hazing death at an AA fraternity)

*

Question: Can I be considered by women as part of the white patriarchy

if I'll never belong to it?

*

Unlike its opposite

the Asian woman who falls for the white GI/soldier/sailor/diplomat

is a tear-jerking romance

as old as the Orient. Or rather,

colonization (*me love you long time . . .*)

*

White whisper: Did you know the only defeats America faced in the twentieth century

were against Asian countries? How the hell did those femmy gooks do it, oh Miss Saigon?

*

dr. david dao dragged down the United Air aisle
screaming "I have patients waiting"

and whether they believed him or not
some of his own people hate him

for saying his being dragged
was worse than escaping from Vietnam

[*trans.: what a bourgeois fuck,*
thinks he's the model minority]

*

Andrew Sullivan in *New York Magazine* assails Clio Chang in the *New Republic*:

> Do you know the real reason Dr. Dao was so brutally tackled and thrown off that United flight? It was all about white supremacy. I mean, what isn't these days? . . . Yes, there is an obvious alternative explanation: The seats from which passengers were forcibly removed were *randomly* assigned. . . .

> Asian-Americans, like Jews, are indeed a problem for the "social-justice" brigade. . . . How have bigoted white people allowed these minorities to do so well—even to the point of earning more, on average, than whites? . . . It couldn't possibly be that they maintained solid two-parent family structures, had social networks that looked after one another, placed enormous emphasis on education and hard work, and thereby turned false, negative stereotypes into true, positive ones, could it? It couldn't be that all whites are not racists or that the American dream still lives?

*

Perhaps Sullivan's headline (oh model minority myth, here we come) should have been:

Dr. David Dao Removes Racism in America, Proves the All American Dream!

—and by being forcibly tackled and removed from a plane, no less!

(hey, we Asians get the job done)[6]

6 Nowhere in her article does Clio Chang say that Dr. Dao was picked to *leave* the plane because he was Asian. Instead, she asks a different question: Did the United workers or the security officials treat Dr. Dao differently because he was Asian? Would they have acted in an *exactly similar fashion* if the person asked to leave were a white businessman in an expensive suit or a pretty young white woman or an elderly white woman or man? Would the United personnel have responded differently to Dr. Dao's explanation if it were coming from a white doctor or someone who did not speak with a Vietnamese accent? Would they have been more patient or empathetic or accommodating with him?

But why would Sullivan be aware of the myriad microagressions Asian Americans face each day anywhere in America? Does he see when I or other Asian Americans are standing in line or at a bar or a counter and are ignored? Does he see when I or other Asian Americans are physically jostled or threatened or when we are insulted both in subtle and not so subtle ways in public spaces? What about the 150% rise in anti-Asian hate crimes during Covid? Or complaints by Asian Americans about the "bamboo" ceiling in corporations? Does he understand why Asian American women have some of the highest suicide rates of any population and why they are stereotyped sexually

*

dr. david dao is no Asian American superhero

neither is

david mura

the raison d'être of

this poem

*

The title of my memoir *Turning Japanese*

echoes the song

slapping some Brit slang

(footnote for U.S. readers: picture slitted—i.e. Asian—eyes

jerking off). So

and treated according to those stereotypes? Does he know how Americans often react negatively to a speaker with an Asian language accent as opposed to Sullivan's British accent? Does he see the racial profiling by police in working-class or economically marginalized Asian American neighborhoods—or do such neighborhoods even exist in his "model minority" myth imagination? But Sullivan either can't conceive of such questions or he doesn't even think such questions are worth considering.

Finally, despite the historical racism Asian Americans have faced, including the internment camps, Black Americans faced far more trenchant and structural racism, a fact that appears nowhere in Sullivan's analysis. Asian Americans also benefitted from civil rights laws that resulted from African American activist movements.

Marc Hayashi

—star of *Chan Is Missing*—

once said to me,

"Every culture needs its eunuchs

and we're it."

Passing thirtysomething white guys in the hotel hall

after their bachelor party: When they think

I'm out of earshot—"Did you see

The Hangover? What's the name of that guy

with the tiny dick?"

*

I can hear many readers, especially AA men, going, *Why the hell go into this?*

"But aren't we as a culture trying not to body shame? And isn't the penis a part of the body?"

"Yeah, David, but did you hear anyone praising the bravery of Ken Jeong for exposing his stubby dick? Or endorsing what he was doing for *body positivity*? Or calling him *our* Tess Holliday or Ashley Graham, *our* Lizzo?"

Oh well.

*

Jon Chu, director, *Crazy Rich Asians*, writing to Coldplay to ask the rights to their song "Yellow":

> I know it's a bit strange, but my whole life I've had a complicated relationship with the color yellow. From being called the word in a derogatory way throughout grade school, to watching movies where they called cowardly people yellow, it's always had a negative connotation in my life. That is, until I heard your song. For the first time in my life, it described the color in the most beautiful, magical ways I had ever heard: the color of the stars, her skin, the love. It was an incredible image of attraction and aspiration that it made me rethink my own self image.

*

And so, I leave you, dear reader, with these final fragments:

*

Message to Whiteness: Racism is stupid. And it makes you stupid.

(Whatever I am, I'm not stupid. I'm Asian.)

*

There is the Whiteness inside our heads. When it's unconscious

we are puppets, yanked this way and that.

When we become conscious, we battle it inside ourselves.

Exorcise it, our freedom begins: we fight

strategically, see its weaknesses, use our cheat codes.

*

Baldwin: “I am not a nigger. I’m a man. If I’m not the nigger here, and if you invented him, you the white people invented him, then *you* have to find out why.”

*

In other words: make the Whiteness in your head smaller

and you begin to

appear

*

On a panel on Asian American psychic health, the speaker said:

“Sometimes what we need to be psychically free

is a simple Fuck You.

It doesn’t have to be loud or angry, just

Fuck You!”

*

Okay, the speaker was me: “You young people,

don’t give power to people

who can’t see you!”

*

Zora: “Sometimes I feel discriminated against

but it does not make me angry. It merely

astonishes me. How

can any deny themselves

the pleasure of my company?”

Race, History, and My Marriage

At a reception, I am talking with two women whom I've just met and who don't know each other—one a tall younger Chinese American woman and the second a slightly older Chinese American woman. I am with my blonde (née brunette) wife. At a certain point, the taller Chinese American woman nods toward Susie and says, "Oh, you're together?!" half-question, half-discovery—meaning, she thought I was with the other Chinese American woman.

Later, on the plane home, my wife is sitting in the middle seat and I on the aisle. Across from us a younger Asian couple is sitting together also, the man in the window seat and the woman in the middle seat. Another younger Asian American couple comes up; the Asian woman has the aisle seat where the other Asian couple is sitting. The Asian woman asks Susie if she will switch seats with her because her husband is sitting in the window seat of our row and she would like to sit with her husband.

Susie says, "I'm sitting with *my* husband," and a look of surprise crosses the face of the younger Asian American woman. She clearly did not think of asking the same question of the Asian woman in the other middle seat.

I've experienced numerous occasions where white people have assumed Susie and I are not a couple. But these two incidents occurred within a day of each other; after the second one, I realized that even Asians/Asian Americans might assume the same thing—that it's unlikely that the blonde woman next to me could be my sexual partner.

My wife is a pediatric oncologist. She served as director of her department for ten years, helped start the hospital's integrative medicine and pain/palliative care programs, and she's now a vice president and chief of pediatric specialties at her hospital. As a pediatric oncologist, she's obviously doing necessary work; she's saving children from cancer. Though she practices less now in her current position, when she was a full-time physician she was known for her almost preternatural ability to comfort and help parents deal with one of the most difficult moments a parent could face ("Your child has cancer") and the even more devastating and nearly impossible to accept final prognosis ("There's nothing more we can do"). She's had mystical deathbed experiences; she carries with her the memory of patients who have died and their grieving parents. But she's also seen the vast majority of her patients grow up to experience healthy and flourishing lives.

When I met Susie in college, she said she was going to become a preschool teacher; she loved kids. But after she moved to Minneapolis, where I was going to grad school, she worked for the state public health department, took a course on epidemiology, and came back saying, "I love the study of diseases." I encouraged her to go to medical school, even though her physician dad had discouraged her in that direction, thinking she wouldn't be happy in the field. But when she first entered medical school, I began to feel threatened and a little jealous. And that, in part, was one of the reasons why I entered therapy in my twenties. I understood my being threatened was my problem, not hers. After that, I encouraged her in each move upwards—to become a pediatric oncologist, to become director of her department, and eventually a vice president of the hospital.

When our children were young, I stayed home with them; I watched them weekends and nights when my wife was on call. I had a more flexible schedule; she made more money. She was able to keep a connection to our kids even while working an intense schedule; I didn't think I would be as close to our children if I hadn't stayed home. And I absolutely loved those years, even though now I wonder how we ever got through them or got anything else done. When my wife won a fellowship to go on several trips abroad, I stayed home with the kids and even held the cast party for *The King and I* while she was away (though I was irked when Tomo, our youngest, asked, "How is Dad going to have a party without Mom to help?").

Like most long-married couples, in so many ways we're in agreement—we share the same class background, politics, sense of humor, taste in music and TV shows; we're not religious, not pet people or nature lovers. Together since college (with occasional intervals of separation), we share decades of memories.

But of course when people first meet us, all they see is a blonde middle-aged white woman and an Asian middle-aged man. Perhaps with a similar sense of style in the way we dress (sometimes going out we have to change because we're both dressed in the same colors). How you read that first impression says as much about you as it does about us.

So what does our marriage have to do with race and history and the basic themes of this book?

Blondes weren't very numerous in my mainly Jewish high schools. But braces and noses shaped by plastic surgery were. I think I was aware and not aware that the prevalence of reshaped noses had something to do with the shape of many of the Jewish girls' noses.[1] I didn't think about how they too were grappling with alien goy standards of beauty. The Jewish kids dominated all aspects of our high school, from academics to band and theater to sports. In that environment, to me the Jewish kids didn't seem to be part of a minority, and certainly not in the way I felt I was. They were simply a type of white person.

Early on I sensed there was an unspoken assumption that I might date another Asian though I don't think anyone actually said this to me—not even my parents. But sensing that expectation, I inwardly protested. Why should I date an Asian girl? The ones I wasn't related to I didn't find particularly attractive, nor did they figure prominently in any of the school's social circles.

No, I thought, I'm as good as a white guy. Just as I was as smart as a white guy or, to a respectable extent, as athletic as a white guy.[2]

1 Later, in college a Jewish girlfriend affectionately dubbed me "no-nose."

2 I played football for three years and lettered in basketball my senior year. I was third string, but I constantly played with my best friend, a white goy who was a 6′11″ All American, and two other 6′4″ white guys, one Jewish, one goy. I was only 5′9″ but I held my own with a decent dribble and a better shot along with twisting and trick layups I learned playing one-on-one against someone 6′11″ (he, in turn, learned how to shoot from twenty feet like a 5′9″ guy—and thus became an All American).

Why should I think of myself as second class?

Of course, I didn't critique my own contradiction. Why did I think dating an Asian American girl made me second class? Did that make dating me or someone like me second class? And who or what created this sexual hierarchy and why? Did anyone in my high school even give a thought to the racial-sexual hierarchies of America? Mainly, they were Jewish Americans; in terms of race and history, they were obviously concerned with the six million Jews who died in the Holocaust, with the racial restrictions, animus, and discrimination their fathers might experience at work, with what the goyim made of them. Why would they even bother considering my racial identity?

In high school, my favorite book was Philip Roth's *Goodbye, Columbus.* The title novella is narrated by a working-class Jewish boy from Newark, and it recounts his brief summer fling with a Jewish girl—and Radcliffe student—from the upper-middle-class suburb of Short Hills. Back in high school, this novella was as close as I could get to something describing what it was like for me to be an outsider of sorts in a Jewish suburb. I identified with the protagonist Neil Klugman's class ressentiment and felt it as a corollary to my own racial ressentiment, though back then I didn't think of myself as Asian, at least consciously. Obviously, I understood that my being Asian could have been part of the reason the Jewish parents rejected me as a suitable suitor for their daughters, but I tended to concentrate on our religious differences—I was raised a Christian—as the basis of my being *treyf.*

Still, race may have been more of a factor in my dating in high school than I knew, as might be intuited by the following story. Throughout high school, I had a crush on a Jewish girl in my homeroom, Jill P., whom I never went out with or asked on a date, but whose house I did visit one evening in the summer before our senior year. When she was a freshman, Jill was a cheerleader, but by that summer she was dressing more like a member of the sixties counterculture. One evening, at one of the typical bi-levels in Lincolnwood, where the majority of Jewish kids lived, I called on Jill with my two other friends, one Jewish, one goy. Her father answered the door and said she wasn't home. We left, and I thought nothing about that visit other than perhaps I shouldn't drop in unannounced to girls' homes.

But years later, after my first book of poetry came out, in my early thirties, I was giving a reading in Philadelphia, and Jill showed up. After catching up on each other's lives, she informed me that she had been home when I visited. After her father sent me away and closed the door, he came into the kitchen and made a racist remark about me. She and her father got into a heated quarrel, and later, after our senior year, her tensions with her father reached such a point that instead of going to college, as almost all our class did, she ran away and lived on a hippie commune for a few years.

Growing up, I did not experience many instances of direct racial confrontation or insult, and I had often wondered how much racism toward Asians existed around me. It was only years later that my father informed me that we moved into our neighborhood in Morton Grove, where our cousins also had a house, because the builder of our house and theirs was the only builder in the area who would sell to "Orientals." Still, back then, neither myself nor my father thought very much about our being the racial other.

And yet, to Jill P. and her father, on differing terms, that is what I was. Certainly, her father would have reacted similarly if a Black teenage boy had showed up at his door asking about his daughter.

A couple of years later, at Grinnell College, I met my wife. I was a junior, an upperclassman from a Chicago Jewish suburb. Susie was a freshman from Atlanta, which was and is both Southern and different from the rest of the South. Her parents were from the North, her father from Grand Rapids, Michigan, her mother from Boston; both traced part of their family trees all the way back to the Mayflower. Her father was a physician and the director of the Centers for Disease Control (CDC), and the family considered themselves part of a racially progressive liberal Atlanta. They attended a Unitarian church and their congregation conducted joint activities with Martin Luther King Sr.'s congregation and heard Martin Luther King Jr. speak there.

When I met her—as if fated, her room was across the hall from mine—she clearly gave me the impression that she had always wanted to leave the South and was determined not to go to college there. And yet she also possessed a love of Doc Watson and Appalachian music and a more than passing acquaintance with Southern rock bands like

Lynyrd Skynyrd and the Allman Brothers. (A friend of hers had hooked up with one of the latter's band members, and Susie remembers seeing Duane Allman shoot up in the back of a van at a concert in Atlanta's Piedmont Park.)

During the first few weeks of her freshman year, her high school boyfriend drove through Iowa on his way back from Alaska to Atlanta. He had a misguided notion that he might persuade Susie to go back with him to homestead in Alaska: in his wooing, he informed her that the country was extremely beautiful, and though she might get lonely, it would be different after she killed her first bear. (He had a mental breakdown shortly after he returned home to Atlanta.) It was clear he had no notion of who Susie really was. Still, he was tall, lanky, and good looking and spoke with a Southern accent, and his family was wealthy and prominent in Atlanta; with his hippie locks and down-home clothing he appeared as if he would have been completely at ease with the Southern boys of the Allman Brothers band—in other words, a recognizably attractive entity.

I of course was something completely different.

And yet how different was not that clear. To me or to Susie.

Both Susie and I had, after all, chosen to go to Grinnell, a top-notch small liberal arts school whose student body and institutional practices were at the vanguard of the changes wrought by the sixties. The school had done away with many academic requirements, had instituted coed dorms with males and females on the same floor and unisex bathrooms. The year before I entered, the college had shut down early because of the Kent State and Jackson State shootings, the mining of Haiphong Harbor, and the nationwide protests against the Vietnam War.

In a way I had gotten to Grinnell by chance. I'd applied to Harvard, Yale, Princeton, and Stanford—schools I knew—and gotten turned down by all. Grinnell was my safety school and I'd never heard of it before my senior year; I'd applied there only because some smart people from my high school had gone there.

Susie, on the other hand, had chosen Grinnell very deliberately. She'd gone through the Barron's book of colleges and crossed off the all-female schools, the schools with "Saint" in their name, and then tried to find the school with the highest board scores and least rules. Grinnell came in first.

So going to Grinnell had already self-selected us as a possible match. We were both smart, our politics similar. We'd grown up in middle-class suburban neighborhoods, and our fathers were both executives working in the medical field, her dad at CDC, my dad at Blue Shield.

Then too there was an obvious source of our mutual sexual attraction: we were both good looking.

That statement, though, isn't as simple as it sounds, at least when it came to myself. Susie certainly had received ample attention from boys in her high school, despite her liberal anti-Southern stance, and this was even more the case in her Unitarian community and their Liberal Religious Youth group. She'd been highlighted in her school paper with a Miss May photo feature for looking sharp, had been featured in a photo from a local Atlanta magazine, and was renowned in LRY for putting off suitors.

As for me, I dated only a few times in high school. I had remained a virgin through my first two years at Grinnell, and only in the summer before my junior year did I lose my virginity to a Grinnell senior from a nearby suburb. In that, I was sexually behind the majority of my classmates.

But Susie says when she met me the first day she arrived and I left her room, she remembers sitting with her friend from Atlanta who was also going to Grinnell, and remarking, "That's the best-looking guy I've ever seen." Her friend nodded in agreement. I was the student adviser for the floor and had deliberately chosen a less popular dorm where there'd be a plethora of freshman women. In the first few weeks of school, rumors spread through the dorm that there were six to eight freshman girls who had a crush on me. Partly this was because I was an upperclassman in a dorm with few upper-class males, but it was also because I had the Grinnell hippie look down pat, with faded bell-bottom jeans and a jean shirt and a room wallpapered with an Indian print sheet and posters of James Taylor and Crosby, Stills & Nash and a sound system that played what Susie's roommate from Fergus Falls, Minnesota, deemed always "the perfect music" for the mood and time of day. I also could play Neil Young and James Taylor songs on the piano along with jazz improvisations that were fumbling imitations of Keith Jarrett and George Winston.

Part of me is not comfortable in detailing all this. I feel it is bragging, and in the remnants of Japanese cultural psychology I've imbibed from my parents, any hint of bravado or crowing is not something one is supposed to do. (There's an old Japanese saying: "The nail that sticks up gets pounded down.") It's certainly easier for me to write of my high school life as a socially excluded Asian American nerd than as a hip college upperclassman whom a group of freshman girls crushed on. But it's clear in hindsight that when Susie and I got together, we were considered one of the cool couples on campus, whatever than means.

So what about the stereotypes of Asian American men? Despite the racist Asian stereotypes in the media that I'd grown up with, in many ways the stereotype of the sexless unattractive Asian male was not quite as prevalent in the culture during the sixties and early seventies as it seemed in the following decades. (Think of the line from the Chinese exchange student Long Duk Dong in John Hughes '80s *Sixteen Candles* to Ken Jeong in *The Hangover* movies or Jimmy Yang in *Silicon Valley* or Raj in *The Big Bang Theory*.) In part this was because there weren't many Asians in the country and certainly in the Chicagoland area. The larger immigrations of Asians following the 1965 Immigration Act and the war in Vietnam had yet to manifest refugees from Southeast Asia.[3]

3 There are political historical reasons for this paucity of Asians in America. As the scholar Juliana Pegues has observed, Asians first immigrated to California, which had a need for a cheap labor force that could be exploited and yet weren't citizens and couldn't reproduce—Chinese women were prevented from immigrating (for those reasons, Blacks and Mexicans did not fit the exact requirements for such oppression and exclusion). Later, as the result of the Yellow Peril campaigns, there came the Asian Exclusion Act of 1924, which stopped official immigration from that continent. Only in 1965, with the Hart-Celler Act, did the immigration laws change to admit Asians and other people of color, and the larger influx of Asian immigrants came with the Vietnam War and an increasing wave of Chinese, Filipino, Korean, and South Asian immigrants.

Having been born in 1952 and growing up before the demographics of the 1965 Hart-Celler Act were manifested, my teenage years were well before Long Duk Dong

But if the Asian nerd wasn't quite a dominant stereotype back then, it is now, and it's hard for me to process in retrospect what happened my junior year in college: an Asian American college upperclassman who has six to eight girls in his dorm with crushes on him, who has a coed lingering outside his class so she can talk to him, who is told that two coeds went outside the dorm to see if his light was still on when another coed was visiting him—that is definitely not part of the image of Asian American men even today. Indeed, it seems, even though I lived it, an impossible image, a situation not to be believed.

And then he, this Asian American dude, hooks up with arguably the prettiest coed in the dorm? How does that happen?

In other words, the self who was attractive to women—that's a self that part of me still doesn't want to recognize. And I have to admit there's something inside me that responds viscerally to Steve Harvey's assertion that Asian men lack sexual appeal: the Asian guy who's attractive to white women—and these were all white women—how *could* that guy exist?

Looking back, I recognize that the conditioning of the negative sexual stereotyping of Asian males was something my psyche has never completely escaped. But there was also the seemingly haphazard nature of who was attracted to me: no matter their race, the women who were attracted to me were not put off by negative sexual stereotyping or racism toward Asian males, and thus they were in some vague

in *Sixteen Candles*—dubbed "the weird Chinese kid" by Molly Ringwald's character, her younger brother, and her mother. This character brought the portrayal of the Asian geek to the social realms of high school and so began a string of such portrayals to plague Asian American guys. This stereotype runs into the present. For example, in the early years of *The Big Bang Theory*, the Indian Raj was completely unable to talk to women, literally unable to utter even a syllable to them, and he's the last of the nerds on the show to get a girlfriend. And yet in real life, Kunal Nayyar who plays Raj, is married to a former Miss Universe from India. In other words, in India he hooks up with the most beautiful woman in the whole country, but in America he can't even speak to a woman and is laughed at for any pretense of sexual attractiveness or mojo. (The fact that there was never an East Asian American character at Cal Tech, where the male friends from *Big Bang* worked, demonstrates how East Asians can be excluded even in a social setting where they might well be expected to be part of the demographic.)

sense different from their counterparts. But on the other hand, that difference didn't necessarily conform to any generalization about their looks or social strata or, as far as I could tell, anything that might group them together.

Certainly, their attraction to me wasn't part of any concerted push toward racial integration, including in the sexual realm, as occurred in some parts of the country between whites and Blacks. No, when white women were attracted to me, I was most likely a racial exception in their sexual history, not the beginning of a preference or attraction to Asian men in general. That saying, "Once you go Black, you never go back" may be problematic, but it's not viewed in the larger culture as an absurd observation or a joke on Black men. But once you go Asian? There's no mojo for whatever could come after that. Because nothing is expected to.

And yet, contrary to Steve Harvey, I was aware very early on that there were also Black women who were attracted to me, from the young Black woman who gave me her number at the Art Institute of Chicago, to my making out my freshman year with a Black coed, to another Black coed who would find me playing piano at the student union and sit and listen, making sighs of appreciation. (My playing was passable, at best.)

When I look at photos of myself when younger, I can recognize that I was attractive, and attractive in a way I couldn't acknowledge back then. At the time, I wanted to think of myself as white, and I didn't understand and frankly didn't want to understand how I looked in the eyes of white American society. I knew both consciously and unconsciously that my sexuality was being evaluated by standards and a framework designed to marginalize and racialize those like me. But it caused too much internal conflict about my identity and place in society for me to contemplate and dissect these issues. Besides, at that time I still did not think of myself consciously as a Japanese American or Asian American or person of color—or at least that's how I presented myself to the world and then to Susie: "Don't call me Japanese or Asian," I said when we first met. "I'm an American. Just like you."

For years, an occasional conversation between me and my wife revolved around why she had chosen an Asian man. Her reply was always, "I don't know. You're you. I thought you were the most attractive guy I'd ever seen."

"But why? Are you saying race didn't have anything to do with it?"

"I met you when I was eighteen," she answered. "I lost my virginity to you. You were my first real boyfriend."

I replied that given my desires for a hallucinatory whiteness, I had grown up desiring to be with a white woman. Why wouldn't her desire possess a racial component?

But Susie would always demur.

Eventually, though, as I began to delve into race in my writing and sometime around when our children were born, Susie's answers to my question about interracial desire shifted and gradually grew more and more complicated. She spoke of growing up with a father who, as head of CDC, traveled widely, visiting public health officials across the globe. He was one of the first Americans to visit Communist China; he had been to Russia. After a trip to Africa, he had brought home a statue of an African smallpox god and placed it on their mantel, and he hung an African tapestry above the fireplace. Visiting physicians and health officials from all over the world came to CDC and visited their house; she had met the Prince of Togo, who was around her middle-school age and seemed to have a crush on her.

Then too she had grown up in the civil rights era, the late fifties and sixties, and she felt many of her white classmates were racists or she suspected them of being racists. Her parents were Yankees from the North, Unitarians and not considered "true" Christians like the Evangelicals and Baptists around her. When she was in second grade, a neighbor Baptist girl hounded Susie to tears on her way home, telling her she was going to hell for not being baptized or going to church. As a young girl, Susie would look in the closets of white friends to see if there might be any Ku Klux Klan garb. She had nightmares about burning crosses on her lawn.

When she was a junior in high school, one Thursday night, Susie was at the home of a white girlfriend; they were jokingly making corsages out of brussels sprouts for the Sadie Hawkins Dance the next night. The television was on, and the news announced that Martin Luther King Jr. had been assassinated. Susie's "friend" snarled, "I'm glad that n——r's dead!" Immediately Susie felt sick to her stomach and left; she never spoke to this girl again. She didn't go to the dance and after that, she removed herself from a lot of the socializing at her high school and instead spent time with the Liberal Religious Youth organization at her Unitarian church.

King's assassination confirmed to Susie that she was never going to college in the South, that she was always going to leave Atlanta. She felt ostracized for being smart—smart girls were not prized most places in America, but the South provided its own particularly severe case of this. That was why, when she counted the votes for her senior class awards and was voted most intellectual, she gave the award to the girl who came in second. She felt alienated from the Southern white boys at her high school, both in terms of their racial views (though in general they weren't as racist as those white boys outside of Atlanta) and in terms of their Southern bro culture; they in turn saw her as somewhat of an other and outsider, a liberal white girl of Northern parents who would never quite belong.

At the same time, when she got to high school, her school district was just being integrated. Early on, she developed a crush on her school's Black quarterback. She began to participate in political activities at her school around integration, in part because she and her parents fervently believed in racial equality and in part because of her crush. But then he moved away, and at a certain point she had the sense that he was too racially other: a relationship with him would have been too taboo.

And then, on her first day at Grinnell College she met me, who was neither white nor Black, who was not aligned with a malignant whiteness nor a taboo Blackness. A blank slate—or seemingly blank slate.

It took a few years for our conversations to ferret all this out, the ways in which her white racial identity had shaped her sexual desires.

A few years ago, Susie and I were having a quarrel—I don't want to get into the particulars here—and she blurted out, "Nothing good ever comes from telling the truth."

I immediately said, "Where did you learn to think that?"

"I don't know," she said. "Obviously it comes in part from being the oldest daughter in an alcoholic family." (Her father's drinking ended when his liver failed and he almost died; Susie was in her twenties at the time.)

"But you said it so strongly. Like it's a belief you acquired very early. Think about it. Who said that to you? Someone taught you that. How old are you when you say that?"

"I don't know. Maybe five or six. Maybe even younger. Four, three."

"And what happened then?"

"I don't know."

"No, I think you do know. You're five or four. What happened then?"

After an hour and half of this—yes, this is how our conversations sometimes go; I can be quite annoying and persistent when it comes to psychological issues between us—this is what came out in drabs and pieces.

"I think of the parties my parents used to have when everyone got drunk. . . . this feeling like I was all alone. . . . I would watch from the upstairs balcony. . . .

"No, it was earlier, we weren't living in Atlanta. We were living in Columbus. . . .

"There was this guy who lived in the same apartment building. He looked a little like Elvis or he had a haircut like Elvis. . . ."

"He took me out in a car, it was a car with fins, and we drove around. . . .

"And then he took a cigarette . . . and he burned me and that's where this scar came from." She pointed to a spot on her forearm and a chill went through both of us.

"I think that's all that happened. But then I told my mother and she freaked. She said we could never say anything about this, that I should never tell my father. . . .

"I think that's around the time I began to think about my father as if he were a foreign spy or a member of the KGB. . . .

"She never told him and I remember we just, my mother and I, we got in our car the next day and went to visit her parents in Boston, and it all happened very quickly. . . .

"I used to have a dream where I was in the back seat and my parents were in the front seat and suddenly they flew out of the car and the car was barreling down the road and I had to figure out how to drive it. . . . and that's why I always hated cars like that, the ones with fins."

Fifty-five years later, and five years after her father passed, this memory comes out, this trauma. Later, in therapy and in our discussions, Susie began to attach this memory to her feelings about Southern white boys and men and to the racial violence of the South during the civil rights period.

Then this year, in a conversation with me, she had another revelation: she recalled that the white man with the pompadour who lived upstairs not only burned her with a cigarette but sexually abused her. And that is what her mother told her never to talk to anyone about—a silence Susie had kept for more than six decades.

In her therapy, Susie has been working to confront this abuse and create a new narrative of her life, one in which the effects of this abuse and, perhaps even more important, her mother's denial of it and her order to Susie to never to talk about it again, were now part of Susie's story. And she has done this with great courage, in the process shifting her sense of how she views her past, her family system, and her sexuality in ways too complex to go into here.

A few years ago, when Susie's mother died, we returned to Atlanta with our children for the memorial service.

At the end of the weekend, late at night, Susie and I talked about her relationship with the South. We were talking about why her brother and her sister stayed in Atlanta and why she always knew she was going to leave the South, that she wasn't going to stay there. At the start of this discussion, I talked about a film based on Pat Conroy's novel *The Prince of Tides*, a film we're both very familiar with.[4] The protagonist, Tom Wingo, who grows up in South Carolina, has to go to New York and meet with Susan Lowenstein, the Jewish psychiatrist of his twin sister, Savannah. Savannah has just tried to commit suicide and the therapist presses Tom for details about their childhood. Their

4 Susie's brother's wife knew Conroy because his third wife was best friends with her mother, and Susie's brother and his wife stayed at Conroy's home in Fripp, South Carolina, on their honeymoon. Fripp was where parts of *The Prince of Tides* was filmed, and when Susie's whole family began vacationing at Fripp, we would watch *Prince of Tides* almost every summer, along with *The Great Santini*, another film made from a novel by Conroy.

sessions eventually stumble into his mentioning and then evading some sort of trauma from their childhood. In the novel and the film, Lowenstein presses Tom to break his silence; she says there's something about their family's history that he's eliding, and she needs that information to help his sister recover. After much prodding, Tom finally releases the truth: it turns out that when he was eight, three escaped convicts broke into their house and raped him and his sister and mother. Through bravery and luck, his mother and his older brother managed to kill the convicts. But then, instead of telling the authorities or even the father, they buried the bodies, cleaned up all the blood, and pretended none of it happened. After recounting these horrific events, the protagonist, played by Nick Nolte, puts on a bright faux smile and says to the psychiatrist, played by Barbra Streisand, invoking the lyrics of an old Southern song and holding up his hands, gesturing like a vaudeville singer, "And that's what I like about the South!"

Susie recalled how in the film Tom's mother orders her children never to talk again about what happened that night. "I swear," he says to the psychiatrist, "the coverup was worse than the rape." Susie and I discussed the implication of her mother's admonition to Susie to never talk about the childhood abuse she had experienced.

Picking up on the Southern setting of *Prince of Tides,* I invoked Faulkner's *The Sound and the Fury,* in which Quentin Compson, of the doomed Compson family, is attending Harvard and he's telling his Canadian roommate Shreve about the history of his family and the South. At one point, Quentin says, almost pleading, "I don't hate the South, I don't hate the South."

"But I do hate the South," said Susie.

"Yes, you hate the South. You hate the racism of the South. But your brother and sister, they hate the racism of the South too, but they don't hate all of the South. You equate hatred of racism with hatred of the South. They don't. The question is why, why do you so hate the South so much more than your brother and sister?"

A long conversation ensued. At a certain point, Susie remembered the time when her parents were living in Ann Arbor and her father was offered the CDC job in Atlanta. Her parents had lived in Columbus, Georgia, and her mother had hated it (and we now know that was where Susie was abused). In Columbus, her mother was the Yankee

Northerner, the outsider, and she always felt excluded by the local white women—and of course she hated the racism. She felt she was never going to be accepted there.

Susie said that at age five, she listened to her parents talking about what would happen if they moved back to the South. It was 1959, the civil rights movement was in full force, and the question of segregation, of ending segregation, and the resistance to that gripped the region. Susie's mother noted that a store-front school had been set up for whites in Atlanta so that the whites wouldn't have to go to school with Blacks. What if the public schools were shut down? They couldn't send Susie to a school with racist segregationists.

Well, said her father, we'll educate Susie at home.

But there was the threat of violence, the very strong resistance of so many Southerners to integration. Why go back to all that?

Eventually her parents decided that they could be part of the movement that was challenging and changing the South. They knew good people at CDC, people who believed in racial equality and integration. They could be part of something new, a force for good.

"Wait a second," I said to Susie. "You were four or five. And you remember these conversations?"

"Yes."

"And you understood them, at five?"

"To some extent. Certainly, I remember them talking about this, very vividly."

I pointed out to Susie that her parents returned to the South in 1959; the years between 1955 and 1965 were the center of the fight against segregation, the most contentious period with violence not just a constant threat but an actuality. A few years before, Emmett Till had been murdered; four young black girls had been killed in a church bombing in Birmingham. Later, Medgar Evers was shot and killed in 1963; the young civil rights workers James Chaney, Michael Schwerner, and Andrew Goodman, were killed in 1964.

"I remember when they pushed to integrate the local pool," Susie said. "My father wrote a letter to the paper saying that Black people and white people swimming in a pool together posed no health risks."

"So your parents were at the very tip of the few whites for change," I said. "Yes, there was a Black vanguard pushing for change, your Unitarian congregation was allied with that, with Martin Luther King

Sr.'s church. But think about what the reaction must have been to your father's letter. That was about as far out there as a white public official in that time could get."

Suddenly, Susie's childhood fears about Ku Klux Klan robes in her white friends' closets, her nightmares about cross burning made more sense to me. She had returned with her parents to Atlanta at the very height of racial turmoil there, and her parents knew it was going to be difficult, perhaps even violent, and her parents understandably feared these threats—and thus Susie feared this violence, too. Whether deliberately or, more likely, inadvertently, they had conveyed that danger and those fears to Susie. At age four or five.

"You know," Susie said, "I never feared Black people. It was the white people I feared, especially white males."

"And then there was that Elvis character," I replied. "The one who burned you with a cigarette."

"But that was before we moved back."

"But when you went South a second time, you moved back into a time and an atmosphere where you perceived white people and white men in particular as the prime danger, not Blacks. And you probably retroactively and unconsciously attached your trauma with that Elvis white guy to what was happening with race all around you, and later, probably also unconsciously, your fear of him was associated with your fear of whites, particularly white males, along with that Baptist girl telling you in second grade you were going to hell and you crying all the way home."

"Yeah."

"Your brother and sister didn't grow up with all that. They came along later when things weren't as tense or violent racially. They didn't grow up with the same fears, with the same nightmares. They didn't listen at five to your parents discussing how dangerous and violent the South was. All those historical circumstances contributed to your psychology, especially since you grew up in the South."

"Blacks were safe."

"But too taboo sexually."

"You weren't."

"In certain ways," I continued, "your understanding of your psychology in regards to race has shifted almost as much as mine. When

I first met you, you seemed much more Southern and you still liked some things about the South like Doc Watson."

"Once I got North, I knew I was never going back."

"And you met me."

"And I met you."

We smiled and hugged. She snuggled into my neck as she often does and said, "Why do I like the way you smell so much?"

"I'm Asian," I said. And we both laughed.

PART III

What VONA Taught Me (Part 1)

My Middle Years

I

In 2001, I was invited by the Lebanese American writer Elmaz Abinader to VONA, the summer writers' conference in San Francisco for BIPOC writers.[1] Elmaz was VONA's artistic director and I'd done a reading with her the previous year at San Jose State University. She was married to the African American executive director Diem Jones. Originally, VONA was to be the West Coast wing of the Hurston/Wright Foundation, which produced a Black writers' conference. But Diem said this was the multiracial Bay Area, and he wanted the conference expanded to all writers of color. So VONA became its own separate entity. In 1999, it was conceived in a collaboration between Diem, Elmaz, the young Dominican American fiction writer Junot Díaz, and Victor Diaz, a Bay area educator and activist.

So there I am, a Japanese American poet and memoirist from the Midwest, starting my first time teaching at VONA. I'm fresh from the expensive cab ride from the airport, wandering into a lounge at the University of San Francisco, into a group of Black, Latino, Asian, and Arab American writers socializing before a panel. The crowd contains far more women than men; some are standing in groups or pairs, some lounging on the couches or in chairs. I'm not sure where I'm to be housed or what I should be doing now, since the session of the conference when I'm teaching doesn't start yet. I'm grateful to see Elmaz, a short Lebanese American woman with luminescent brown eyes and long eyelashes and wavy shoulder-length dark brown hair; she's wearing a brightly colored summer dress and she's talking to a beautiful young woman, with streaked-blond wavy hair, sharp angular cheeks,

1 The full name is Voices of Our Nations Arts foundation (www.vonavoices.org).

and a prominent equally angular nose, her body thin and lithe and her demeanor and speech animated with an energy and demotics straight out of the multiverse of Brooklyn. I would later learn this was the Palestinian American spoken word poet Suheir Hammad, who'd performed on Broadway in Russell Simmons's *Def Poetry Jam*.

I'm nervous, still wondering if I belong in such an eclectic group, one I can't imagine occurring anywhere else but in either the Bay Area or New York. Elmaz looks me up and down—I'm wearing a black leather jacket, a black shirt and jeans—and she turns to Suheir and says, "Rock star," and Suheir smiles and nods.

Suddenly I think, *Maybe I just might belong here.*

Though there was certainly a touch of irony in Elmaz's remark, I read it also as a positive. I realized that I was suddenly in a space where not only was my writing respected—after all, I was being asked to teach there—but where my body was no longer regarded as alien or abnormal, as associated with the negative stereotypes regarding Asian American masculinity. Simply to know that there could exist such a world shifted something in my psyche in a profound way. If you did a survey of the American public and asked what words do you associate with Asian American males, *rock star* would not be anywhere near the top ten on the list. (Of course, this was way before BTS.)

So there I was teaching at a conference for writers of color, and the writers I was mingling with were the likes of Willie Perdomo, well known at the Nuyorican Poets Café and whom I'd seen on PBS performing his "Nigger-Reecan Blues"; Suheir, the Broadway Def Jam spoken-word artist; the young Dominican American and eventual Pulitzer Prize fiction writer Junot Díaz, whose *Drown* had signaled for so many a new and distinctive voice in American fiction. Later I would be joined on the faculty with award-winning writers like Cristina García, Chitra Banerjee Divakaruni, ZZ Packer, Quincy Troupe, Staceyann Chin, Chris Abani, Mat Johnson, M. Evelina Galang, Reyna Grande, Patricia Smith, Terry McMillan, Colson Whitehead, Martín Espada. VONA's director, Diem Jones, had done album covers for George Clinton and toured with Clinton and had encounters with musicians like Sly Stone. (Diem once tossed Sly's weed into the toilet after warning him not to bring it into his office.)

Slowly, gradually, I became a part of VONA, all the while being impressed and challenged by this array of talent and diversity of backgrounds, and energized by the faculty reading among so many well-known writers of color. There I was teaching at a conference where social justice and arts activism were treasured values, and the traditions of BIPOC writers were deemed essential and centered in our pedagogy.

Sometimes, yes, I wondered, *Do I really belong here?* I grew up in a white middle-class Jewish suburb, not in a multiracial hotbed like the Bay area, not amid urban multiverses like Suheir's Brooklyn. Unlike most of the writers at VONA, I didn't grow up among my own; I wasn't raised by my parents and neighborhood to be ethnically or racially conscious, and I didn't encounter more than a handful of people of color until my late twenties. And for the first few years at VONA, I did suffer from my own version of imposter syndrome.

To be clear, nothing anyone said to me at VONA made me feel like an imposter. Indeed, from that first moment with Elmaz and Suheir, I was welcomed by the VONA community, and my being Asian American didn't make me suspect but instead was regarded as an asset. Still, from the beginning I was aware that I had come from a more privileged and white suburban background than the majority of the other writers and students, who grew up in urban ethnic and racial communities. But it wasn't just where I had grown up. Many of the urban BIPOC artists at VONA were far more hip and conversant with other BIPOC cultures and communities than I was. Over and over, I felt I was rushing to catch up.

What saved me, though, was that I was willing to learn. No, I was eager to learn. The diversity of writers and students and knowledge and talent around me was like nothing I had encountered in English graduate school or my MFA program. As I taught, I was learning along with my students what it meant to be a writer of color and to practice my craft as a writer of color. I learned this in part by teaching these diverse students; I learned by simply listening and asking questions and being constantly confronted with my own ignorance, which only made me want to listen and learn more.

So VONA helped me to develop as a writer, artist, and teacher, and this essay and the next recount that process. But for readers in the time of Trump and his attacks on DEI, please note: the diversity I encountered at VONA, the myriad histories and backgrounds, is *America's* diversity. My VONA experiences illuminate how complex today's America is compared to the America I grew up in. Which means, white writers who cordon themselves off into all-white or mainly white spaces do not know and cannot adequately address what our nation has become.

II

One of my early VONA memories took place in the living room of our University of San Francisco housing, the highest elevation in the city, rising on a hill just a few blocks above the Haight-Ashbury district. The famed Frisco fog was rolling in, and Elmaz and Suheir were talking about their visit to the West Bank and the ways they were hassled and harassed at the Israeli checkpoints into Palestine and made to wait hours, over and over questioned about who they were, what their purpose was in traveling there—though they were there simply to give poetry readings. As a Palestinian, Suheir spoke of her family's property, which was no longer in their possession and her father's bitterness about losing his land; she then went into the ways the Israeli settlers were seizing chunks of the West Bank for their settlements. Elmaz spoke about the Palestinian refugee camps in Lebanon. Junot added to the critiques of Israeli policy, likening it to a form of colonialism and apartheid.

Having grown up in the Jewish suburb of Skokie outside Chicago, I had imbibed the image of an embattled Israeli Jewish populace, carving out a democratic state in their ancient homeland, reclaiming the land from the British colonizers, and establishing a safe haven for Jews after six million were slaughtered in the Holocaust. One key text in my high school had been Leo Uris's *Exodus*; everyone knew the film, starring Paul Newman, made from the novel. *Exodus* starts with the Jews held in the Karaolos internment camp in Palestine and their attempt to smuggle past a British blockade. The film then moves on to the fighting between the Jews and Arabs over the establishment of Israel.

In that room at VONA in San Francisco, more than twenty years after high school, talking with Elmaz, Suheir, and Junot, I realized that I had grown up hearing only one side of the story of the conflict between

Israelis and Palestinians. Indeed, I had a lot of work to do if I was going to catch up. Fifteen years later, I traveled to Palestine and Israel as part of the Palestinian Literary Festival, invited by the Palestinian American writer Nathalie Handal, who has also taught at VONA. (I'm still working on my account of that trip.) During that trip, I recalled my bewilderment back in my sophomore year in high school when Sheila Levine said to me that after graduation that she was going to Israel to live on a kibbutz. *But you're an American,* I thought naively and ignorantly. *Why would you want to do that?* Back in high school, I didn't even know Palestinians existed.

On the trip with the Palestinian Literary Festival, I not only learned how methodically the Israeli state was trying to take not just Palestinian land but also Palestinian sources of water, how the moniker *settlements* did not do justice to the high rises and infrastructure being put up on the West Bank. I met Palestinians who were nothing like the terrorist caricatures in Western media, Palestinians whose relatives had been killed by Israeli forces or settlers but who would not use the word *hate* when referring to the Israelis; instead, they often spoke of how they were determined not to let the injustice of the Israeli occupation keep them from living lives that were not solely rooted in suffering and rage. After I read a poem about an Issei community leader imprisoned by the U.S. government behind barbed wire, a Palestinian father and daughter came up to me and told me how strongly they related to the poem—just as I had responded to Joe Sacco's brilliant graphic novels of Palestinians surrounded by barbed wire, which could not help but invoke the internment camps for me.

But again, back in the early aughts, I knew nothing about the Palestinians or many other subjects and issues; there was so much for me to catch up on.

I ended up rooming with Junot Díaz, from the first year on. Junot's a compact, lean-muscled, bespectacled Dominican with a shaved head, mustache, and goatee, and his speech flows with intellectual and literary references, nerd culture and sci-fi, urban street and hip-hop, bilingual lacings and references to Dominican culture—the mixture of languages used by Junior, the narrator of his *The Brief Wondrous Life of Oscar Wao.*

When we first met, Junot told me that he had read my memoir, *Turning Japanese,* and thought, "Well, if this dude can be that honest, I'd better be too."

As we got to know each other, Junot educated me with tales of growing up in Santo Domingo and the poverty there. He recounted the terrors of the Trujillo regime, the ways Trujillo kept the country sealed off from the rest of the world and created a dystopia where any hint of dissent resulted in prison, and where Trujillo, like a mob boss, had his hand in every cookie jar; like a medieval king, he would even claim for himself any woman he fancied, no matter if they were the daughters of the people who worked for him—so that some would try to hide the existence of their daughters from the dictator, as does the father of the cursed family in *Oscar Wao.*

Junot frequently said you can't get through a Third World childhood without a sense of humor, and his stories were often filled with both hilarity and pain, with the emphasis more on his cutting humor. He talked about his beautiful older brother, who always picked on and pummeled him, whom his mother and all the girls in the neighborhood loved, and who died young of cancer but then became a character in Junot's fiction. Later, when I started working on my novel, *Famous Suicides of the Japanese Empire,* about the son of a Japanese American No-No Boy, I made my protagonist, Ben Ohara, a single child. But Junot said I should give him a brother. That way Ben would have someone to talk to about what was happening in his family—his father's growing depression, his mother's increasing desperation and anger. Once I gave Ben a brother, the novel took off with a whole new energy and plot.

In what seemed at first rather odd to me, Junot informed me he had always had Asian friends. In part this was because back in Santo Domingo when he was growing up, the theaters could not afford American films but instead rented gangster or chop-socky martial arts films from Hong Kong, like the ones that made Bruce Lee famous. As a result, Junot had grown up seeing Asian faces on the screen. Then, too, he was a nerd from his teenage years on, and when he immigrated to America, he could always find Asians who shared his nerdy passions.

Eventually Junot began to turn his prankish sense of humor and razor wit on me. More than once, he seemed to delight in making me feel uncomfortable, especially how straight-laced and proper I seemed to be, how little I swore, how much I didn't know about current culture—and not just hip-hop, but nerd culture or, in a more serious vein, science fiction, and I would try to hide my ignorance of figures like Samuel Delany or Octavia Butler or I'd try to keep up using whatever knowledge of hip-hop I'd gleaned from my adolescent sons. After *Harold and Kumar Go to White Castle* came out, I sometimes thought of myself as the uptight straighter Harold to Junot's Kumar.

Sometimes, Junot would add a particular ethnopolitical context to this ribbing. When we would go to Korean barbecue places—something that became a tradition with us—he would introduce himself and then announce to the staff there, "And here's my Japanese friend, David," thus putting me square in the sights of the very understandable dislike many Koreans harbor for the Japanese and their brutal colonization of Korea. He would do the same thing when we went to Chinese restaurants. At one of those restaurants, the House of Nanking in North Beach, like the kid from the Jewish suburb I am, I ordered fried rice and chow mein. The waiter-owner, a severe-looking older Chinese man with close-cropped white hair, whom Junot dubbed "The General," barked, "You don't come to my restaurant to order chow mein and fried rice. I order for you!" To which Junot quipped, "Man, you just got your Asian license revoked!"

Often late at night, Junot and I talked about literary matters, such as the use of vernacular and swear words in his prose ("Students don't realize a little goes a long way," he remarked) or the ways Edward Said opened up a whole new way of contextualizing and evaluating global literature ("There's before Said and after Said") or the use of Nathan Zuckerman as a narrator in Roth's American trilogy (both Roth and Junot grew up in New Jersey), which in certain ways served later as a model for Junior, the narrator of *The Brief Wondrous Life of Oscar Wao*. This discussion of the narrator's voice set us on to talking about the precedent set by Conrad's and Marlow's narration in *The Heart of Darkness* and *Lord Jim*.

When Junot mentioned the latter, I talked of how once the Chinese American poet Li-Young Lee related to me that when he was younger, he read *Lord Jim* identifying with Marlow and Jim. But then Li-Young had this sudden realization: he was identifying with the whites in the book and not the Malays. I linked Li-Young's epiphany with Chinua

Achebe's similar experience reading *The Heart of Darkness.* Following his British colonial education, like a good scholarship boy, Achebe was identifying with Kurtz and Marlow contemplating the unintelligible savages on the banks of the Congo River. But then Achebe came to the realization that those unintelligible savages were like his great-grandparents: *Do I think my ancestors were uncivilized savages?* he asked himself. This realization prompted his writing *Things Fall Apart,* that seminal African novel about an Ibo villager just before and after the Europeans came to Nigeria.

Moving deeper, our conversation would then tumble into various aspects of postcolonial lit and theory, such as Junot's reading of Patrick Chamoiseau's *Texaco* (centered on the period when slavery ended in Martinique and from whose text, and not David Foster Wallace, Junot got the idea for the footnotes in *Oscar Wao*); we'd move on to Said's reading of *Mansfield Park* and how the novel ignores the West Indies slave labor that provides its wealth; or the dictators of Latin America and how the Trujillo's dictatorship came out of the legacy of Spanish colonialism and was one of the models for Márquez's *The Autumn of the Patriarch.*

I had known almost nothing about the DR before I met Junot, but I did know something about postcolonial and Caribbean lit. From a list I'd gathered searching for literary confrontations with Whiteness, I talked about all those scholarship boys who came from Britain's colonial empire and their first encounters with actual Brits. There was Salman Rushdie and the semiautobiographical character in *The Satanic Verses* trying to eat a breakfast of many-boned kippers the first time and his white British classmates laughing at his clumsy primitive efforts.[2] There was Derek Walcott's initial reading in London and how,

2 "One day soon after he started at the school he came down to breakfast to find a kipper on his plate. He sat there staring at it, not knowing where to begin. Then he cut into it, and got a mouthful of tiny bones. And after extracting them all, another mouthful, more bones. His fellow-pupils watched him suffer in silence; not one of them said, here, let me show you, you eat it in this way. It took him ninety minutes to eat the fish and he was not permitted to rise from the table until it was done. By that time he was shaking, and if he had been able to cry he would have done so. Then the thought occurred to him that he had been taught an important lesson. England was a peculiar-tasting smoked fish full of spikes and bones, and nobody would ever tell him how to eat it. He discovered that he was a bloody-minded person. 'I'll show them all,' he

when they applauded his first poem, he thought that meant the reading was over, and so he left the stage; when he was told his mistake, he was so embarrassed he refused to go back on. When Walcott went to Westminster Abbey where many famous British poets are interred, he wondered if he and his poetry would ever have a place among them.

In a perhaps more deluded case, in his semiautobiographical novel, *The Enigma of Arrival,* a young version of V. S. Naipaul takes a plane from Trinidad to New York for a boat to Britain. Naipaul had his own British colonial education, and on that flight his autobiographical protagonist is romantically imagining how he's going to write stories like Evelyn Waugh about English country houses, thoroughly unaware of the multiple absurdities in his imbibing such an ambition. But then the young colonial lands in New York and gets cheated by a cabbie. He relates how he had the Indian fear of eating other's food and so he'd lugged a chicken in a paper bag on the plane; then, at the hotel he didn't know how room service worked and was afraid to ask. Without a plate or utensils or napkin, he ate the chicken holding it in his fists, with the juices dripping, hunched over a wastepaper basket in his hotel room—an act that Naipaul describes as eating like a "savage," despite his romantic Brit-lit fantasies.

Moving on from the scholarship boys, I talked about how my friend, the Twin Cities Indian director Dipankar Mukherjee had dreamed as a young man in Kolkata of directing Shakespeare in Britain. But when he finally got to London, during the first days someone yelled "Paki" at him and he thought, "I'm not Pakistani, I'm Indian"; it took him a while to catch on to British racism. That racism wasn't only out in the streets with working-class louts; in his residency at the Old Vic it became clear that the white Brit theater people didn't think he had the proper background or chops to direct Shakespeare—after all, listen to his accent. Dipankar has told me that one of the things that helped him in Britain with a way out of Whiteness was coming upon my memoir, *Turning Japanese.*

At some point in my talks with Junot, we got back to Junior, the narrator of the novel Junot was working on. When I asked whom Junior

swore. 'You see if I don't.' The eaten kipper was his first victory, the first step in his conquest of England."—Salman Rushdie, *The Satanic Verses.*

imagined as his audience, Junot said it wasn't a white audience but Junior's Dominican community. This led us to a discussion of how we could bypass centering the white audience and speak directly to our communities, and in that, we could change the narration's economy of explanation. Where there were things we might have to explain to the white reader, we didn't have to do that if we were speaking to our own communities. (Later, our conversations about narrators would influence my essay "Four Questions of the Narrator" in my book on creative writing, *A Stranger's Journey*.)[3]

Late one night Junot and I were smoking weed on the balcony. He was pondering how he could unite the different strands of the novel, from the father who had been imprisoned by Trujillo, to the daughter who immigrated to America, to her son, the Oscar Wao of the title, who'd grown up to be a nerd of color, to his rebellious sister who runs away from home. Junot had all their stories, but he wanted them to somehow cohere more. As he talked about them, I suggested that once Trujillo imprisoned the father, the family had been cursed and that curse was handed down through the generations. Immediately Junot saw how this might work; there was even a Dominican word for curse, *fukú*. In the end, he decided to open *Oscar Wao* with a discussion of curses in Caribbean culture as Junior positions his tale as a *zafa*, a counter-spell to ward off curses.

In so many ways, VONA was a world-class education for me, not just about literature but the world.

VONA was where I heard M. Evelina Galang describe her interviews with the Filipino "comfort women," who were brutalized and raped by Japanese soldiers during World War II, and yet the Japanese government still refused to recognize the war crimes perpetrated by its military. Evelina would detail how hard it was for these women, these *Lolas*, to recall what had happened to them, the horrors they endured, and yet they were so generous to Evelina, knowing she would tell their tales to the world, as she became part of their family.

3 The four questions are: Who is the narrator? Whom is the narrator telling the tale to? When is the narrator telling the tale (in relationship to the events of the narration)? Why is the narrator telling the tale?

VONA was where I heard the jazz guitarist Tony Khalife talk about "manning" a gun post at fourteen during the Lebanese civil war. He'd been hanging out at a café where some of the fighters gathered, and one day they needed a replacement and the next day there he was, stuck behind sandbags with an AK-47. Later, as his teacher, I read his writings about that experience and the ways the abnormal conditions of war can create a new normal, can become for its participants, no matter how young, just what is.

In the faculty dorm, I would have late-night talks with Chris Abani, the Nigerian writer, who informed me that his Blackness was never a question or problem when he was growing up—or, rather, if it was a problem, it was because he had a Scottish mother and so this became the source of his difference among his peers in Lagos. In distinguishing the complex parameters of his identity and history, Chris talked about his ability to adopt a more upper-class British accent, which served him well in encounters with the British police when he was living in Britain. And yet the same accent was read as uppity by American police. As an African, Chris had a different take on race in America, and this in turn helped prepare me for my students—at VONA and in the Twin Cities—who were Black immigrants from the Caribbean and Africa.

When a teenager, Chris had written a novel about a revolution in Africa, somewhat in the vein of novels like Frederick Forsyth's *The Dogs of War*. When this novel gained a certain readership, the government read Chris's novel as encouraging subversion and revolution, and so the government arrested and imprisoned him. Chris's experience as a teenager in a Nigerian prison was something I could barely take in. Given the terrors and brutality of that experience, I could not imagine how he was sitting before me, calmly talking about it (though he acknowledged the difficulty of getting those experiences into poetry, much less a more extensive prose account). In prison, Chris said, he was regularly ordered into a pit of urine and shit, and several times he and the others were awakened and lined up and informed they were going to be shot—only to have the execution called off at the last second. I couldn't even begin to contemplate what this experience must have been like for Chris, who was seventeen or eighteen at the time, and I was amazed at the strength in him and how he was able to keep his sanity in the face of such trauma.

Chris's imprisonment became one of the ways I would come to measure any difficulties in my own life or as a writer: nothing I would ever suffer would approach what Chris had gone through; the least I could do was be grateful for never having to endure such imprisonment, and I should make less of whatever problems I might be going through as a writer and view them proportionately.

One of the things I loved about Chris's fiction was that in certain ways he didn't posit a norm or any sort of universal, and yet, conversely, he presented a world where the universal was everywhere. For instance, seen from a certain light, any place can be strange, exotic, and at the same time normal, whether it be Lagos, London, Los Angeles, or Las Vegas. His novels are peopled with those at the fringes—Nigerian Siamese Twins and freaks from a circus show; a Nigerian–El Salvadoran living in Los Angeles who falls in love with a black trans stripper; a crazed South African doctor conducting horrifying medical experiments in Las Vegas; a young Nigerian Elvis impersonator trying to elicit contributions from tourists in Lagos; a child soldier in an endless African war. Chris searches for and discovers what is beneath the surface appearances of his characters. I took this in part as a counter to how he as a heavyset Nigerian immigrant—he's built like a defensive lineman, solid, wide—who is a brilliant novelist and thinker, is so often misread in America. One example is a story Chris told me about being a new hire at Northwestern University. When he came to his first faculty meeting, he kept waiting for the meeting to start and when he asked about this, the professor next to him said they were waiting for Chris Abani. He let this go on for a while, and then, after he revealed that he indeed was Chris Abani, he asked, "So how often do you let random Black men attend your departmental meetings?"

Rooming one year with African American novelist Mat Johnson, I listened to his stories about his growing up as a very light-skinned Black in New York and the ways he has had to navigate his body through a world that often misidentifies him or tries to pigeonhole who he is. Matt told me the story about how when he was younger he tried to manipulate his appearance—such as shaving his head—so he would more often be perceived as Black. But he became so discouraged by how often he was still perceived as or mocked as white that he let his hair grow. Then walking down the street with a light-skinned

Latina in New York, a Black man walking by muttered, “Passing motherfucker,” and Mat felt a sense not of shame but of joy; his racial identity had been recognized. Some of this sense of what it means to be a light-skinned mixed-race Black man went into Mat’s brilliant novel *Loving Day,* about a protagonist with similar qualities and his mixed-race daughter.

From both Chris and Mat, I learned more deeply that any positing of an essentialist identity for any ethnic or racial group belies the reality and complexity of that group. If some might find my credentials as a person of color suspect because I was Asian, Chris and Mat had had to confront suspicions or exclusions of their own—for Chris in Nigeria, England, and America; for Mat within Black America. And yet at VONA we were all colleagues, fellow writers and teachers, friends. And part of the basis for this was we had all rejected the tenants of Whiteness, whether in configuring our own identities or in our writing and teaching.

VONA was the alternative grad school to my white-dominated MFA and to the all-white literary community in the Twin Cities I’d once belonged to. Over and over there I was struck by how dull, limited, myopic, and uncreative the white writing world looked in retrospect, how absurd its claims to universality. But even more important, I became aware not just of the growing diversity of America and American literature, but through both the faculty and my students I learned how to view that literature in the context of world literature.

III

When I was coming up as a young writer, no older white writer took me under their wing; I always felt this indifference from them, and this indifference began to be mixed with a coolness as I became known as a race man. Aside from Asian American writers like Frank Chin, Jeanne Wakatsuki Houston, and Wakako Yamauchi, the older writers who greeted me with warmth, as if I were one of their own, were Lucille Clifton, Gwendolyn Brooks, and Quincy Troupe. I could not help but be struck by how these three took to me even though I was not a Black writer.

So I was pleased that for a couple of summers Quincy was part of the VONA faculty. A friend has called Quincy the Black Zelig, since

Quincy seems to know so many famous Black people, and listening to Quincy's tales was like getting a free class in African American history. VONA was where I heard Quincy talk about traveling with Muhammad Ali to Zaire for the Rumble in the Jungle, how Ali transformed the whole nation into his posse as he ran through the city for his training. Quincy described meeting Sartre in Paris who told him he should keep a diary and thus began Quincy's writing career. It was in Paris that Quincy first met "Jimmy." Quincy conducted James Baldwin's last interview where he proclaimed, "I was not born to be defined by someone else, but by myself and myself only."[4] In that interview, Baldwin talked about his friendship with Miles Davis, whom Quincy collaborated with in writing Davis's autobiography. Ever the raconteur, Quincy had stories about his friendship with Miles that were replete with a dead-on imitation of Miles's raspy voice, often cutting Quincy down to size. He described the time Miles and Prince jammed together, two periods of African American music interweaving in ways I wish I could have heard. The next moment Quincy would be talking about his father's days in the Negro baseball leagues, Quincy sitting in the dugout and meeting stars like the legendary Josh Gibson. Or Quincy would tell about going to a football game with Danny Glover or his shooting hoops at Grambling, or he'd disparage "Master" Danforth, the white conservative senator from Missouri, who'd championed Clarence Thomas's nomination.

Then there was the time Quincy told me about teaching at Staten Island and how in the hall a white professor questioned Quincy's learning and literary chops—it was clear Quincy had read everything. Quincy, at 6′4″ and probably 230, took the guy by the scruff of his neck, hauled him up against the window, and said "If you ever talk to

4 From my thirties on, I've quoted from that interview in my teaching: "You see whites want black writers to mostly deliver something as if it were an official version of the black experience. But the vocabulary won't hold it, simply. No true account really of black life can be held, can be contained in the American vocabulary. . . . the only way that you can deal with it is by doing great violence to the assumptions on which the vocabulary is based. But they won't let you do that. And when you go along, you find yourself very quickly painted into a corner; you've written yourself into a corner. Because you can't compromise as a writer."

me like that again, motherfucker, I'll throw you out the damned window!" It was another lesson for me in not taking shit from white guys, not letting them think they were capable of measuring who you are when they have no fucking idea who you are. Both physically and by temperament, I'm not capable of throwing anyone out the window or threatening such, but I could still refuse to give power to those who cannot see me.

This was a lesson that deepened with each year I spent at VONA. Not only did VONA complicate the ways I viewed my own racial and ethnic identity, it also transformed how I viewed my own work. For instance, my first memoir, *Turning Japanese: Memoirs of a Sansei,* related the narrative of my yearlong stay in Japan, the land from which my grandparents emigrated at the beginning of the twentieth century. While this memoir was widely praised, white critics focused on the book's descriptions and stories about Japan and the Japanese; they praised the vividness and specificity of the prose, the description of Japanese settings and Japanese individuals. During the 1980s, at the time I wrote the memoir, many Americans viewed Japan as an economic and political threat to America; there was the Detroit auto crisis, books like *The Coming War with Japan* by George Friedman and Meredith LeBard, and Michael Crichton's book and subsequent film *Rising Sun.* In other words, it wasn't me as a Japanese American, but the falsely perceived, racially animated rivalry with Japan that made Japan important to these white critics.

As for my life story? Almost in passing, the white critics mentioned my investigation into my family history and my questioning of what it means to be a third-generation Japanese American. But to the white critics, this aspect of my memoir was more a sidelight, something minor to be easily passed over.

In contrast, all of the Asian American reviewers understood that my memoir was an investigation into my ethnic and racial identity; Japan was the lens and mirror through which that investigation took place. The Asian American reviewers realized that the book investigated a dialectic between my own story and the history of my family in America on the one hand, and on the other, the Japanese culture and the Japanese people I encountered during my visit. The Asian American reviewers understood how my visit enabled me to see my grandparents and parents more clearly, to detect where and how Japanese cultural values still manifested themselves in my family and even in me. In short, these Asian American critics saw how Japan sparked me to ask questions about Japanese American history and my family and the effect of the internment camps on all three generations of my family. How it led me to imaginings of moments in the lives of my Nisei relatives, as they dealt with racism and imprisonment.

But then I published my second memoir, *Where the Body Meets Memory: An Odyssey of Race, Sexuality, and Identity,* which explored my own life and the lives of my parents and grandparents and, at the same time, explored my own struggles dealing with my sexuality as an Asian American male. As a rule, white writers can be celebrated and romanticized for their accounts of neuroses and melancholy and sexual escapades—think here of Sylvia Plath or Robert Lowell or John Berryman, or today, of Karl Ove Knausgård or Annie Ernaux, Rachel Cusk or Rachel Krantz. In contrast, here's the way the anonymous reviewer in *Kirkus Reviews* characterized *Where the Body Meets Memory*:

> More tediously self-absorbed reflections on the emotional torments of a lost-and-found soul from the author of *Turning Japanese* (1991). A third-generation Japanese-American (sansei) who remains vaguely discontented with his heritage, albeit endlessly fascinated by his place (or lack thereof) in contemporary US society, Mura (who turns 44 this year) offers a discontinuous memoir that draws on the lives of those close to him as well as his own experiences. . . . Mura comes nowhere near his stated objective in the flights of fancy he has patched together, and the egocentric text is remarkable only for its modest shock value.

To such a reviewer, the idea that my writing about myself involved a way of investigating not just my own life and context but the history and psychology of Japanese Americans or Asian Americans was nonsense. To view my life within the context of my ethnic or racial group was decidedly not a legitimate literary or cultural question, much less a political question.

My teaching at VONA and what I learned from my fellow teachers and students helped me see more clearly the egregiousness of that *Kirkus* critic. Within such a safe community, at VONA I was able to confront a version of my own wounding—that I didn't belong, that I was a freak, that no one was interested in my story, that I would always be the anonymous look-alike Asian with no individuality or visibility. Because the other VONA faculty and the VONA student emerging writers had had similar experiences, I realized I was no longer an exception; instead, I was part of a community, a community that shared a certain understanding and context for who I was, an understanding and context I never found in any white-dominated workshop I had attended as a student.

One lie of white supremacy is the lie of sameness, the lie that the past is not complicated or contradictory or filled with trauma, is not suffused with and lived amid real *difference*, that there is only one normal. Given the vast differences—and commonalities—I encountered at VONA, I know this is not the case. And in such a community, I may or may not be a rock star, but I do belong.

What VONA Taught Me (Part II)

Teaching

A couple of years ago, a Black writer friend recounted to me an experience in her MFA program. On the first day of class, the white professor took my Black friend aside and advised her that she should go over to the remedial English center for some instruction since there were grammatical errors in her poems. My Black friend explained that the poems were written in Black vernacular. The white professor, tenured, a distinguished chair, later a MacArthur Fellow, responded that if my friend continued to write in that way, her poems would not be published.

I shouldn't have to add this, but my friend not only went on to publish poems and complete her MFA; she also earned a Ph.D. in English literature, later worked internationally for the U.S. government, won literary prizes, and she's now a college professor. My friend was acutely aware of the differences between Black speech and the conventions of white literary and professional language. On the other hand, her white professor's ignorance of the tradition of African American literature or, say, of critical works like Henry Louis Gates Jr.'s *The Signifying Monkey* or Toni Morrison's *Playing in the Dark* was not an issue that my friend, as a student, felt she could bring up.

In his introduction to *Dismantle: An Anthology of Writing from the VONA/Voices Writing Workshop,* Junot Díaz critiques the damage done to student writers of color in MFA programs and breaks down the racism and ignorance of their professors and fellow students:

> I've worked in two MFA programs and visited at least 30 others and the signs are all there. The lack of diversity of the faculty. Many of the students' lack of awareness of the lens of race, the vast silence on these

> matters in many workshops. I can't tell you how often students of color seek me out during my visits or approach me after readings in order to share with me the racist nonsense they're facing in their programs, from both their peers and their professors. In the last 17 years I must have had at least three hundred of these conversations, *minimum*. I remember one young MFA describing how a fellow writer (white) went through his story and erased all the "big" words because, said the peer, that's not the way "Spanish" people talk. This white peer, of course, had never lived in Latin America or Spain or in any US Latino community—he just knew. The workshop professor never corrected or even questioned said peer either. Just let the idiocy ride. Another young sister told me that in the entire two years of her workshop the only time people of color showed up in her white peer's stories was when crime or drugs were somehow involved. And when she tried to bring up the issue in class, tried to suggest readings that might illuminate the madness, her peers shut her down, saying *Our workshop is about writing, not political correctness.* As always race was the student of color's problem, not the white class's. Many of the writers I've talked to often finish up by telling me they're considering quitting their programs.

In our society, the divide between how whites and people of color regard the social reality around them is always present. Often, though, this divide remains invisible or obscured, especially in classes like science or math. But creative writing involves the very description of our social reality, and so the gulf between the vision of whites and of people of color is present right there on the page. Moreover, the judgment of these descriptions can also reveal a gulf between whites and people of color. Conflict then ensues. Such conflict is societal, not individual, though creative writing's focus on the individual writer may camouflage or obfuscate this. This is what Richard Wright meant when he implied that Black and white America are engaged in a struggle over the description of reality.

In other words, what the MFA student of color experiences in a predominantly white institution is not simply an obscure or numerically insignificant occurrence. Instead, it is symptomatic and revelatory of the ways the voices and consciousness of people of color are suppressed in our society.

This is exactly the reason why VONA was created—to provide a pedagogy and community where the concerns, theory, and literature of BIPOC writers are not ignored or marginal or forbidden but instead are given primary focus.

At VONA, everywhere I turned, I could find not just the amazingly talented BIPOC faculty members but also emerging student writers with incredible potential, which afterwards blossomed like Danez Smith, Tayari Jones, Saeed Jones, Melissa Rivero, John Murillo, Kali Fajardo-Anstine, Patricia Engel. My simply being part of such a faculty and community said something to me about the respect I myself had earned as a writer. As Mat Johnson said to me, "When I teach white students at a university, I know in some sense I have to prove my intelligence, my bona fides to them. At VONA, my ability and credentials to teach are assumed."

In 2019, I published *A Stranger's Journey: Race, Identity, and Narrative Craft in Writing*. The book argues that the issues of race and identity are now essential to the teaching of creative writing to all students in America, regardless of their color, but particularly for BIPOC students. From the book's basic principles to my use of short stories from VONA faculty ZZ Packer and Junot Díaz, much of that book came out of my experiences at VONA. In 2015, I had also used what I learned at VONA to teach a class of eighty-five BIPOC writers at the Loft, a literary organization in Minneapolis, which previously had not been able to fill even a class of twelve BIPOC students.[1]

1 When the Loft first asked me to teach there in order to increase their diversity, I had a class of eleven white women and a Japanese immigrant I knew. So obviously my teaching there did not automatically diversify the class. I told the Loft they should get funding to make the class free, and I would design it so each class did not depend on the previous class. I then said we needed to pay representatives from the communities to spread the word, and I did three introductory sessions before the actual class—one on the North Side at the Urban Center, one at the Center for Hmong Arts and Talent in St. Paul, and one at a café in the multiracial Phillips Park neighborhood in Minneapolis. The Loft had first proposed a twelve-student class, but I told them I wanted to use the auditorium. We had 145 people sign up for the class, and 85 BIPOC writers attended the first class. When mainstream organizations say they want to diversify, they think they can do the same thing they've always done and BIPOC will show up. They don't

In my VONA classes, I started using not only literary texts but theoretical writings on culture, race, and postcolonialism—Frantz Fanon, Edward Said, bell hooks, James Baldwin, Toni Morrison, Frank Wilderson, Antonio Gramsci, Michel Foucault. I began to understand more deeply how becoming a writer of color involved dismantling the cultural and political forces and ideology that had repressed and shaped our communities, from colonialism to Jim Crow to white literary standards that eschewed social justice and the political, and whose canon dismissed and occluded writers of color. After a preclass assignment where I asked the students to write on their identities, I would start the first class with these readings and a discussion of the issues of race, identity, the canon, and political writing. Many students expressed that they had never engaged in such discussions in any of their creative writing classes.

And yet at VONA I often felt I was learning as much from my students as they were from me. I had the good fortune to work with students like Daisy Hernández, Maurice Carlos Ruffin, Lisa Ko, and Ingrid Rojas Contreras, all just about to become celebrated writers in their own right—or my friend from Minneapolis, Frank Wilderson, who had lived in South Africa and become a member the ANC and whose theories of Afropessimism deeply influenced my thinking on race. Over and over, in working with my students I had to expand and complicate my own thinking and identity to incorporate their experiences and writings.

I recall an undocumented Chicano student who talked about his family's need to keep their immigration history a secret to everyone outside the family. This caused him to lie about his identity and where he was born, even to other Chicanos, and this hampered his personal relationships and for years kept him from letting anyone get close to him. Instead, from childhood on, the keeping of secrets became a central foundation of his psychology; he had to work many years to undo this and was still working on it through his writing. At the same time, his story made me think anew of how my parents and their generation

realize they have to change their relationship to the communities they are trying to attract—or, rather, they have to start building a relationship with those communities.

decided to not tell their children about their imprisonment during World War II, and again I wondered about how their internment and silence had affected my Sansei generation and our psychology.

At VONA, I taught students from a variety of ethnicities and all the racial groups, and I worked to prepare for these students from the moment I chose their manuscripts and the students as members of my workshop. If I had a student from Trinidad, I would have to bone up on Caribbean literature. If I had another student from Trinidad who had a Ghanaian mother, I had to do research into that background.[2]

Sometimes this research was both particular and complicated. From his writing sample and the introduction I asked students to write, I knew that my Muslim South Asian Indian student had grown up near San Jose in the South Bay area (Bombay in the South Bay, they dubbed his neighborhood). But further back, in the 1920s, his family had immigrated to Tanzania from Gujarat.

In 2002, after dealing with the aftermath of the first Gulf War and then 9/11, my student wanted to escape from America and the overwhelming antipathy displayed to someone who looked the way he did. So he thought he would travel to his ancestral home in Gujarat. He arrived there just before the outbreak of the anti-Muslim riots in Gujarat where more than two thousand Muslims were killed. As a journalist, he made a decision to stay and report on what was happening, an experience that left him severely traumatized. During that time, he interviewed Narendra Modi, then governor of Gujarat and now India's Prime Minister, who was banned from the United States for failing to stop the anti-Muslim riots. (That ban has been rescinded.) After interviewing Modi, my student remarked to a friend, "I have just met a prototypical fascist."

I knew nothing about Gujarat or these riots, but before we met for our conference, I read about the riots and read the journalism this student had written about them and the situation of Muslims there.

2 When my friend the Korean American adoptee actress Sun Mee Chomet came to the head of her graduate program and complained that she was only doing plays by white authors and asked if they could do some Asian American plays, her teacher said, "Well, if you can find them, I'll consider it." The same teacher told her that as an Asian American, Sun Mee would always be relegated to minor roles.

It gave me a picture of the religious conflicts in India and where they might lead, though I didn't foresee that Modi would become prime minister and do everything he could to ratchet up Hindu nationalism and anti-Muslim sentiment.

And yet, ultimately, after working with this student, I helped him see that a key to his development as a creative writer was not what happened in Gujarat, as important as those events were. Instead, the key lay in his own story of growing up as a Muslim Indian American kid and going to high school just after the first Gulf War when he experienced all the typical stupid racism that many Arab and Indian Americans faced during that time (and ever since). As a journalist, this student could access a language to describe what was happening in Gujarat, the public displays of hatred and violence and ethnic cleansing; in that task, he was using the language of political reporting, as he'd been trained as a journalist. At the same time, in India the identities of Hindu and Muslim Indians possessed a semantic certainty that his identity as a Muslim Indian American did not.

In other words, while he possessed a language to describe and refer to Hindu and Muslim Indians, what he didn't possess was a language to describe himself, someone who loved typical American things like the LA Lakers; he possessed no language to describe how alienated he felt, how much he wanted to blend in, in ways that seemed barred to him; he had little language to express his own ethnicity, race, and family history, how he fit and did not fit into America. The pain and trauma he experienced in Gujarat did scar him and was certainly horribly real, but the pain of being a Muslim Indian teenager in America after the first Gulf War was something that he was afraid to access, that he did not have the language to access and would rather have avoided writing about.

But of course, that was precisely—if unconsciously—why he came to VONA: to find that language. Certainly, I could identify with the difficulties he was facing; I myself had gone through my own reluctance to examine my ethnicity and racial identity, to claim my body not as something to be excluded from my writing but something that could center my writing. I understood intuitively the psychic blocks he was avoiding. As his teacher, then, my job was to challenge him, to help him push back his denial or marginalization of his own past, to push him toward discovering the language that would allow him to describe himself, his feelings, and his experiences. Pointedly, I told him this was not a language he could find in the works of white authors he had read, but a language that other BIPOC writers were constantly in the process of creating.

At VONA I pushed my students to delve deeper into their own experiences, even if they were painful or difficult, and I was able to do this in part because I had gone on my own journey uncovering my ethnic and racial identities. For instance, I had a student whose mother was Russian and whose father was Chinese African. She didn't grow up with her father, though, and her mother was a large, opinionated woman whose love of things Russian was a constant presence in her daughter's life. In her novel, my student transposed her Russian mother into a Cuban American who had inculcated a love of Russia while growing up in Communist Cuba, and the character she created was marvelous and larger than life, a flamboyant, imposing figure in the mind of the daughter in the novel. In contrast, the daughter seemed a bit pale or flat, uninteresting, even though she was going out with a white juvenile delinquent who had spent time in state-run institutions. Then, during our two-hour-long conference—part of the way I teach at VONA is to spend a lot of time with the students one-on-one—this student revealed that her actual high school boyfriend was indeed white but also a white *supremacist.*

She began then to tell me tales of going to parties/dances out in the countryside with young white supremacists with racist heavy metal blaring into the night, and she wasn't alone in such passing. She knew a few other kids of color who also tried to pass and go to these parties, in the process risking being discovered and beaten or worse.

"So why didn't you write that story?" I asked.

"I'm too ashamed," she said. "I was so stupid and blind. I don't want people to know I dated a white supremacist."

"And that," I said, "is precisely why you need to write about it. When I read your piece, I was feeling like the daughter as a character didn't have the energy the mother has in the prose, and now I know why. Having the daughter date a white supremacist—that truth of your own life—is what you should put down, and when that happens the novel is going to take off into a whole new direction. It's going to have an energy it didn't have before."

I then went on to explain how often our most powerful writing comes out of our deepest wounds, but we have to be willing to reenter those wounds, to dig them up and hold them to the light. We have to fight past any shame we might have over those wounds. I told her that so many children of color in America are taught, are conditioned, are reinforced to deny who they are, who their families are, and where they come from. Yes, she might feel shameful about her past with the white supremacist boyfriend, but she was not the only person of color who experienced such shame about their ethnic and racial identities or racial self-hatred. Rather than running from that shame, I said, she should seize that shame and examine it, excavate, dissect it, and certainly, not hide or bury it. Exhume it, I exhorted her, make it yours, because it already is; if you do, you'll find the daughter in your novel will have her own interesting tale to tell, a tale just as dramatic and as interesting as her mother and her mother's immigrant tale.

Aside from a postgraduate learning experience, it was the psychic changes I experienced at VONA that were the most profound. At VONA, I was suddenly in a space that centered not just the work of writers of color but also our bodies. I witnessed how, in a such a space, so many other writers of color were able to open themselves up emotionally and psychically with their peers. In ways they had not experienced before, they were able to speak and write about their traumas and emotional responses to the wounds they had received in their families and in a white supremacist society.

Such pedagogy and such steps in their development went far beyond the standard operation of white writing workshops; certainly, this could not have occurred for these writers within a white-dominated space. Free from the white gaze, from white literary, cultural, and racial assumptions, the writers of color entered and occupied their bodies and freed their creativity in ways many of them had never experienced before. For many, VONA became either a preparation for the ignorance and racism of a white-dominated MFA program or a postgraduate recovery space from their white-dominated MFA program. Where in white workshops BIPOC writers are often met with critiques that display an ignorance of BIPOC literary traditions or the communities the writers come from, the VONA faculty and students could make knowledgeable critiques; if they called a writer on their shit, the writer could more readily trust that critique and listen to it. The writer would know that the workshop wasn't trying to other or exclude or compete with the writer; the workshop was trying to help the writer, because the writer was part of the VONA community.

Not surprisingly, this new emotional and psychic freedom was bound up with the progress of their work, with their increased ability to express their own stories and those of their families, with their recognition and expression of their own truths.[3] And when these writers of color read their work to their peers of color, the energy in their bodies and in the room was powerful and palpable; it expressed itself in open vocal expressions of anger and grief, in applause and shouts of encouragement, in tears and laughter. Whatever the emotions, those voicings arose from a sense of liberation and acceptance that came from being with other BIPOC writers, outside the alienating gaze and ignorant critiques of Whiteness.

The faculty readings were certainly amazing, with so much talent, but it was the student readings that affected me more. So many of the students felt, some for the first time in their lives, that they were *not* crazy; it was the world *outside* the space, outside VONA, that was crazy. Though I was a teacher and not a student, I too felt all this, more in my emotions and my body than in my intellect; I also witnessed similar transformations with the particular individuals in my workshop, who often opened up in their writing emotionally and personally—and thus, artistically—in unprecedented ways.

I have gone on to teach the past nineteen years at VONA, and I often say to people, VONA saved my life. Other members of the VONA community say similar things.

In addition to still being on the faculty, I've served on the board of VONA for six years and served as its board secretary and volunteer

3 The writers who attend Kundiman, an Asian American writers' conference; Cave Canem, an African American writers' conference; and Macondo Writers, a Latino writer's conference, also experience something similar to this.

director of development. More than 2,600 BIPOC writers have attended VONA, and more than 500 have published books and won major prizes and grants. And in this way, VONA has literally changed the faces of American literature.

“Racial Melancholia, Racial Dissociation”

I

Amid 1960s cookie-cutter bi-levels and ranches, I grew up in a solidly middle-class Jewish suburb of Chicago. Most of the grandparents had immigrated from Europe, but a few parents, like the parents of my friend Gerry Horn, had escaped from Germany or Eastern Europe, before and during World War II. The Jews in my high school were highly cognizant of their history: we read Anne Frank, Elie Wiesel, and *The Merchant of Venice* in our English classes; everyone had seen the films *Exodus* and *Fiddler on the Roof*; the Six-Day Arab-Israeli War was a traumatic event for my classmates and their families.

As I’ve often said, in high school I knew more about the Holocaust and the Jewish concentration camps than the Japanese American internment camps (and more Yiddish language than Japanese). As for the non-Jews, the white goyim were definitely the minority, not the Jewish kids. And in a high school of 3,200, there were ten Asians and I was related to half of them. (In that era of de facto segregation, no Blacks lived in the northern suburbs near the lake, with the exception of Evanston.) In high school, I did not date much, did not go to prom or homecoming; with the handful of girls I dated, two stopped going out with me after the first date because their parents found out I wasn’t Jewish.

Growing up, from adolescence to my late twenties, I had to battle depression; part of my depression, I see now, stemmed from feeling out of place in high school, a feeling that I sensed was in part racial and ethnic but didn’t have any language or desire to investigate.[1] But

1 In *Mona in the Promised Land,* Gish Jen’s protagonist seems to enjoy much more social acceptance and sexual interest in a fictional version of Scarsdale, the Jewish suburb where Jen grew up. Her character Mona not only has a Jewish boyfriend but at one

part of the source of that depression was clear to me: it stemmed from my family system. In those years I reacted strongly to what I felt was my parents' constant criticism, their lack of approval or display of affection. This had many manifestations, and yet those manifestations often did not seem to me cultural or Asian. This lack of an Asian cultural context was in part due to my parents' conscious and unconscious decision to let go of their Japanese culture roots after their imprisonment in World War II. As I often explain, "If you're put in prison for shoplifting, after you're released, you don't shoplift anymore. But what if you're imprisoned for your race and ethnicity? What if that is your crime?" My parents' answer: try as best you can to blend in with white people.

I too was part of this assimilation, and this meant adhering to my father's conservative white Republican vision undergirded by a (never labeled *Japanese*) stress on endurance and hard work. According to my Asian tiger dad, my goals were first an Ivy League school and then law school, also preferably Ivy League. To my adolescent psyche, he seemed filled with critiques and demands for absolute academic perfection, the occasional B+ noted as a highly questionable blemish. (He also criticized just as harshly my performance on, say, the football field.) Ironically, my weakest grades were in English, and since he wrote speeches and press releases for a living, he'd red-mark drafts of my English papers, muttering "How could you be so stupid!" (My calculus class was beyond his math abilities.) By my senior year in high school, he and I were engaging in boiling arguments on issues like my applying for conscientious objector status, my opposition to the Vietnam War, my leaving our Episcopalian church, my leftist politics

point converts to Judaism, much to the consternation of her Shanghai-born parents. What determined the differences in our experiences—assuming Jen's novel is somewhat true to her own high school experiences—is up to question. Perhaps Jen simply possessed a more winning personality than mine. Or perhaps, as an Asian female, she was regarded differently from how I was. Or perhaps Skokie/Lincolnwood were different in certain ways from Scarsdale. But Jen did use as an epigraph to her novel a line from *Turning Japanese*: "I knew more Yiddish than Japanese." At any rate, our experiences were quite different from, say, a Japanese American growing up in Gardena, California, or a Chinese American growing up in Chinatown or Monterey Park.

that ran so counter to his fervent Republicanism. My hippie clothes and long hair and my devotion to what he deemed outré rock music were just toppers to this list.

After my freshman year, driving me back from college, seeing I had let my hair grow, even before we reached our home, my father drove me straight to the barber to cut my shoulder-length hair. Afterwards, I felt humiliated, defeated, ugly. We had a huge fight in our living room where I shouted I didn't want to be depressed like I was in high school—to which my father said, "I didn't know you were depressed," and my mother replied "Oh Tom, you knew."

Then in my senior year I decided to go to English grad school and declared my intention to become a poet—whatever the hell that meant—and I doused my dad's dream of a lawyer son. When I told him I wanted to apply to English grad school, he replied, "Well, I'm paying for your applications so you have to apply to law schools, too." I wasn't strong enough to push back on this; instead, my rebellion was to get drunk and party the night before the LSATS (and I was not a drinker). Ironically, I got into better law schools—Stanford and Yale—than English grad schools.

Eventually, my political arguments with my father receded with the cultural and political changes of the late 1970s. What's more, he did come around to approving my career choice, even becoming proud of my being a writer.

Still, it was only years later, after I traveled to Japan, that I would wonder about my parents' Japanese cultural roots and their effects on our family. It gave me a context for my mother's disapproval of my writing, which made public what she deemed private family issues; more significantly, I began to understand the cultural roots to their never saying directly "I love you" or providing physical affection, their never saying "I'm proud of you." Most likely, if I had grown up in Japan, these traits would have seemed to me no different from the other families around me, and I would have read and reacted to them differently.

Despite not quite understanding all the cultural and political roots of my family's psychology, in my late twenties I entered therapy, and I got to a point where I could forgive my parents and let go of my anger toward them. Indeed, after therapy I stopped viewing myself as a depressed person and I stopped seeking from my parents the approval and displays of affection I felt they would never give me.[2]

But my racial identity? In therapy we never touched on that.

No, my recovery from the racism came through other means, starting with reading Frantz Fanon's *Black Skin, White Masks*, which examines how race shapes the psychology of whites and Blacks. A Black psychiatrist, Fanon grew up in Martinique and was educated in the French colonial school system, and he closely analyzes the effects of that system upon his own sense of identity:

> In the Antilles . . . in the magazines, the Wolf, the Devil, the Evil Spirit, the Bad Man, the Savage are always symbolized by Negroes or Indians; since there is always identification with the victor, the little Negro, quite as easily as the little white boy, becomes an explorer, an adventurer, a missionary "who faces the danger of being eaten by the wicked Negroes." . . . The black school boy in the Antilles, who in his lessons is forever talking about "our ancestors, the Gauls," identifies himself with the explorer, the bringer of civilization, the white man who carries truth to savages—an all-white truth. There is identification—that is, the young Negro subjectively adopts a white man's attitude. He invests the hero, who is white, with all his own aggression—at that age closely linked to sacrificial dedication, a sacrificial dedication permeated with sadness.

I read this passage and said to myself, "Oh shit, that's what I've been doing"—identifying with "an all-white truth . . . a white man's attitude." I was never going to be a white person, so who was I? I started reading Black writers like James Baldwin, Alice Walker and Toni Morrison, and through these writers I learned a language to examine the issues of race, a language I never found in the white writers I'd read in my English Ph.D. program. I had to investigate what it meant for me

2 In his later years, in various and remarkable ways my father apologized for how he treated me in adolescence and our political fights; in fact, he wrote me a couple of letters apologizing for how scared he was of the cultural changes in the sixties and seventies in America and how he was not brought up to say directly that he loved me. And I see now he too was struggling with his own bicultural values all through his life.

to be a Japanese American, a person of color, and gradually, through Asian American artists and my writing, I began to understand and articulate my own ethnic and racial identity.

Unfortunately, many Asian Americans are never exposed to such writings and art and never learn how they might begin to examine their racial identity.

II

The title of Korean American Wesley Yang's *The Souls of Yellow Folk* doesn't quite represent the book's content; indeed, some have criticized the title both for being overly pretentious and something of a trick. In a *New York Times* book review, the Vietnamese American Pulitzer Prize–winning novelist Viet Thanh Nguyen complains, "One expects the book to be about 'yellow folk,' or Asian-Americans. As it turns out, only three of the thirteen essays address issues related to Asian-Americans. Three other essays talk about race and whiteness."

Still, in his essay on Asian Americans and "success," first published in *New York Magazine,* Yang opens with a contemplation of his own face:

> Sometimes I'll glimpse my reflection in a window and feel astonished by what I see. Jet-black hair. Slanted eyes. A pancake-flat surface of yellow-and-green-toned skin. An expression that is nearly reptilian in its impassivity. I've contrived to think of this face as the equal in beauty to any other. But what I feel in these moments is its strangeness to me. It's my face. I can't disclaim it. But what does it have to do with me?
>
> . . . Here is what I sometimes suspect my face signifies to other Americans: an invisible person, barely distinguishable from a mass of faces that resemble it. A conspicuous person standing apart from the crowd and yet devoid of any individuality. An icon of so much that the culture pretends to honor but that it in fact patronizes and exploits. Not just people "who are good at math" and play the violin, but a mass of stifled, repressed, abused, conformist quasi-robots who simply do not matter, socially or culturally.
>
> I've always been of two minds about this sequence of stereotypes. On the one hand, it offends me greatly that anyone would think to apply them to me, or to anyone else, simply on the basis of facial

> characteristics. On the other hand, it also seems to me that there are a lot of Asian people to whom they apply.

Yang exhibits here what sociologists have called stereotype threat—an awareness of the negative stereotypes surrounding the group you belong to. These negative stereotypes can center on race or gender or orientation or class or any number of other groupings. Stereotype threat can affect both academic performance and general psychological well-being. At the nadir of this threat, the individual is not only aware of the negative stereotypes but begins to believe them, to incorporate them into the way the individual looks at themselves. The individual may even view the negative stereotypes as a kind of fate or destiny; they can't be anything else.

How, then, as an Asian American do you search for an alternative fate, a way of healing your psyche from these racist stereotypes?

Back in my middle thirties, in the late 1980s, when the Japanese American playwright Philip Kan Gotanda visited the Twin Cities, we talked about our trips to Japan. Philip said he was severely depressed before his trip, even plagued with thoughts of suicide. But when he got to Japan, his suicidal ideation disappeared. Eventually he wrote a play, *Fish Head Soup,* where a Sansei like him appears to commit suicide but instead ends up traveling to Japan. At the time he disappears, this Sansei is the golden boy of the family, a smart, seemingly typical young Asian American who has done well at school and is expected by his family to go on to greater things. But clearly all this is on the surface; from the play's beginning, when he returns to his family who are understandably shocked and angered by his reappearance, it's clear the model minority surface of his family is belied by psychological dysfunction and the negative effects of the internment and the racism of American society.

As he wrote the play, Gotanda was well aware of the wave of anti-Japanese sentiment during the 1980s; in an article in the *LA Times* just before the play's premier, he said, "Given the rise in anti-Asian sentiment and Japan bashing, nothing surprises me anymore in what I read about and what I experience in terms of being Asian. The consciousness is raised at the same time you have the most ugly, overt forms of racism in your face." But in Japan, Gotanda had felt emotionally lifted up; certain feelings of self-hatred began retreating from his psyche. He wanted to know if I had experienced something similar.

In reply, I talked about how I grew up in the Midwest in an era when there were few Asian Americans living there. When I first went to San Francisco in my midtwenties and got on a streetcar and was surrounded by Asians, it unsettled me: *Who are all these people who look like me?* a voice inside me asked.[3] So my experiences growing up were different from Gotanda's, who was raised in Stockton and then lived in San Francisco and thus resided in places with significant Asian and Japanese American communities. I explained that back then I was very white identified and didn't like to be associated with Asians; this was in part as a rejection of the stereotypes surrounding Asians and in part because of my parents' conscious and unconscious desire to have me assimilate into a middle-class white identity.

But then, in my late twenties, after reading Black authors, I began to see myself as an Asian American and Japanese American, and indeed, this was part of why I applied for and received the U.S.–Japan Exchange Fellowship from the NEA. When in my early thirties I got off the plane at Narita Airport and everyone looked like me, I felt elated and a sense of psychic comfort and freedom I'd never felt before. I realized I had not understood how alienated I felt in American society until I experienced living in a country where my body was not an oddity and did not carry the burden of racialized Western stereotypes, where I could turn on the television or go to the movies and even to a baseball game, and everyone was Japanese, everyone looked like me.

In Gotanda's *Fish Head Soup,* prior to the play's beginning, when the main protagonist is in Japan, the Sansei does a porn film with a white American porn actress. The feeling that he could be a star, if only in a porn film, inspires him to return to the States to write a play that centers on a Japanese American family like his own—an ambition his parents can hardly contemplate, much less approve of. Given my own examination of Asian American sexuality and race, I understood

3 A psychiatrist friend who lived in St. Louis once talked to me about her Asian American female patients who expressed the feeling that going out with an Asian American male felt to them somehow "incestuous."

intuitively why Gotanda linked this "good Japanese American boy" with depression and suicide, with struggles with his own body and sexuality, and his desire to create a different relationship with his identity and his family's past. I even remembered during my time in Tokyo reading articles about a blonde American porn start who came to Japan, and I understood how Philip picked up on this and linked her visit with his Sansei protagonist.

In my talk with Gotanda I suddenly felt less alone and more of a sense that I wasn't the only one dealing with the issues that show up in my writing. He and his writing were confronting the same racialized psychological knots I'd been trying to unravel. In his *The Souls of Yellow Folk,* Wesley Yang seems to be facing stereotype threat all by himself, as he looks at the mirror; in contrast, I was meeting Asian American artists and community members both locally and nationally and learning I was not alone. I wasn't only seeing my face in white America's cultural reflection; I was seeing myself reflected in other Asian Americans, particularly Asian American artists and activists.

Still, I do feel for Wesley Yang. I too have felt similarly to his description of looking at himself in the mirror.

For Asian Americans, there are external forces that we face—the image of the Asian American nerd or the model minority myth or the anti-Asian sentiments that arise any time America views a country in Asia negatively. But internally, there's the personal burden of these phenomena that almost all Asian Americans must deal with or at least acknowledge.

Here we come to issues of our psychological health—from depression to the rates of suicide, especially for Asian American women, to culture clashes within our families and with the mainstream white culture. To me, it's clear that the place and reception of the Asian body have a great deal to do with our struggles with mental health, even though the field of psychotherapy has failed in so many ways to admit, much less deal with, the issues of race—and certainly with the Asian American body.

III

In *Racial Melancholia, Racial Dissociation: On the Social and Psychic Lives of Asian Americans,* the literary critic David L. Eng and the psychologist Shinhee Han describe the problematic reactions by Asian

Americans to the hostility, negativity, marginality, and invisibility that Asian Americans, their bodies and psyches, face in American society. The book comes out of a long collaboration between Eng and Han and it makes use of Han's case studies of individual Asian American subjects/patients. In their introduction, they argue that psychotherapy has bracketed race as outside the arena of psychoanalysis; in analysis, the focus is on "a patient's personal family history" rather than "the subject of (racial) history writ large": "Put otherwise, psychoanalysis is focused on the mother but rarely considers the motherland; it is attuned to family dynamics but rarely thinks about the family of nations."

Eng and Han point to how almost all psychotherapy, as it is currently practiced, eschews the issues of race. This is in part because its practitioners, who are predominantly white, generally have no training in how to deal with clients of color. But it's also because these white practitioners—and indeed therapy itself—excludes race as being beyond consideration in addressing the psychologies of individuals (not dissimilar to the banishment of race as a subject in white-dominated writing workshops). White clients don't come into therapy and talk about the "problem" of being white, nor do their therapists consider the race of their white clients an issue. So why would they think otherwise when dealing with clients of color? Yes, feminist issues can be dealt with in therapy, but the effects of structural racism on the psyches of clients of color? That's political, not psychological, according to the implicit model. It's not a problem individualized therapies are designed to address.

In Freudian psychology, *melancholia* designates a failure to mourn properly, thus a mourning without ending. Such mourning is placed in contrast to a healthy or adequate mourning, which emotionally processes a loss and then moves on from that loss. Part of this unhealthiness stems from the fact that often the mourner has come to see what is being mourned as part of the self rather than separate from the self; the result is that the mourner can never properly separate from their object of mourning. One can see how this works, say, with a mother who has lost an infant or a child who loses a parent. But how does the concept of mourning function racially with Asian Americans?

Eng and Han locate the nexus of melancholia in Asian American subjects in the loss of a social acceptance and place in American society; this is an acceptance that is granted to whites and not granted to people of color. So, argue Eng and Han, what Asian Americans are often mourning, even if they do not realize it, is their being outside of Whiteness. From birth, we are excluded forever from a white identity and all that that identity provides white people—acceptance, a sense of normalcy and power, a confidence and sense of belonging. This sense of normalcy and power is what others who are not white—BIPOC—are judged as lacking or are forbidden from experiencing, however much they might want to be regarded otherwise:

> To the extent the ideals of whiteness for Asian Americans and other people of color remain unattainable, processes of assimilation are suspended, conflicted, and unresolved. The irresolution of this process places the concept of assimilation within a melancholic framework. . . . The suspended assimilation, the inability to blend into the American melting pot, suggests that for Asian Americans ideals of whiteness are perpetually strained—continually estranged. They remain at an unattainable distance, at once a compelling fantasy and lost ideal.

Today, as I wrote down this quotation, my immediate reaction was "Fuck whiteness!" Why try to belong to an entity I could never be part of?

One of the benefits of my entering racial arguments with and then losing most of my white artist friends in my early forties was that I recognized in a new and powerful way that I was never going to be white. Just as important, I shouldn't be so fearful of pissing off white people. I would hold to my own truths and those of my community in face of this opposition. Yes, I was upset and deeply saddened by the loss of those white friendships, but those losses made possible other friendships with people of color—and as my friend the Black novelist Alexs Pate said to me, it was only when I started upsetting and angering white people that Alexs began to feel he might trust me, that we might truly become friends. In this process, I threw away the dream of assimilating into Whiteness—what Eng and Han point out is an impossible goal—and thus I abandoned a perpetual mourning for the loss of white acceptance. Whiteness wasn't a part of who I was nor would it ever see me as part of Whiteness.

Eng and Han distinguish melancholia from psychological dissociation, which centers on the subject's inability to find or feel they possess a true self. This is a tricky concept and requires explanation: given the various demands of human interactions, each individual is always facing situations that challenge the self, that call for accommodation or adaption or imitation or camouflage, in order to function in society. We speak and act differently with our boss than with our fellow employees; we speak and act differently at work than with our families and differently with our friends or lovers. In these shiftings, we may concoct a different or seemingly false self to engage and deal with social situations or individuals who may be unaccepting or hostile to us. But within these shiftings, the healthy and adjusted individual feels and acts from a sense that a true self exists beneath. That true self anchors the psyche and gives the individual a sense that they are, in the end, one person; that singular uniqueness provides the self with a sense of autonomy, authenticity, and continuity. This allows the individual to go out into the world, interact with others, adapt to the demands of the social world, and yet maintain a sense of stability, balance, and wholeness.[4]

But with dissociation, the individual feels that there is no true self, no anchor, no psychic center of authenticity; each possible self or projection of the self is false, fake, a sham. As explained by Eng and Han: "Unmodulated, pathological manifestation of false self ultimately hides the True Self even from one's own self, resulting in feelings of fraudulence and phoniness, the absence of 'true experience,' the affective incapacity to feel real, spontaneous, authentic, or alive. Sensations

4 This is one reason why the Captain, the double agent in Viet Thanh Nguyen's *The Sympathizer*, is not just a character who embodies many of the conflicts of the Vietnamese people and their diverging views of the war. The Captain also suffers from racial dissociation, in part because he is mixed race—his father is a French priest—and in part because he is constantly playing a role, adapting his character and views to whomever he is speaking to at the time. In many ways, he is always in disguise, and eventually he feels he has lost any sense of who his true self might be. In this he also mirrors what it means to be Asian American.

of wasted life—of emptiness, futility, and hopeless—overshadow all social interactions and relations."

What does it mean to be Asian in America? It's not just that others may feel my body is foreign to this country, but that I can also feel that way about my own body. And yet such dissociation from our bodies is not an easy topic to address or talk about with others, especially if we don't understand the reasons why we may feel this way.

For many Asian Americans, psychological dissociation may often center on their perception of their bodies or their lack of a place in American society where they feel they can truly be themselves and, in turn, where they are seen and understood for who they are. The individual Asian American may present what they feel is a facade in order to be accepted by others or not regarded as un-American. Or the Asian American individual may be constantly attempting to fit in with the whites around them and even, as I did, deny any ties or associations with other Asians Americans. Whether consciously or unconsciously, the individual may also want to avoid acknowledging or claiming ownership of their own faces and bodies because it is their face and body that mark them as outsiders, as unattractive or unacceptable, as foreigners and strangers—as Other. Wesley Yang's discomfort with and alienation from his own face is one manifestation of this, again one I myself also know too well.

Not surprisingly, it is to the prime psychoanalyst of race, Frantz Fanon, that Han and Eng turn to illustrate the racial aspect of psychological dissociation:

> Frantz Fanon's *Black Skin, White Masks* (1952) contains a famous description of feelings of dread while he sits in a darkened movie theater waiting for repugnant images of himself to appear on the silver screen. Often interpreted in terms of a racialized Lacanian mirror stage, Fanon's critique of the racial stereotype in this parable of race relations underscores how the black male subject, rather than joyfully tipping into and identifying with the mirror image of this scene, would work hard to keep as much distance as possible between himself and these idealized images, between his bodily ego and these racially disparaged images. "In the white world the man of color encounters difficulties in the development of his bodily schema," Fanon writes. "Consciousness of the body is solely a negating activity."

If you live in a society where the images and narratives of bodies like yours are marginalized, denigrated, and negatively stereotyped, it is often extremely difficult for you as an individual to integrate your psychological sense of yourself with your own body. This is especially true when the only images of bodies like yours are almost always negative, substandard, deficient, alien.

Thus, in the society that surrounds you, your own body signifies distorted or harmful meanings you cannot control, meanings that others thrust upon you. Through these meanings, others interpret who you are and react accordingly; indeed, these negative stereotypes might even become part of the way your own psyche evaluates your self. Those hostile meanings and reactions can easily create in you a sense that you are not your body, and a dissociation with your body ensues. This can make it extremely difficult to create and possess a sense of your true self, since any self you formulate will be disassociated from your body (e.g., back in high school when I wanted my friends to say to me, "I think of you, David, just like a white person"; or my concentrated pursuit of white women).[5]

Fanon is talking specifically about the Black body, but his description can be applied to the Asian body in America. Now there is no doubt that the negativity projected onto the Black body is markedly greater than that projected on the Asian body, and in this way, the potential for dissociation within the psyche of individual Blacks may in many ways be greater. At the same time, though, most Black Americans grow up within an African American culture and a family that recognizes their African American heritage as an integral and essential aspect of their identity; that culture has been formed in part from a history of contending with and combating Whiteness and the racialization of the Black body in America for four hundred years. In other words, African American culture provides a Black subject with a context, precedence, and history to process their greater racial trauma.

In contrast, Asian Americans often grow up without a sense of

5 In the book Fanon describes a Black patient who constantly sleeps with white women and asserts that this patient believes on both a conscious and unconscious level that sleeping with white women will make him white.

their racial identity or how that identity and the history of that identity might be articulated.[6] Their immigrant parents may tell them they are Vietnamese, Hmong, or Indian like their parents, but their parents do not understand what it's like to grow up within and to try to fit into American culture and society. Their parents grew up in Asia; their parents have not gone to an American high school with all its racial assumptions. So for some Asian Americans, all this prevents them from being able to contextualize their own body within a politically resistant cultural and historical background. For Asian Americans, our identity is not only based on the ethnic culture of our families but also on the ways that culture and our bodies are regarded by American society—and that is a political question.

It would seem understandable, then, that for many Asian Americans, their racial trauma might lead to melancholia—a mourning without end for an unachievable Whiteness—for the racial source of the trauma cannot be articulated without a theoretical, political, and cultural analysis of racism toward Asians. Conversely, it can only be articulated by understanding what exactly the individual Asian American is mourning—to assimilate into Whiteness, a goal that is ultimately impossible. In order to escape these psychic dilemmas, the individual Asian American must acknowledge that such an assimilation is impossible. This dilemma is neither their fault nor an essential defining aspect of who that individual actually is; nor does it determine what their potential for happiness and achievement might be.

Of course, this is not to say that once the Asian American individual realizes the pursuit of Whiteness is an impossible goal, everything will be fine. The individual will still encounter the racial barriers and negative stereotypes. But the Asian American will now understand that they can live and thrive without, to use Eng and Han's words, the motherland's approval. This is similar to the ways an individual therapeutic patient might have to acknowledge that their mother will

6 This is why I would contend that trauma from the racialization of the Asian body within American society contains an element that is not dissimilar to gay theorist Alex Ross's description of the realization by the young gay male of his difference: "a trauma without visible cause."

never approve or completely approve of them and that they can thrive without their mother's approval. In addressing racial melancholia, the individual can then abandon their mourning for the impossible object—Whiteness.

A similar process must occur when their racial trauma leads to dissociation—a sense that there is no true self or that one's sense of self is at odds with or cannot absorb the meaning of one's body. The individual must understand that the racism of American society projects negative stereotypes onto the individual's body. But those negative stereotypes are neither true nor valid evaluations of the Asian American's body or who they are as an individual; nor do these stereotypes completely determine what others must always think that the Asian body signifies. Obviously, in Asian societies the Asian body is not seen as inherently negative or a sign of racialized negative stereotypes. And within an Asian American community and sometimes in other BIPOC communities, the individual can find themselves and their bodies perceived as normal, part of the community, and accepted in ways Whiteness does not.

In short, reclaiming your Asian body from the negative stereotypes of American culture and society obviously cannot occur without a racial reading of how Asians are regarded in our culture and society. It involves finding or creating a space where who you truly are and your body can be unified, aligned, and accepted. But that is a reclamation few white therapists are trained for, since the basic premises of a white-defined therapy don't acknowledge or address racial issues.

IV

Internment Camp Psychology

circa 1945

Just after his release Mas took a psychological test.
Three questions he never forgot: Do you think
people are out to get you? Do you feel you are
being followed? When you see a crowd of strangers
walking toward you, do you try to avoid them?
To all three he answered yes.
And knew he sounded insane.

V

In *Red, White & Black: Cinema and the Structure of U.S. Antagonisms*, the Afropessimist Frank Wilderson writes:

> When I attended the University of California at Berkeley, I saw a Native American man sitting on the sidewalk of Telegraph Avenue. On the ground in front of him was an upside-down hat and a sign informing pedestrians that here they could settle the "Land Lease Accounts" that they had neglected to settle all of their lives. He, too, was crazy. . . . [But] to what does the world attribute the Native American man's insanity? "He's crazy if he thinks he's getting any money out of us"? Surely, that doesn't make him crazy. Rather it is simply an indication that he does not have a big enough gun.

Wilderson argues that *sanity* is not simply a psychological term; it's also a political term. The definition of *sanity* and the power to enforce that definition stem from the difference in power between the Native American and those non-Natives who pass him by. If he possessed a bigger gun—that is, more extensive tools of violence—he could not only enforce his "Land Lease Accounts"; he could also imprison those who did not comply with his wishes; he could label *them* insane. But whatever psychological designation he could place on them would not simply be a Platonic term regarding how the human mind is actually structured; no, it would constitute a term whose definition and power stemmed in part from military might and violent force, and would be therefore political—and thus, this is also the case with the judgment by whites that he, the Native American, is the one who is crazy for thinking white Americans have stolen Native American land and should pay reparations for that.

In terms of therapy, the very definitions of healthy and sick, sane and insane come into play for Wilderson in the political arena.[7]

7 In a *New York Times* magazine article, "America's Hidden Racial Divide: A Mysterious Gap in Psychosis Rates," Daniel Bergner writes: "As a growing body of research reveals, Black people in the United States suffer the hallucinations and delusions of psychosis—the voices that seem to emanate from outside a person's head, the visions, the paranoias, the breaks with common reality—at a rate roughly twice that of white

In therapy in 2024, gender roles can be discussed, whether you are a man or a woman, trans or nonbinary or gender-fluid, single or in a couple. However, if you are a white person in therapy, Whiteness will never be part of the discussion because Whiteness is never viewed as being significant to the white person's identity or their mental problems.

In the mind of the white person—and it is white people who have devised therapy—Whiteness only comes into play when they encounter a person of color. Otherwise it is neither an essential part of their identity nor essential to the way they look at the world or instrumental to understanding their psyche and their behavior or their experiences. (And yes, this parallels the way many men view feminist issues.) This is one reason why white authors never feel they need to designate their characters as white—unlike the practice of most BIPOC authors. For these white authors, Whiteness is the universal default; it is people of color who are the exceptions. To the white author, race is not important to their white characters, to their identity or experience. Needless to say, this is not the assumption of many BIPOC readers; we understand that the identities and lives of white people are affected by race, even if white people deny this.

As an Afropessimist, Wilderson argues that on the ontological level, the categories of white and Black cannot be separated; from the very start of America, the human is defined as Whiteness and Blackness is defined as nonhuman and slave.[8] Therefore, in therapy, because

people. In Europe, racial disparities regarding psychosis are yet wider. Even after researchers control for socioeconomic factors and address issues of diagnosis, the alarming racial gaps remain.

"Studies suggesting a link between minority or outsider status and psychosis run back about a century. A 1932 study looked at hospital admissions for psychosis in Minnesota. It found that Norwegian immigrants were admitted at twice the rate of native Minnesotans or Norwegians in their home country." Certain individuals may possess a genetic predisposition for schizophrenia but, explains Bergner, social conditions can determine whether that predisposition remains dormant or is ignited and inflamed.

8 According to Wilderson, whites created and then enforced the ontology or meaning of Whiteness and Blackness: white is human, and therefore whites are citizens and members of a nation. Black is nonhuman, and therefore can never be a citizen or member of a nation. To enact violence upon the white body requires either that

Whiteness has been defined as determining what is human, there is no reason to discuss or question this. Whiteness is one and the same with humanity. Why would a therapist discuss whether you the white person are human or not? That would simply be discussing a tautology.

But that tautology doesn't exist solely by itself—though white people sometimes act as if and often believe this is so. Originally, that equation established its meanings because there was something that was not white and not human—the Black slave.[9]

According to Whiteness then, Whiteness can't be a problem. The problem, as W. E. B. Du Bois recognized, is supposed to be the Black.

When a person of color enters therapy, the white therapist may or may not understand that the person of color is experiencing problems that are racial. But even if the white therapist acknowledges these racial problems, the therapist generally has had no training on how to address these problems or what the patient of color's viewpoint might be. But there's a deeper level to this: would the therapist attribute these problems to the ideology and culture of Whiteness? That is not

whites break the law or when war is declared between nations. In contrast, violence can be wreaked upon the black body without need of justification. Whites can own property. Blacks are property and are thus fungible and can be owned and sold. Whites have natal rights—that is, the right to their own children. Blacks do not possess natal rights. Wilderson argues that although these ontological definitions were created and first enforced centuries ago, they still structure American society today. Certainly, the many videos of police beating and murdering Black citizens in recent years attest to the rule that violence can be wreaked upon the Black body without actual legal justification—i.e., Blacks do not enjoy the rights of white citizens to be free from violence from the state, except when they break the law.

9 It's not surprising that the first formal legal distinction between whites and Blacks took place after Bacon's Rebellion in 1676 when Colonial Governor William Berkeley refused Bacon's demand to drive out Native Americans from Virginia. In that rebellion the working-class whites, including indentured servants, joined with indentured, enslaved, and free Blacks. The white colonial elites were alarmed by this coalition. After two other such uprisings, they passed the Virginia Slave Codes of 1705, which legally proclaimed the different status of whites and Blacks, making them two distinct groups, with only the whites possessing the rights of citizens. As President Lyndon Johnson once explained, "If you can convince the lowest white man he's better than the best colored man, he won't notice you're picking his pocket. Hell, give him somebody to look down on, and he'll empty his pockets for you."

how the white therapist understands their own identity—as a question or a problem, as an ideological construction. The political is thus forbidden from entering the therapeutic space.

When I've talked with Wilderson about these issues, he maintains that Asian Americans do not exist within as deep, rigid, and destructive a designation as Blackness functions for African Americans. For Wilderson, we Asians don't occupy a separate ontological category from whites. But I would disagree; our ontological category is not exactly the same as whites. Asians in American are forever regarded as an alien presence and can never be completely considered as true Americans; instead, we are seen always as a potential fifth column, an invasive presence, perpetual outsiders and Other (inscrutable). Certainly, the World War II imprisonment of my parents, who were natural-born citizens, and my grandparents, who were forbidden from becoming citizens, comes out of such categorization; the same categorization led to the rise in anti-Asian hate crimes during the Covid pandemic.

Wilderson argues that we cannot wish or even think ourselves out of these ontological categories. They are not simply embedded in the language, they *are* the language; therefore, they determine the structures of our thought, the very means through which we think.

The poet Audre Lourde famously observed that the tools of the master cannot dismantle the master's house. For many people of color, therapy is still the master's tool.

Owning My Asian American Body

In both my writing and my life, I have constantly felt the lack of mirrors and models. I did not grow up in a culture where Asian Americans were famous poets and novelists, protagonists in television shows and movies, celebrated in documentaries and political figures on the news. Addressing this absence, my colleague the Chinese American photographer Wing Young Huie has remarked, "You can look in the mirror every day and never really see yourself."[1]

If nobody sees you, are you still there?

If you grow up as an Asian in America, it's so easy to look at your own face and feel, "Well, that person doesn't belong here. That person can't be the hero or the protagonist. That's the face of an alien. A foreigner, not an American."

Here I want to make an uncomfortable admission: in the past few years, I've begun to force myself to stare at the mirror and say to myself, "Look at that person. That person is you." My feelings when I do this are complex. Obviously, I know that face is mine; I am actively trying to own the face I have. But at first glance I often have this fleeting sense of seeing my face through the eyes of white American culture, since white American culture resides within me, and so, according to those dictates, the face before me—mine—is not the usual face of

1 In a series of moving and brilliant photography books and exhibitions, Wing Young Huie's work helps center BIPOC in the Twin Cities and Asian Americans both locally and nationally: *Frogtown: Photographs and Conversations in an Urban Neighborhood*; *The University Avenue Project Volumes 1 and 2: The Language of Urbanism: A Six-Mile Photographic Inquiry*; *Lake Street, USA*; *Chinese-ness: The Meanings of Identity and the Nature of Belonging*; *Looking for Asian America: An Ethnocentric Tour.*

an American; it doesn't quite fit with the other ways I feel absolutely American.

Thinking back, I know that after months of living in Japan, I didn't look at my face in the same way I do in America. Surrounded by Japanese faces, I was aware that culturally I was very different from those faces; I didn't think like the Japanese around me, I hadn't grown up with the same values or rules of behavior. But the fact that my face looked like theirs, that I could blend in on the streets, made it a bit easier to own my face, to not see it as a foreign element—even though I was a foreigner in Japan. And so when I'm staring at the mirror in America today, I'm trying to approach something like that feeling, a sense of natural ownership of what is staring me back in the mirror: "That person, that face, is me."

Similarly, sometimes I go back over my life, especially my sexual life, and in direct contradiction to the way Asian American males have been portrayed in popular culture as sexless buffoons, I say to myself, "Remember these memories, inhabit them, relive them, they are yours, these sexual events happened to you."

In short, after almost five decades of writing, I still struggle to see myself. I still have trouble looking at my face in the mirror and recognizing that face as my own and feeling good about that; I still have trouble thinking my experiences are significant, that they can be those of a protagonist, that I can be a hero of my own life. Racial disassociation.

In so many obvious ways, American culture and society center and privilege the white body. That is one reason why many whites don't have to think consciously about being white. But if you're an Asian American, you have to seek and consciously construct a space where the Asian body is centered and accepted and not marginalized or burdened by negative stereotypes. For me, this has come in large part from the development of Asian American community and the work of Asian American artists; it also came from living in Japan for a year; it has come from teaching and organizing within a community of BIPOC artists, both locally and at an organization like VONA. And it has stemmed from a conscious effort to create and live in a multiverse where my Asian body is the norm.

In 2010, I was chosen to play the King in a local production of *The King and I.*[2] I had acted before, mainly in performance pieces I had written or co-written, and I'd also played the poet Li-Young Lee's father in an adaption I wrote of his memoir, *The Winged Seed.* As a writer who constantly presents his work to audiences, I was a practiced and accomplished public speaker.

Still, this was a classic Broadway musical and I was the lead. But I had never undergone any formal training as an actor. So before the rehearsals started, I took an acting workshop at Theater Mu, the Twin Cities Asian American theater company. The instructor, Filipino American actor Randy Reyes, assigned this exercise where we would go to the local mall and observe someone walking and then come back and imitate their body movements. I first chose an older Somali woman, but she quickly entered a beauty salon. I then saw a group of young white men, not big enough to be football players but bigger than normal; I thought they might be baseball teammates; some of them sported baseball caps. They walked with arms outspread, chests forward, in long loping strides, taking up as much space as they could. They sauntered past me as if they owned the mall.

Back at the workshop, as we did the exercise, I realized that I moved through the mall with a slight crouch, hunched over as if always on guard, my head tilted down, always wary of where some attack or challenge might be directed my way—as if I were an alien presence. As with many people of color in America, my first concern, which emanated from my body posture, was safety, protection; both consciously and unconsciously, I felt I had to be attuned to any potential negative forces and threats around me.

With the help of director Rick Shiomi and my acting instructors, Randy Reyes and the African American actor Harry Waters Jr., I realized I couldn't play the King of Siam with my normal body posture or movement. I had to stand and move and enter my body in a new

2 Ironically, my cousin Paul Nakauchi, who is an actor and a singer, has played the King in several productions of *The King and I*—at Lincoln Center, in London, in a touring version, and in L.A. I like to tell people we're the only family that's had two Kings, but of course Paul's version is one of a highly accomplished professional.

way; I had to believe not just that I could be the king of a country, but that I *was* the king of my country. I should not just project power and strength, I had to embody power and strength. I had to imagine a country where there was no racism against Asians, where my body had never been invisible or marginalized, where I was always destined to be the king.

To play the king, I also had to improve my vocal projection, to breathe in and out from the bottom of my diaphragm, to speak from deep in my core. I had to be loud and towering, projecting to the far rows of a three-hundred-seat theater. I had to own the stage, to take over the audience.[3]

Embodying such a figure every night changed me. At the opening we received a standing ovation, and we played to full houses and standing ovations throughout the run. One of the reviews referred to me as a theatrical veteran, a status both my wife and I chuckled over.

There are times still when I lose the King's sense of strength and power and relationship to my body. But I have known it; I have enacted it on stage before crowds of hundreds. I have taken over the stage and owned my body. I know how that feels.

As an Asian American, then, I am trying to find that state where the negative stereotypes American has created of us do not enter my psyche and distort my image of myself. In this struggle, this journey, I search for and keep talismans, objective correlatives to help me. *Crazy Rich Asians* is one of them—as it has become for many Asian

3 My friend the Korean American actor Sun Mee Chomet has told me about what happens when she teaches women, especially Asian American women, to breathe and project properly, from the core of their body; suddenly, these women feel the power emanating from their voice and body, power and emotions they've been holding in, who knows for how long. Often they break down weeping. So many repressed emotions are stored within the core of our bodies, and in getting in touch with our core and the voice it produces, a complex of emotions is released; under Sun Mee's training, the women feel a strength—and yes, including the pain of past wounds and denial—that they did not know existed within them. This example is just one of the many reasons Asian American parents should encourage their children in the arts, rather than focusing solely on STEM classes.

Americans. Now I'm aware of all the criticism toward its worship of wealth and the less than one percent, so yeah, it's a guilty pleasure.[4] But what I was struck by in that film was this: the Chinese in Singapore don't give a fuck about white people or Whiteness. They don't even think about them. When they are confronted with white racism, it doesn't faze them, it doesn't affect how they think of themselves.

Take the flashback that opens the movie. Nick Young's mother, played by the magnificent Michelle Yeoh, and the child Nick and his sister are visiting London. Coming in from a cold rain, they are confronted by the white hotel staff. Upon seeing that Mrs. Young is Asian, they lie about her reservation and say there are no rooms available. The manager, with a smiling snarl, suggests she look for accommodations, "say, in Chinatown." But Nick's mother doesn't go home and nurse her wounds, she doesn't break down and weep. Instead when the staff refuses to let her use their phone, she walks out in the rain to a pay phone, calls her husband, and has him buy the hotel! (How often when I was younger and tried to get into a hot club in Chicago and was turned away by a white bouncer did I want to do the same.) The mother reenters the hotel with an air of triumph, and in the lobby, as the staff tries to shoo her out, she is greeted by the eponymous owner of the hotel, Lord Calthorpe, who lives there. He informs the staff that Eleanor Young is now the hotel's owner. At this declaration, the look on the hotel manager's face is priceless—well, not exactly priceless, but to my Asian American ressentiment, it's an absolute delight.

A few nights ago, my wife and I watched the Chinese movie *The Last Tycoon*. The film tells the story of a Shanghai gangster of the 1920s and 30s, who's modeled after the (in)famous Big-Eared Du. The gangster is played by Chow Yun-Fat, probably best known to American audiences from *Crouching Tiger, Hidden Dragon*. I've been told I look a bit like Chow Yun-Fat, and this not only by Asian Americans but Chinese

4 White people, consciously and unconsciously, derive their self-image and identities from all areas of the culture and society, from the high-minded to the seedy, from political and religious leaders to gangsters, rock bands, and porn stars. Why must I as an Asian American be limited only to politically correct correlatives?

Chinese, so perhaps there's something to it. And yet to own that I look like a Chinese movie star is still a bit hard for me to grasp as an Asian American.

At the start of the film, Chow Yun-Fat is sitting alone in the center of the upper-tier balcony looking down at a Shanghai theater, just before a performance. From the stage the announcer tells the audience that tonight's opera performance has been sponsored by the renowned businessman, Chen Daqi. Chow Yun-Fat stands up in a gorgeous white silk cheongsam and the audience stands, turns their heads to him, and applauds; the camera starts from behind him, looking down at the audience, and then switches to the audience's view of this man who rises regally, imperially, above the crowd: in his case, he literally owns the theater, and, indeed, the city of Shanghai.

To a Chinese audience, a Chinese man playing the protagonist, a figure of power and prestige, is a natural given. But to me, an Asian American, such a charismatic figure, such a lead, almost feels like sci-fi, a far-flung multiverse where faces and bodies like mine are the norm, central and significant, a place where Whiteness does not intrude.[5] No stereotype threat here, no racial melancholia or racial dissociation.

To see myself in such a realm, I have to let go all the negative images and tropes surrounding Asian Americans; I have to make and see myself as central, commanding, and, yes, normal. I have to regain what my friend the writer and educator Alexs Pate calls innocence, a radical innocence that is absolutely free of the diminishing negative stereotypes of the white gaze. And to accomplish all this, I have to imagine myself in this alternative multiverse, I have to live inside it and thus

5 My use of multiverse here obviously stems in part from *Everything Everywhere All at Once*. The film depicts ordinary Asian Americans, two immigrant parents from China and their American-born daughter, as secretly being superheroes, and it imagines a myriad of existences, skills, and selves they live in other multiverses. The battles they fight both span the galaxies and yet are rooted in their working-class Asian American lives. Most major reviews did not view the film through an Asian American lens. But for Asian Americans, part of the delight in the film is the implicit affirmation that in our daily lives, our struggles and successes, and yes, our failures, *are* heroic, even if so often it's a heroism no one, and sometimes not even we ourselves, truly sees.

inhabit my chi in a totally different way from what I have learned and experienced growing up in America. I have to liberate myself into a different David and claim my power.

And sometimes, in meditation, in my teaching or readings or performances or interviews and certainly in my writing, I'm actually able to do this, to project myself into that multiverse and breathe its liberating air.

Activism, *Miss Saigon*, and the Arts

I. *MINOR FEELINGS* AND ANTI-ASIAN HATE CRIMES

In Cathy Park Hong's book of essays *Minor Feelings: An Asian American Reckoning,* she recounts a racial incident when taking the New York subway with two white friends, her roommate and the roommate's boyfriend. As they walk down the stairs to the subway, a white guy passes them singsonging, "Ching chong ding dong." Her white friends say nothing, and Hong is worried about making "them uncomfortable." When they get on the subway, the white guy is in their car, sitting with what appears to be his Black wife and their biracial toddler. Hong decides to confront him: "I not only called him a racist but I also hissed that he was setting a horrible example for his baby."

But then the white guy gets up, comes up to her, and points to her roommate's boyfriend, and says, "He's lucky that he's not your boyfriend, because if he was your boyfriend, I'd beat the shit out of him."

What's striking to me about this incident is not the racist white guy—there are racist white guys all over America—but the reaction of Hong's seemingly liberal companions. Hong also stresses the reaction of her so-called friends:

> My roommate's boyfriend kept saying, "I wish I said something." Then it was our stop. As we were getting off, the guy shouted at me across the crowded car, "Fucking chink!"
>
> "White Trash motherfucker!" I yelled back.
>
> When we were on the platform, my friend, who had failed to say much during the train ride, burst into tears.
>
> "That's never happened to me before," she wailed.
>
> And just like that, I was shoved aside. I was about to comfort her and then I stopped myself from the absurdity of that impulse. All of my

> anger and hurt transferred to her, and even now, as I'm writing this, I'm more upset with her than that guy. We walked silent back to our apartment while she cried.

Most readers, I hope, won't need a breakdown on why Hong is so angry here, but perhaps it's useful to delineate how her friends' reactions exemplify white fragility: Hong is the one who was attacked with a racist insult and threat, not her white friends. But the white male friend is preoccupied with his own cowardice; the white female friend is preoccupied with her even being in the proximity of a racial attack—that is, with having her white bubble of racial security approach what people of color experience all the time and must be on guard for constantly. The white female is in tears and seems far more emotionally upset than Hong.

Here white fragility merges with white narcissism. Neither white friend is capable of saying to themselves, "Yes, this is upsetting to me, but who is the real victim here? Who was really insulted and in danger? Whose needs at this moment should take precedence over mine?" Both whites cannot even formulate this thought because they presume that their needs will always take precedence over those of any person of color. And that is one of the rules of Whiteness and white supremacy, despite Hong's friends' presumably—*presumably*—liberal leanings.

In contrast, after the incident Hong doesn't break down; she steels herself, indeed so much so that she even has the impulse to comfort the white friend, a gesture neither white friend contemplates for her. Neither white fragility nor white narcissism is a luxury afforded to Hong or other people of color. Most people of color recognize that indulging in such fragility will not help them survive a racist society; that's reserved for white people. This is why James Baldwin, for instance, writes about whites as if they were children, who cannot grow up and face the truths of the world they themselves have created—and thus, the truth about themselves. And because whites cannot see the truth about themselves, they are incapable of seeing people of color clearly. Whites live and thrive in a dream of what they believe the world to be, not what the world actually is. Often trying to tell them they live in an illusion, implies Baldwin, is like telling a very young child Santa Claus does not exist.

What Hong doesn't say is whether she remained friends with this white couple after this incident. It's a dilemma so many Asian Americans face with white friends: How much do your white friends understand about your experience as an Asian American? How strongly will they have your back when race comes up? Obviously, Hong's white friends fail in this regard, but oftentimes we Asian Americans forgive white friends or choose not to see how much these white friends don't have our backs; it's part of the price we pay for acceptance in white society (which, as a rule, is also the price of the ticket for thriving in a white-dominated corporation or organization).

I don't know if Hong ever confronted her white friends about this incident. The way she tells the story it doesn't appear as if she did. But then she wrote about it in *Minor Feelings*, and whether she said it directly to those white friends, her recounting this anecdote is certainly her version of "Fuck you" to them. That she was probably afraid to say it to them at the time is understandable; many of us Asian Americans feel our position in this racialized society is already precarious. But what seems clear to me is this: at least at this time in her life, Hong did not see herself as part of a larger Asian American community or, rather, an Asian American activist community that might have supported her in ways her white friends—or, rather, companions—did not.

If the reader thinks Hong's racist encounter is merely a "minor" matter, something that doesn't occur with any frequency, just plug in Covid-19 and Asian Americans into your search engine. You will find article after article of how there have been nearly three thousand incidents of anti-Asian hate crimes in all fifty states in the year 2020–21.[1]

1 As many have pointed out, almost all Asian Americans know someone or they themselves have experienced anti-Asian remarks or violence in recent years. In responding to these attacks, activist Amanda Nguyen, co-founder of Rise, a sexual assault survivor advocacy organization, has created a viral Instagram video on the rise of anti-Asian violence. The video includes the surveillance clip of eighty-four-year-old Vicha Ratanapakdee, a Thai man, being shoved to the concrete by a masked assailant on a street in San Francisco. Ratanapakdee later died as a result of his injuries. Nguyen told *USA Today*: "When I made that video, I was tired of living in fear and I wanted to scream. It's so absurd that I have to say, 'Stop killing us.' . . . We are literally fearing for our lives as we walk out of our door, and your silence, your silence rings in our heads."

Obviously, this anti-Asian phenomenon needs to be contextualized as caused by Trump's rhetoric (in his first term) of the "Kung Flu" and the "China virus" as well as the continued linking of any Asian in America with any country in Asia. More broadly, there's his constant push of anti-immigrant views, racism, and xenophobia. All that needs to be viewed through the lens of white fears about their coming racial minority status and the racist toolbox that has been in the arsenal of white supremacists throughout our nation's history.

In one survey during Covid-19, one third of adult Asian Americans said they have experienced anti-Asian remarks, bias, and harassment. In a 2024 survey, 32 percent of Asian American parents said they feared their children might be subjected to racist bullying. Beyond this, the 150 percent rise in anti-Asian hate crimes during and after the pandemic points to a rule about Asians in America, one Japanese Americans know all too well: whenever there is trouble between America and a country in Asia, Asian Americans will be transformed into aliens and a threat to the country, a fifth column element or a disease that must be rooted out and sent back to Asia or to concentration camps, our citizenship and rights abolished. If you as an Asian American have any acquaintance with Asian American history, you know that your citizenship is not permanent. In many ways, you are never going to be truly part of America; your being American is always contingent and subject to revocation by the white majority.

II. *MISS SAIGON* REDIVIVUS AND ASIAN AMERICAN ACTIVISM

When St. Paul's Ordway Theater announced it was bringing back *Miss Saigon* a third time in 2013, local Asian Americans organized the Don't

In February 2021, on a New York subway, an assailant slashed the face of Noel Quintana, a sixty-one-year-old Filipino man, with a box cutter and left him bleeding. Quintana told ABS-CBN News that the attack seemed to him to come out of nowhere, from the man next to him: "He started kicking my bag, actually it's a tote bag, and I don't see any reason why because I don't think it even touches him or something. And when I said what's wrong with you, and I moved away from him, that's when he slashed me." It's difficult to view the interview with Quintana or photos of him with a huge scar running across his face and not instinctively flinch.

Buy *Miss Saigon* Coalition, made up of local artists, scholars, and activists like Juliana Pegues, Margie Andreason, Bao Phi, Eric Sharp, Anna Min, Ed Bok Lee, and others. As we first began gathering, I was so impressed with the talent and political vision in the room, the various skills and experiences we brought to bear on our organizing, from artists to political activists to educators to administrators to those in corporations. I understood that room was a result of the work done for a couple of decades by the Asian American Renaissance and Theater Mu and other arts organizations like the Center for Hmong Arts and Talent, Pangea World Theater, and the Ananya Dance Theater. I'd known many of the artists and activists, like Juliana, Bao, and Ed, through my work as artistic director of the Asian American Renaissance, when they gave some of their first public readings and performances in their twenties; I'd taught them in classes, worked with them in theater pieces for Theater Mu, and seen them grow into significant voices in our community.

The Coalition would meet at the Loft, a local writing center where Bao, a slam champion, ran the spoken word series or in meeting rooms at the Wilder Foundation, which was headed by MayKao Hang, who had worked at AAR as an intern. (Community builds connections!) Sitting around the table at these meetings with a circle of younger Asian Americans, I spoke about how in the early 1990s I had angered many of my white artist friends with my views on *Miss Saigon* and how that led to my ostracism from the white writing community. I told the group how much it meant to me to be part of this coalition of Asian Americans from many ethnicities, how it was proof that we could organize as a community and speak not just against *Miss Saigon* but against the racism we Asian Americans face in our society and culture. I was no longer the lone angry Asian, I said one night to the group. "Indeed," I smiled, "some of you are more angry than me. I'm the mild old man."

Naming ourselves a coalition was not an accident. We worked with the local Asian American theater, Theater Mu, and other local theaters and groups and other artists of color, to organize against the Ordway; we wrote grants and my friend Dipankar Mukherjee's Pangea World Theater served as our fiscal sponsor. We designed a website with articles about *Miss Saigon* (including by respected academics Josephine Lee and Kim Park Nelson)—on Orientalism, on transracial adoption (our community has many Korean adoptees), on human trafficking.

We put up a petition and statements by local political, cultural, and education leaders condemning the musical. We set up a national Tumblr site, Miss Saigon Lies, with photos and testaments by Asian Americans around the country. We put online photos by the great Corky Lee of the original New York protests of *Miss Saigon*. Later a couple of members created a tool kit on organizing.[2] After our calling for help from the BIPOC community, the Puerto Rican artist-activist Ricardo Levins Morales designed a brilliant poster, calling the Ordway "Ignoreway," displaying a white man and a Vietnamese woman in a pose like the posters for *Gone with the Wind*, alluding to America's racist portrayals of its racist past. Theater Mu organized a series of educational forums, the last of which was attended by personnel from local foundations. And after listening to dozens of Asian Americans of all ethnicities testify about the inaccuracies, distortions, lies, and stereotypes in the musical, one foundation officer said to me, "That changed me as a human being." Later that officer's foundation turned down a grant to the Ordway.

As part of our campaign, we contacted local theater reviewers and educated them on the Orientalism and historical inaccuracies of the musical. When the musical came to the Twin Cities in the early 1990s, it had been greeted by positive reviews. But in 2013, the local reviews were all decidedly negative. One reviewer opened with his preconception that it couldn't be "that bad," despite all the fuss from the local Asian American community, but he ended with the conclusion that it was "that bad." Another reviewer even referred readers to our webpage and my critique of *Miss Saigon*. Of course, we held a political demonstration at the opening of the musical, with support from artists from other communities of color, but we had done that the two times before when the Ordway presented *Miss Saigon*. The difference this time was in part the internet ("How did you organize protests back in the day? Before the internet?" one young activist asked), in part the experience garnered from our past organizing, and mainly the development of a community of Asian American artists and activists with myriad artistic and political connections developed over two decades of work.

2 The Don't Buy *Miss Saigon* Coalition website and the tool kit are online and can be used by other communities (https://dontbuymiss-saigon.com). Again, pass it on.

Through all of this, we observed the wisdom of Sun Tzu and his *Art of War*: we did not fully reveal our purposes or tactics; we worked behind the scenes; we did reconnaissance; we had contacts who worked within the Ordway; we knew more about our enemy than our enemy knew about us; we let them underestimate what we were capable of. When local arts foundation personnel showed up at Theater Mu's public gathering, the Ordway administration freaked out and objected, but there was nothing they could do. They hadn't realized that we had contacts in the funding community. (In part, this came from my time serving as board president of one of the local foundations.)

We didn't stop *Miss Saigon* from coming, but our work continued.

A couple of months after the last performance, our coalition met with the Ordway staff and its board members. The Ordway in no way wanted this meeting. But it was arranged by a local feminist multiracial dance troupe, the Ananya Dance Theater, whom the Ordway wanted to present; in order for this to happen, ADT had demanded that the Ordway meet with us as a condition of their performing. Though the Ordway didn't know this, I was on the ADT board and the Coalition was collaborating with ADT and their artistic director, Ananya Chatterjea, on their demands.

At that meeting with the Ordway board, we demonstrated that we knew more about the history of their organization and the previous protests by the Asian American community of *Miss Saigon* than their staff did. We knew that back in the 1990s the organization had not heeded warnings and admonishments by two Asian American advisory groups not to present *Miss Saigon*. We knew that their staff had hidden from one Asian advisory group the Ordway's plan to bring back the musical a second time, and the advisory group only found out secretly through an Asian American employee. (So much for asking for "advice" from the community.) Neither the current Ordway board nor its staff knew this history.[3]

3 The Ordway's ignorance of its own history of its relationship with the Asian American community is symptomatic of Whiteness. Whiteness consciously and unconsciously wills itself to forget its own history of racial relations, its acts of oppression, and its rejection of the concerns of people of color. Whites then are angered when we remember that history that they want to bury. Thus, according to Whiteness, the problem is

At a certain point the president of the Ordway remarked that she had underestimated the negative reactions of the Asian American community. On hearing this, I pulled out the Asian American political science text *Asian American Resistance in the 1990s* (I've got an essay in it), and I pointed to Corky Lee's cover photo of the New York city *Miss Saigon* protests. "So what you're saying," I told her and her board, "is that you are ignorant of our political and cultural history. You don't realize that our most famous Asian American playwright, David Henry Hwang—our August Wilson—wrote two plays concerning the controversy over *Miss Saigon, M. Butterfly* and *Yellowface.* You don't know how important the *Miss Saigon* protests were to Asian American activism. So you don't know our political and cultural history, you don't know our theater, and you don't even know the history of your own organization with our community. And yet you presume to present us with this awful musical to help spark conversation about racial issues in our community?" (This was one of the arguments the Ordway pushed when they first became aware of our community's negative response to the musical.)

After I spoke, one white-haired white board member—the board was almost all white and mainly from the corporate world and elites of St. Paul—admitted, "I think he has a point."

A short while later, the Ordway issued a formal apology to the Asian American community and promised never to bring the egregious musical back to the Twin Cities again.

I can imagine some might wonder, Why all this fuss about a Broadway musical? And isn't this censorship or at least "political correctness"?

People who ask these questions usually aren't actually asking a real question; they're not willing to admit there are other points of view. First, theaters all the time decide not to present material; no one today is going to do a remake of, say, W. D. Griffith's *Birth of a Nation* or a minstrel show. But no one calls that censorship. Second, the people who created *Miss Saigon* aren't being censored; they're rich enough

not what whites have done to people of color but that people of color keep remembering what whites have done—and that somehow oppresses whites. As I point out in my book *The Stories Whiteness Tells Itself,* this is the psychology of an abuser.

to put the show on themselves if they wanted—as opposed to a local St. Paul theater that purportedly wants to relate to an increasingly diverse local community and receives funds from the state arts board and local foundations. Third, there's a difference between *political correctness*—however that term is defined—and an insistence on truth, accuracy, and equal opportunity in the arts.

Let me explain briefly. This musical represents the ways white artists and culture have for so long felt they could freely portray Asians and Asian Americans in any way they wished. Indeed, they could do so without regard to inherent racist and colonial assumptions, without critiquing their use of stereotypes, and without feeling the necessity to include actual Asians or Asian Americans in the work of portraying and representing us, our culture, and history. This of course starts with the yellowface casting in the original Broadway production, but there's so much more that's egregious about this work. *Madama Butterfly* was created by an Italian not a Japanese, and yet this opera about the "Orient" was used by the creators of *Miss Saigon* to concoct a plot not about Japanese but the Vietnamese. (All dem gooks must be the same.) When Kim kills herself so that her mixed-race child can live with her white father in America, Japanese seppuku becomes generalized to an all-Asian tradition of suicide, and the message is: "Those gooks don't care about life like we Westerners. Certainly, it's better off to be with your white father and having a dead Asian mother than being raised by your Asian mother in, yuck, Vietnam." Following the colonial tropes of Western soldiers in Asia, the love affair between an adult soldier and a seventeen-year-old girl forced into prostitution would only be seen as romantic if the adult is a white male and the underage female is Asian. Just imagine how American audiences would respond to a "love" affair between a Communist Chinese soldier, who is occupying America, and a seventeen-year-old white American runaway prostitute—would any see this as romantic?

In its echoes of colonialist ideology, there is no positive portrayal of any male Vietnamese in the musical; they are cruel and brutal Communists, sexist and cruel South Vietnamese, pimps. (Compare this with the far more nuanced and individualized portraits of a wide political spectrum of Vietnamese in Viet Thanh Nguyen's novel, *The Sympathizer*.) In contrast, Kim is mainly seen as positive because she falls in love with a white GI—the only attractive aspect of

Asian colonial natives are the women who side with and sleep with the colonists. (Yes, she has other qualities, such as courage, tenacity, and love for her child, but these are only positive because she's not a Communist, she's not against the Americans.) In the original Broadway run, not only did they practice yellowface casting, but when the actors portraying the Vietnamese performed a religious ceremony, the director and producers didn't even bother to use the actual Vietnamese language but had the actors mumble gobbledygook, thus demonstrating how little the team that created this mess cared about the Vietnamese or their culture.

In the various protests of *Miss Saigon* over the years, what we and other Asian Americans were objecting to are the rules of Whiteness: white people can portray people of color in any way they see fit; they don't have to do the necessary work to portray us accurately and without distortions; they don't have to examine and critique the stereotypes *they* have created, their own racial and colonial assumptions about who we are. Certainly, they don't have to listen to *us* tell our own stories; they don't even have to recognize our right to tell our own stories. (The producer Cameron Mackintosh called the original *Miss Saigon* controversy "a tempest in an Oriental teacup.")

All this is the legacy of racism, colonialism, and what Edward Said dubbed Orientalism, but this legacy is something white Westerners supposedly don't have to consider, any more than the colonial powers had to listen to the Asian natives they ruled over and colonized (or in the case of the Ordway, its Asian American advisory groups). The white West always knows best for us Asians.

Moreover, as I pointed out to the Ordway board, this Orientalist concoction, this kitschy wedding of *Madama Butterfly* to the Vietnam War, marked a turning point in the artistic careers of many Asian American artists. So many Asian American artists, as I myself did, quarreled with fellow white artists and institutions over the yellowface casting in the original production of *Miss Saigon*. Some, like me, lost friendships over this controversy.[4]

4 In the time since *Miss Saigon* was created, a number of Vietnamese American writers and artists have begun to penetrate the American psyche with a different version of what the Vietnamese call "the American War." In 2019, in the *New York Times*, Viet Thanh Nguyen, author of the Pulitzer Prize–winning novel *The Sympathizer* and

What we all have been working for is not simply to relegate *Miss Saigon* to the historical trash heap of racist artistic productions, but to change the institutional and critical landscape of the arts to be more inclusive of Asian American artists and our community. We were working to change white-dominated arts institutions in their approach to race and culture, to get them to actually hear our voices and stories, and not solely their versions of our voices and stories.

Finally, I want to make a key point here that many do not understand about such protests. The purpose of activism is not simply to confront and change those outside one's community or to address any particular issue; no, its purpose is also *to change those inside our communities.* In the Twin Cities, the Asian Americans who participated in organizing against *Miss Saigon,* whether back in the 1990s or in 2013, were transformed by their work. We gained a sense of our own power; we saw that our voices mattered; we found in ourselves a strength and a willingness to speak out that would embolden and empower us in any endeavor we engaged in afterwards. We accomplished something no other Asian American community in the country has done—as an ad hoc volunteer group, we got a powerful white institution to apologize for putting on *Miss Saigon* and to promise never to bring it back.

co-producer of the HBO miniseries based on it, wrote an op-ed critiquing the musical: "Some people who are irritated by these criticisms of *Miss Saigon*'s enduring popularity will say, *It's only a show, nothing more.* But the enjoyment of the show's fantasy is precisely why the show matters. Fantasy cannot be dismissed as mere entertainment, especially when we keep repeating the fantasy. Fantasy—and our enjoyment of it—speaks to something we deeply want to believe. The enjoyment of this show is based on the privilege that the audience feels, the privilege of not being that Asian woman who kills herself, the privilege of seeing the world from the viewpoint of the powerful white male savior who can both be so attractive that a woman would kill herself over him and be so paternal that he can adopt the mixed-race child who will stand in for childlike Asia, in need of Western benevolent guidance. . . . Should *Miss Saigon* therefore be censored or canceled? The question is a distraction from the real answer, which is that censorship or cancellation does little to address the inequities of Broadway and Hollywood. Perhaps those of us who detest the musical would not be so upset if there were other stories about Asians or Vietnamese people that showed their diversity." Case in point: *Miss Saigon* was the only work the Ordway Theater has ever presented about Vietnamese people.

As I recently said to a group of Asian Americans at the University of Minnesota on a panel about our mental health, sometimes what we need is to say "Fuck you" to Whiteness, to the silencing and neglect of our communities, to our continued marginalization in this society. Protest requires inner strength, not just outward resources; it requires acknowledging our own powers, powers we may have not previously recognized or known we possess. It requires working together with other members of your community, supporting and befriending other members of your community. Through this process, activism creates community and makes all in the community feel less alone and more empowered. All this is something that individual therapy cannot do. In order to address our psychological issues as Asian Americans, the link between activism and our mental health is real and valuable; that too is what our protests demonstrated.

III. BUILDING LEADERSHIP, BUILDING COMMUNITY: OUR FEELINGS ARE *NOT* MINOR

Recently, I attended a fundraising luncheon for members of CAAL (Coalition of Asian American Leaders), a Minnesota organization whose mission has been to build a network of more than five thousand Asian American leaders and to advocate for our community and other marginalized communities.[5] CAAL holds training seminars to develop local Asian American leaders; commissions demographic, economic, and political studies; lobbies for Asian American causes in city and state government and in education and business. As in many urban areas, there are class and ethnic differences among our communities. Certainly, the large refugee Hmong community has been more working class than, say, the more professional Indian community; but the mainly Hmong leadership of CAAL has made a concerted effort at outreach, and all our communities are represented in CAAL's membership and board.

I've spoken to CAAL's leadership development cohort for the past two summers; two weeks before the luncheon, CAAL honored me

5 CAAL is in Minnesota, a place not known for its concentration of Asian Americans. The numbers reflect the tremendous activism of the Twin Cities BIPOC community and of visionary leaders like Hmong American Bo Thao-Urabe. So much for Jay Caspian Kang's "the Loneliest Americans."

as one of the elders in the Asian American community. My daughter Samantha is the head of 826 MSP, a creative writing/tutoring organization for marginalized K-12 students, and she was one of the table monitors designated to collect contributions at the luncheon; she's now secretary of the CAAL board.

More than three hundred Asian Americans attended the luncheon, which presented various speakers and recognized new leaders, all of whom described the ways CAAL helped them to find their own voices and empowered them to act in their field. The point was: leaders aren't produced spontaneously; they have to be mentored and nurtured by the community.

At the end of the luncheon, the Board President Margie Andreason, a Korean adoptee and a key leader in the Don't Buy *Miss Saigon* Coalition, related a telling anecdote. One summer evening she was walking in a park with her partner in St. Louis Park, a Minneapolis suburb. They passed a group of white teenage boys who began making "ching-chong" sounds and speaking in mock Asian accents. It was the type of racial harassment that so many Asian Americans, like Cathy Park Hong, are all too familiar with.

Andreason said that before CAAL she might have just gone home, feeling furious and hurt and sad and kept those feelings to herself (as Cathy Park Hong did). But empowered by CAAL, she called up her city council representative and the mayor. She told them about the incident and she asked what the city was going to do to improve racial relationships in their community. Both answered back and began to work with Andreason on a program to fight racial intolerance in St. Louis Park. At the end of her speech, Andreason pointed to the city council member who was attending the luncheon.

The lesson here is clear: Asian American organizations are necessary, necessary not only to enable us to take collective action, but also to empower us as individuals. In her lifetime, the great Asian American activist Grace Lee Boggs worked both with the Asian American community and her husband's African American community in Detroit. She wisely observed, "Building community is to the collective as spiritual practice is to the individual."

Over and over in my life, I've felt the wisdom of Grace's observation.

Conclusion

Writing and the Long Game

The earliest essay in this book was published in 1992, when I was forty. Back then, my wife and I had only one child, Samantha, three years old. I am finishing this book at seventy-one. My son Tomo is twenty-eight, my son Nikko thirty, and Sam, thirty-five, is a representative in the Minnesota legislature and mother of Tadashi Sencermura-Witzig, my two-year-old grandson.

A year and a half ago, my mother, Terry (née Teruko), died at ninety-one; two months ago my father, Tom (née Katsuji Uyemura), died at ninety-seven. In the past few years, all my Nisei relatives, my parents' generation, have passed. I am now the oldest in my extended family. The elder.

Unlike in traditional Asian culture, I've resisted this appellation till now. My friend Alexs Pate still resists it. And yet at dinner a few nights ago, even he admitted that over the past five years, with the isolation that came on with Covid-19, he's been feeling a certain diminishment of his energies. He's still heading Innocent Technologies, an educational business that now has programs all over the country, and they're about to make a leap into online programs for educators, but he too understands that he and I are in what most consider old age.

In so many ways, though, I don't feel old. I still do my runs and weight training four or five days a week, though the speed of my runs has become tortoise-like. On the road along the Mississippi, every runner passes me and younger joggers speed by at a brisk clip. I am still able to beat my sons at golf by ten strokes or more, and I'm dreading the days when they'll begin to beat me (which I tell them is a long way off). But it's been many years since they first beat me one on one in basketball.

I don't think I look as old as my age; like many Asians, I can take ten or fifteen years off and people would believe it. I often jokingly refer to that saying, Black don't crack, brown don't frown, and yellow stays mellow. Lately, I've taken heart from the late-career successes of Michelle Yeoh, who seems more famous than ever and finally duly recognized for her immense talent. She certainly now is a respected elder, whose beauty is acknowledged and who has received her due. But if I share Michelle's younger Asian looks, there's a difference between us: unlike Michelle, I still feel significantly underrecognized. Of course, in this I share the ressentiment of most authors, whatever their age.

Still, I try not to dwell on such feelings. I don't have a lot of time left. I have a goal of at least fifteen books, and this one is my twelfth. I'm aware Philip Roth publicly quit writing at seventy-eight. Alexs and I have talked about a Black male novelist who was an integral part of the Black Arts movement, but when Alexs interviewed him in later life, that novelist was profoundly bitter and biting about his lack of recognition. As a great admirer of this writer's work, Alexs understood the man's bitterness; Alexs could taste it on his own tongue. But Alexs said he never wanted to become that full of rancor. It discourages the writing impulse rather than helps it, and he's steeled himself against such resentment.

And so have I. That's not always been an easy task. If you come from a marginalized community, in order to evaluate and address that marginalization you have to focus in many ways on scarcity, on what your community does not receive—resources, privileges, power, physical and psychic safety; you have to address the forces of oppression, aggression, and insult. But this can induce in either you or the community a psychology that makes it harder to address progress or plenty, to acknowledge ways in which you are now less marginalized. You think if you admit there's been progress or improvement or any sort of bounty, that means that you or the community hasn't suffered in the past or that you are no longer marginalized. Moreover, inveighing on the injustices of the past feels more empowering than admitting those injustices no longer occur or occur with less frequency. On an individual level, your group's marginalization can, in certain ways, foster a personal psychology where you focus on what you don't get rather than what you have received. Such a psychology can indeed become a block to your own personal happiness or prevent you from being properly grateful for what you have. I speak here from a personal knowledge of how I've been shaped by a psychology of scarcity.

That said, I know I've led a privileged and fortunate life, and in so many ways I do feel lucky and grateful. I've been able to publish my work, if often at smaller presses. While the couples on either side of our house have gone through divorce, I've been with the same woman for more than fifty years. I have a close-knit family; my children, their partners, and Susie and I get together every week for dinner. Susie and I have our grandson, Dash (shortened from Tadashi), overnight once a week and I tell people, "It's so much easier and fun being a grandparent." (Admittedly, I've had to get used to referring to myself as a grandfather.) Summers, I go golfing with my two sons and my daughter Sam's partner, Lance, and it's great fun to watch them razz and trash-talk each other. As for the rest of my social life, I have fewer literary contacts than I used to, but I live in a marvelously diverse and supportive community of BIPOC artists in the Twin Cities, where I'm considered, as they say, a "respected elder."

In short, I have been multiply blessed.

Despite all this, this past summer I fell into a three-month-long depression. Some of it had to do with my disappointment that my last book hadn't broken through in the ways I'd hoped, though it garnered strongly positive reviews. Given that the book challenged the fallacious premises of white narratives and the dismissed truths of Black narratives in nonfiction and fiction, perhaps I was still guilty of being disappointed by a lack of white acceptance; but I had also thought the book might have been picked up by a larger portion of BIPOC readers.

Still, my depression also involved more directly personal causes than my literary career. My mother's death in 2022 had been both expected given her age and yet not expected—at the time she was more spry and mentally alert than my dad, and the cause of her death, bleeding ulcers, was not one we'd expected given her and her family's medical histories.

As a pediatric oncologist, Susie has been present at a significant number of deaths, most of them children; both her parents are gone. In contrast, until my mother passed, I had only been present at one deathbed. The ugliness and pain of my mother's death from her ulcers' perforations, the blood that was being sucked up and foaming on her lips through a tube in her mouth from her stomach, her whispering to me, "I want to die"—all that struck me in a way that nothing in my life has ever hit me.

After my late twenties and the years of therapy when I was breaking from my family system, my mother and I had gotten along fairly well. I had long ago forgiven her for any of the things that bothered me about my childhood and the ways my parents raised me. But beneath the surface, buried for the most part, was an underground vein of resentment and disapproval on her part, mainly because she hated my writing, hated that I had written of private matters in my family.

I see this disapproval as stemming partly from my mother's particularly private sense surrounding family matters and partly as cultural. When talking about my mother's disapproval of my writing with the Japanese American writers Garrett Hongo and Karen Tei Yamashita a few years ago at an Associated Writing Programs conference, Karen told us of the time in her twenties when she was living in Brazil and her short story was accepted in the annual *Rafu Shimpo* Christmas literary supplement. (*Rafu Shimpo* is a bilingual Japanese American newspaper that has been publishing in L.A. since the 1920s.). When Karen's mother learned of this in a letter, she had her father drive her to the *Rafu Shimpo* office, where her mother went in and demanded that the story be retracted, even if it was already in the presses. "Geez," I replied to Karen, "my mother may have disapproved of my writing, but she never actually went down to the press and tried to stop my work from being published."

You keep family matters private: that's a rule of Japanese culture. Having a writer in the family? How could my mother—or Karen's mother—support that? In my mother's viewpoint, my refusal of silence or discretion came in part out of arrogance and selfishness, and so my writing was another mark against my character, a judgment she occasionally voiced in indirect and direct ways: "David, you think too much of yourself," was a frequent refrain from high school on.

So this past summer I was also mourning my mother, and I guess I am still being affected by her disapproval, which made my mourning less than clean. Then too I had begun writing about her death and my reaction to it, something she would have severely disapproved of. I was upset and saddened and thrown by the abruptness of her passing; I missed her and broke down several times afterwards. But none of this dissipated my mixed feelings about our relationship or how I felt she regarded me.

Then too I realized in writing about her death, I was also writing about my own mortality, my own coming death. My predicted end seems much more imminent now that I am the oldest in my family.

Of course, my unfamiliarity and lack of attention to death are part of my privileged first-world life. I'm a baby boomer, the generation who proclaimed, "Don't trust anyone over thirty." We never imagined our later years, despite that Beatles tune "When I'm Sixty-Four." In the past few years, I would sing to my wife that Bebe Rexha chorus, "We are never growing older, we are never growing older." Susie and I still go out to clubs, still go out dancing with crowds of young people at the Gay '90s. But no matter how many years I've insisted I wasn't growing older, I've come to a point where the knowledge of my age can't be denied. And so, like Hopkins's poem to Margaret, it wasn't just the leaves passing or in this case, my mother's passing, that I was mourning—it was my life.

Looking over my depression last summer, I feel now that I had to, in some hard way, come to terms with the fact that I was seventy-one: I didn't have several decades left. Yes, my health is good. But I could drop any time in the future—a month, a year, five years, certainly ten years—and no one would say it was a surprise; people would regard my passing as inevitable and unremarkable.

With my father's death two months ago, my sense of my mortality hit even deeper, even if I had come out of the depression from last summer. During the time just before my father passed, I'd take dictation from him about his life. His and my mother's deaths have spurred me back into writing about our family's past and Japanese American history. Though my parents tended to avoid speaking about their childhoods and their incarceration by the U.S. government, in their last couple of years something shifted in them, and they began to speak more about their past.

As the oldest member now in my extended family, I realize I am now a keeper of our history, its vessel and voice. Watching over my sleeping father, a couple of days before his death, I was reading *Lament in the Night,* a novel by Shoson Nagahara, a Japanese immigrant of his father's generation, which tells the tale of a poor Issei worker who is trying to scrape out a living in Little Tokyo around 1925, a year before my father was born. I looked across the room at a photo of his mother and father, probably when they were married, and I thought of them making love in that year to make my father. Suddenly, I felt I could see the streets of Little Tokyo and my grandparents in a way I've never been able to, as living vividly in history, as palpable to me in a way they've never been. I could acknowledge their importance not just to my history but to American history. I could see them as the center of the screen, not restricted to the peripheries.

Recently, at the Associated Writing Programs conference, I had an inspiring conversation with the Black Minnesota writer Shannon Gibney about the Black poet Robin Coste Lewis's *To the Realization of Perfect Happiness,* which pairs poetic texts with her grandmother's photographs. Looking at that book I realized the family photos that I and my sibling perused after my father's death are now historical documents. Here's what Shannon wrote on her Facebook page about our conversation:

> David and I were talking about artifacts you find of your family(ies) as you age (if you're lucky), and then you realize those stories and experiences will die unless you, the writer, decide to work with them in some way. I was also reminded of Bao Phi's observation that creative writers from historically marginalized communities are often the first historians our people have, as mainstream dominant culture usually has little interest or investment in our stories. And will approach them with a different, often problematic perspective.

I've been writing for many years about my family and their past, but I realize that this next book will probably be the last time I do so. Because of this, because of my age, the task is different now. I don't know what exactly this difference will be; I'll have to discover it in the writing. But I know it entails the vantage point I'm telling it from—my parents are gone, and soon I will be too.

My friend, the poet Garrett Hongo has suggested that part of this next book needs to be about love—the complicated and sometimes difficult love between my parents and me, the five decades' long love between my wife and me, my love for my kids and now my grandchild, Tadashi. And I realize this means somehow I must become a different sort of writer, one willing to address more directly feelings and emotions in ways I've kept at bay, perhaps through the political, perhaps through the theoretical, or through some preconceived notion of literary rigor.

In what ways do I love my parents differently now that they are passed? In what ways does that love help me to see them differently, perhaps in a more forgiving light? Is there a deeper love I'm now allowing myself to feel for them, and as I do, does love become for me something greater? Do I love the world more now that I'm more aware I will soon leave it? Is it love that will help me to see my parents and their parents more palpably, more truly, to inhabit or imagine their psyches and lives in ways I haven't allowed or enabled myself to before? And what part of those barriers were the forces of cultural marginalization and race, and what barriers were those in my own psyche and my refusal to more deeply love or find a greater love for them?

That I find myself asking these questions is surprising to me. Just this week I sat on a panel of BIPOC grandfathers. On the panel one of the things I said is that at my age your position in the world has drastically changed. You're no longer the most important generation, you're not at the center of things. Your kids and your grandkids are the center stage now. You know even more viscerally, new pain by new pain, new med by new med, that you're not immortal. As Philip Roth observed, "Old age isn't a battle, it's a massacre." You're on the losing side of time. And so you have to redefine yourself as a man. Young men are always ready to fight, but contrary to Dylan Thomas, it's ridiculous for an old man to think like a fighter, to always be ready to put up your fists and strike a blow. You have to find another place to stand, another way of regarding yourself. As a result of aging, your ego should get smaller, whether you want it to or not. That allows you to see the world through a very different lens.

I've been a writer for almost fifty years. For most, when you're in your twenties or early thirties as a writer, it's hard. You don't know if you have it. You haven't published much. You're consumed with doubt, which you often mask with arrogance or self-promotion. But at this stage of my life, I've done my work, the work I wanted to write, and I think I have a reasonable sense of what I've achieved.

In an article in *The Atlantic,* "You Might Be a Late Bloomer," David Brooks looks at the careers of late-blooming artists like Cezanne, Grandma Moses, or Morgan Freeman or those late successes from others fields like Copernicus or Darwin, and how they are different from those who flourish early in their careers. Where the younger successes like Picasso or Sylvia Plath make revolutionary and groundbreaking conceptual innovations in their twenties or early thirties, the late-blooming artists must take a more seemingly indirect and wandering journey. They're less motivated by external rewards and less likely to fit into hierarchies or gather mentors and benefactors (hence in part their longer path to success and recognition). They're more likely to stray into other fields: "Nobel Prize winners are 22 times more likely to spend large chunks of time as an amateur actor, musician, magician, or other type of performer than non-Nobel-winning scientists are." When I read this I thought, *Oh, I play the piano, I've acted, I've done performance work.* Late bloomers are often mainly self-taught learners with great curiosity and at the same time characterized by "epistemic humility." (*There's a lot I don't know.*) After years at their craft or field, they're at a point of mastery of their skills where they can push in new directions, where they can attack the canvas with boldness and confidence. They find themselves suddenly penetrating through veils of doubt; insights can occur to them that clarify and simplify, that come after years of experience and seem what some would call wisdom.

I see something of myself in Brooks's description of late bloomers. But who knows? Inevitably, I and my writings will eventually, if not quickly, descend into a deeper obscurity that comes with time passing. I have to recognize now that this is simply how things are, how things have always been. You are not important, you are dust—or as Joni Mitchell sang, "stardust"—but in any sense, you're not immortal, you're not going to live forever. Yes, people close to you may be sad at your passing, but to the rest of the world, it will mean nothing, you won't be remembered, and in that you're no different from anyone else, despite whatever fame or immortality you hoped to attain with your writing.

But Sam, Nikko, and Tomo will remember me. Dash and yet-to-come grandchildren will remember me. My paternal grandfather was born in 1880, came to the States in 1898, and Dash will hopefully see the year 2100. I am now a bridge between three centuries, between five generations, and that is where I write from.

Susie, whose grandmothers both lived past one hundred, will probably survive me. And there will be my books, somewhere out there in the digital world, even if libraries eventually vanish.

And Asian Americans? Certainly, the center of Asian America has moved in part from the East Asian Japanese and Chinese to Koreans, Filipinos, Southeast Asians, and South Asians (now the largest group). But eventually perhaps they too will diminish, or at least the stories of those Asian Americans alive now, mostly immigrants and the children of immigrants. By the third or fourth generations, they'll have intermarried, they'll be less and less distinguishable from other Americans, though whether that will be in a democracy or an autocracy is still a question to be decided. Whether a significant number of new Asian immigrants will be arriving here in the future is still a question.

Despite my age, I'm not done with writing by any means. As I've said, I'm working now on a memoir about my parents, their lives, and their passing. Although my father had disapproved of my career choice when I was in college, he eventually came around. He himself had wanted to be a writer when he was younger, and he made a living writing speeches and doing public relations. Eventually, unlike my mother, he grew proud of my accomplishments, and while my mother never read anything I wrote after my first memoir, my father read all of my work, even my last, fairly difficult book, *The Stories Whiteness Tells Itself: Racial Myths and Our American Narratives,* not necessarily a book meant to delight an elderly Republican. Perhaps that's why my loss of him and the pain of his last days—in all his limbs and back—and his suffering with the indignities of incontinence have so affected me. (In the span of a few days I changed my grandson's diaper and my father's diaper: the smell of his urine will stay with me forever.) My mourning for him feels clearer and cleaner than my mourning for my mother.

Then too my father's death process was less chaotic and sudden than my mother's. My siblings and I were all able to be present at his passing, and he got to say goodbye to all his grandchildren on Facetime and even to Dash, his great-grandson. My father had decided he wanted to die; he said he was in too much pain, he wasn't going to get better, and he had thought long and hard about it. It was a profound and sacred lesson to all of us about facing mortality and death. Before he began taking the morphine and tramadol, on his last day he was calm, accepting his end. One of his last sentences was, "I'm going to see my beautiful wife."

In his calls to his grandkids, I was impressed with how he talked to each one slightly differently, adjusting his conversation to who they were as individuals. I didn't know my grandparents and so I did not speak to them on their deathbeds. I think of my children talking that day to their grandfather, knowing he was going to die, and I realize we are always talking to loved ones who are one day going to die. Mortality is built into our existence; we just don't always sense its bones inside us or feel it pumping through our veins. We are all passing through.

And so, I too am preparing to go. Word by word. I look out my window, from my office where I've been writing for these thirty years, and the air is unseasonably warm for March in Minnesota, even if the trees are still bare and won't sprout leaves for several weeks. It's a day of mild sun, a little overcast. I'll go running out there along the river road in an hour or so, trying to stave off time and the body's decay. I'll think of this piece and this book I'm finishing. I'll be thinking of the next book, and the next. It's what writers do. I'll feel this pain in the soles of my feet that's more frequent now; I'll be aching a bit in the knees and afterwards with tingling in my calves and feet. I'll worry about the neuropathy that's only gotten worse in the past few years or my recent A-fib diagnosis. My body is signaling me—your warranty's over, nothing more guaranteed. You've racked up the miles, only a few left. But I love the fact that I can still run and still write and I feel lucky I'm still here. And as she has for decades, Susie will be waiting for me when I return from my run, as will the next page on my computer.

Once, years ago, I became a race man. Others made different choices. Indeed, most Asian Americans don't think about race as much as I do; it doesn't occupy their consciousness in the ways it does mine. Part of this stems from my being a writer, but part stems from something stubborn and inquisitive in me, something uncompromising, or, some might say, a too-judgmental streak. So be it.

The Manichaeans believed that if the world were not evil, every choice would not constitute a loss. But that's not the whole story. The choices I've made are my own, for the life I was meant to live.

It's been a good, no, a great life.

Appendix: Endnotes to "Fragments in Search of Asian American Masculinity"

I. STEREOTYPES OF THE ASIAN MALE BODY AND THE RISKS OF WRITING ABOUT THEM

Years ago, my friends the poets Li-Young Lee and Garrett Hongo were talking to a famous Asian American male academic; when my name came up, the academic replied, "Yeah, he writes all that stuff about sex. Is that what we want our young people to be reading?" Similarly, I can hear readers of all races, but particularly Asian American men, saying, *Really, David, what dignity is there in speaking of the stereotype of small-dicked Asian males?*

But then why should I, as an Asian American male, assume I'm afforded any dignity?

Boogie is the 2021 film Eddie Huang wrote and directed about a Taiwanese American high school basketball player; it presents our version of Jesus Shuttlesworth (see Spike Lee's *He Got Game*). Early in the film, Boogie ends up going out with Eleanor, the Black ex-girlfriend of his Black basketball rival, Monk. Boogie is a virgin, and in an awkward moment, just before he and Eleanor make love for the first time, he mutters that "my dick might be trash." Eleanor reassures him and they make love. In the end, it's not his dick that fouls up his relationship with her but his insecurities, his jealousy, and self-pity—i.e., his character. But as reviewer Justin Chang notes in the *LA Times,* "Boogie knows he's up against years' worth of racist below-the-belt stereotypes. 'Boogie' the movie knows it too."

Asian Americans, both men and women, have reacted to this stereotype, generally in this way: they point out that there are Asian men who are well endowed—Keni Styles, the Thai-French-Brit former porn actor, for instance—or they point to themselves or their boyfriends and say their dicks are certainly up to par or better. (Recently I heard a story attesting to the huge member of a famed Asian American writer.) So this means the stereotype is not true, though such claims are generally anecdotal and are not part of any legitimate scientific study. Nor do they dispel the stereotype and its persistence.

Moreover, as people often forget, certain claims of stereotypes can be true, even if the explanation or context for the stereotype is misleading or false.[1] You can have a 7′4″ Yao Ming in the NBA and still maintain that at least certain Asian populations are shorter than certain African or European populations. What this says about penis size, of course, is another matter.

There are Asian American men who probably wish I wasn't going into these sexual stereotypes. Some might contend that I am merely reifying or reinforcing the stereotype by writing about it. Silence, some might feel, is the way to go.

When I was an adolescent, the size of my member was not something I thought a lot about, nor do I think most Asian American males of my baby boomer generation thought about this issue much either. I'm pretty certain the Asian Americans of my father's or his father's generation did not as well. But as porn became more prominent in the culture, so did certain racial stereotypes about penis size. For Black males the stereotypes became more established in one way and for Asian males in the other. Given the increasing ubiquity of porn—and the absence of Asian/Asian American porn stars in hetero

1 There is, for instance, a disproportionate number of Asians who get into elite colleges, despite evidence of a bias against us. But the ways such a stereotype is rationalized or explained or interpreted or acted on in society can at the same time be inaccurate or false and, therefore, racist. For example, does the evidence of high Asian American academic achievement mean that Asians are genetically smarter than other races? No. There are many other possible reasons for the high academic achievement of Asian Americans: they work harder; they study in groups; Asian cultural norms emphasize academic study and persistence; the class and education of Asians who immigrate to America; Asian American parents pour more money and time into their children's education; the lesser amount and type of overt prejudice and racism faced by Asian Americans as opposed to those faced by other people of color, etc. There is a myriad of other factors that might be considered. So stereotypes can be true and not true and distorting at the same time.

porn—younger Asian American men like Eddie Huang grew up in a culture that denigrated our masculinity not just in terms of behavioral stereotypes but in stereotypes about our endowment.

So when did the stereotype of the lesser-endowed Asian male begin?

But wouldn't that mean the white patriarchy actually noticed Asian men and the size of our dicks?

Perhaps there's a footnote about this somewhere in Said on imperialism (jk).

Certainly, those imperialists colonizing Asia had all sorts of ideas about the sexuality of Asian women, including the tightness of their vaginas and their sexual worship of white men—*me so horny, me love you long time* is how the *Madama Butterfly/World of Suzie Wong/Miss Saigon/Full Metal Jacket*/2 Live Crew/Thai sex tour refrain goes. The sexually submissive and exotic Asian female readily submits to the colonial and superior masculine great white West—whether the colonial powers or individual white men. And their bigger dicks.

White feminists readily join Asian American women in critiquing such stereotypes about Asian women. Not so much though for the stereotypes of Asian men and our sexuality. Louis C.K. might joke that we're all women, but that's not how white feminists perceive Asian American men. They don't see us at all as part of an oppressed group.

When I talked about these issues with a Black friend, he observed: white men like Louis C.K. love the stereotype of the short-dicked Asian guy because it helps them with their discomfort and insecurities over the porno stereotype of the big-dicked Black guy (BBC).

This same Black friend pointed out that though porn certainly brought this stereotype to the surface of the culture instead of on the down-low, the oversized sexually voracious and predatory Black male was a deep stereotype during slavery and has existed in the culture for hundreds of years. It was embedded in the fears of the white master and in the lynchings of Black males accused of assaulting white women.

Still, this Black friend often expresses to me reservations about my even writing about these subjects. You're setting yourself up, he says. He wants to protect me from some of my own impulses as a writer. But he also knows me well enough to understand my answer: this is who I am as a writer; I make readers—and even myself at times—uncomfortable. And when people are made uncomfortable by the message, they attack the messenger.

So be it.

II. ANOTHER TABOO TOPIC: PICKUP SEMINARS AND ASIAN AMERICAN MEN

As seen by the above, all this talk of Asian men's members and white patriarchal definitions of who is attractive can lead one into other various untoward and politically dicey topics. For instance, Eddie Huang's complaint about how Asian men are considered unattractive is not unrelated to the seminars of JT Tran for Asian American men on how to meet, pick up, and bed women. While much of the rhetoric of Tran's seminar echoes white patriarchal misogyny, the problem or questions behind these seminars are, I think, worth considering. In his essay "Paper Tigers," which provides the quotation below on Tran, Korean American writer Wesley Yang points to the ways some Asian American men might be baffled by or ignorant of the dominant white traditions of masculinity:

> What if you missed out on the lessons in masculinity taught in the gyms and locker rooms of America's high schools? What if life has failed to make you a socially dominant alpha male who runs the American boardroom and prevails in the American bedroom? What if no one ever taught you how to greet white people and make them comfortable? What if, despite these deficiencies, you no longer possess an immigrant's dutiful forbearance for a secondary position in the American narrative and want to be a player in the scrimmage of American appetite right now, in the present?

Obviously, there are problems here. Are the lessons taught in gyms and locker rooms about masculinity what we want to teach young men? Of course not. Is the purpose of life to dominate others in the boardroom or the bedroom? No. Should our purpose as Asian Americans be to make white people comfortable? No.

And yet, is knowing how white American men think and practice masculinity useful in guiding one's way as an Asian American man through American society? And since white norms still are the most influential in the society and culture, wouldn't the way white American men think of and present their masculinity influence what white woman or even BIPOC women think is attractive?

Again, we live in a culture and society where white patriarchal norms rule. Might such knowledge of the rules of white masculinity have prevented some of us from being bullied or ridiculed as adolescents? Can knowing how our body posture or voice or social banter is interpreted by non-Asian men and women be useful, especially if your body posture or voice or banter convey to them a message you are not aware of? Is knowing what makes white people both comfortable and uncomfortable useful? (Which is different from wanting or trying to make them feel comfortable.)

On another more subterranean and defiant plane: isn't dominance or submissiveness in the bedroom a complicated and contradictory subject? Wouldn't it be useful to know what constitutes either submissiveness or dominance in sexuality and where one might fall within that spectrum? Wouldn't such knowledge help you as an Asian American to make an informed decision about where your own sexuality might fall in this context and what you might do about this? Wouldn't most Asian Americans have to get that knowledge outside of whatever little their family may have taught them about sexuality?

To be clear, there are ways for Asian American men to grapple with our insecurity and doubts that cannot come out of a pickup seminar. The goal certainly isn't to become an asshole white guy.

And yet, what JT Tran and his seminar are addressing, in however misguided an approach, is a very real issue: as is abundantly clear, in the realms of heterosexual attraction and dating, women can smell a lack of confidence. Moreover, confidence in America is generally associated with aggressiveness, an ability to project an air of power, a self-assumption of one's own attractiveness and importance, a willingness to dominate conversations. For white men, such qualities are in part reinforced and supported by white supremacy; as the T-shirt saying goes, "Lord let me have the confidence of a mediocre white man." In contrast, Asian American men live in a society whose culture has generally pictured us as unaggressive, even meek, ever so silent and retiring—in short, unconfident, unattractive, powerless.

In her CNN *This Is Life* series, in an episode on pickup artists, Lisa Ling points out that in some of these seminars what the men learn is less a misogynistic attitude toward women and sex; instead, it's more a message of simply having confidence in themselves and learning how to present themselves in ways that don't seem desperate and off-putting. Such a seminar focuses less on the woman and more on the men's lack of belief in themselves.

Here "coolness" comes in, a quality that derives certainly from confidence, but it's more complicated than that. When one watches the cool of Denzel Washington in, say, *The Equalizer* or Toshiro Mifune in *Yojimbo,* their lack of reaction is also strategic. Certainly, with Denzel and Toshiro, their characters are letting those threatening them know they're not scared. But they're also camouflaging their intentions. They're sizing them up, letting them react to show themselves; they're reading the room. Often the opponents are overconfident, and that leads to mistakes and errors of strategy.

Cool also comes from knowledge and mastery, but what does that mean in the heterosexual realm? Certainly, there's the difference between being experienced and unexperienced; as the Singapore-born porn actor James Bang explains on the Fung Brothers podcast, you become good at fucking by fucking a lot (which puts the guy without experience in the quandary of how do you gain such experience?). Bang points out that he grew up in a culture where Asians ruled the social hierarchy, even when encountering whites; that gave him a confidence that he doesn't always see in Asian American men.

But what's missing from most heterosexual porn is blatantly obvious—the point of view of the woman, what she is feeling. You can't know women, how they think and feel, if you think they're inferior or if you think they should submit to you, and if you're not really interested in them. (And so many men have very little interest in the complexities of real, actual women—that's why they'd rather watch porn.) Indeed, you ought to want the women in your life to empower themselves, to have opportunities to maximize their talents and abilities. Fear of that isn't masculine in my book; it's cowardly—and stupid. That's the contradiction in patriarchal values. Men want competition in sports: Magic Johnson wanted to compete with the best in Larry Bird, and Bird felt the same about Magic. They wanted their teammates to be at their best. But somehow patriarchal men don't want women to be at their best, whether competing with them or being on their team.

It is here mastery comes in, and it's not mastery over women: it's mastery over yourself, which is essential for "coolness." A lack of confidence leads to overeagerness, too overt displays of attraction or need. And that stems in part from a lack of belief in yourself, which means you haven't mastered yourself, you haven't learned to be detached, to understand what you can and can't control when you are in a sexual situation or a potential sexual situation with a woman.

Part of that, again, comes from experience. But for Asian American and other men, your problem may also be that you're so concerned with your own insecurities you can't see the woman, the person in front of you; you're not interested in her—and in so many heterosexual encounters, women sense this. If you're regarding her simply or primarily as a sexual object, you're not seeing her, too, as a human being, with strengths and foibles and insecurities, with complex motives and thoughts and desires. You're not listening to her; instead, you're listening to your own insecurities and needs and fears. One Asian American woman I know, who's dated men of different races and body types, explained, "It's so hard to find a guy who will listen to you. I can't worry about how they look."

At the same time, in a conversation in a sexual setting, there's a dance one does between listening and speaking, between allowing the other person space to tell you who they are and then doing the same back. This dance isn't always clearly marked out or easy, and there's a fine line between opening yourself up honestly and opening yourself up too quickly or too openly. Having grown up in an Asian cultural family, we might have to work to overcome our reticence to speak about ourselves or—conversely—we may overcompensate by speaking too much about ourselves. Having someone with more experience help you in this process isn't necessarily a bad thing.

In the end, you can't manipulate someone into being attracted to you. You can't control that. What you can control, what you can work on, is yourself.

III. SHOULD ASIAN AMERICAN MEN BE REGARDED AS MEN OF THE WHITE PATRIARCHY? (EVEN THOUGH WE DO NOT BELONG TO IT)

The Filipino Canadian-born *New Yorker* columnist Jia Tolentino is aware of the differences between the ways American society views the sexuality of Asian/Asian American women and Asian/Asian American men. But for Tolentino, the major—and understandably major—consideration in regards to the incel movement is the patriarchy and misogyny:[2]

> On a recent ninety-degree day in New York City, I went for a walk and thought about how my life would look through incel eyes. I'm twenty-nine, so I'm a little old and used up: incels fetishize teen-agers and virgins (they use the abbreviation "JBS," for jailbait), and they describe women who have sought pleasure in their sex lives as "whores" riding a "cock carousel." I'm a feminist, which is disgusting to them. ("It is obvious that women are inferior, that is why men have always been in control of women.") I was wearing a crop top and shorts, the sort of outfit that they believe causes men to rape women. ("Now watch as the level of rapes mysteriously rise up.") In the elaborate incel taxonomy of participants in the sexual marketplace, I am a Becky, devoting my attentions to a Chad. I'm probably a "roastie" too—another term they use for women with sexual experience, denoting labia that have turned into roast beef from overuse.[3]

2 We need to distinguish the "incel" movement or its ideology from the actual lived state of being involuntarily celibate or not experiencing sexual attraction from women. Yes, the *incel* moniker is associated with a noxious misogynist ideology that often deplores the advances women have made in terms of rights and powers; the incel movement proffers a retrograde view of gender as the solution or antidote to involuntary celibacy. But one can be involuntarily celibate and reject the incel label. In such a case involuntary celibacy is a state shared by a larger number of men, a portion of whom don't know about or may even reject the incel ideology but still experience a lack of sexual companionship. While we may deplore the incel movement and the anger and blame it directs toward women, we can also have sympathy for those who have not found sexual or romantic partners and want to change that for themselves. It doesn't mean we need to approve all their efforts at change, but we can empathize with their unhappiness at their state and their desire to change it.

3 My jejune reaction: "Can a hetero Asian American man be regarded as a Chad? What is the male equivalent of a "roastie? Can an Asian American dick turn raw (oh Portnoy of my youth) from overuse? Would that be a roasted dog—or sashimi? Maguro? Yellowtail? Perhaps Unagi—roasted eel? Once long ago, I too was an "incel," now I'm Mr. Futomaki—a short tasty vegetarian roll?"

But what happens when we bring race into any consideration of feminism? As Mikki Kendall writes in "Feminism's Toxic Twitter Wars" in *The Nation,* feminism can often tacitly or unconsciously leave out an intersectional racial perspective: "Feminism has a mammy problem, and mammy doesn't live here anymore. I know *The Help* told you 'You was smart, you was important, you was special.' *The Help* lied. You're going to have to deal with anger, you're going to have to deal with hurt." Kendall wasn't specifically referencing issues of sexual desirability, but she argues that the ways white women, Asian women, and Black women are viewed in this society, including sexually, must take into account the factors of history, colonialism, power, and race. So why wouldn't that be the case for Asian American men?

And yet when it comes to issues regarding sexual desire and desirability, we Asian/Asian American men are still considered by most feminists of any race as de facto part of the white boys' club; we're indicted as full participants and soldiers—though never generals—in the white patriarchy's misogyny (or Asia's patriarchy, even though we do not live in Asia and, indeed, some of us have never even been there). We don't share the privileges or power or prestige or sexual aura of white men, but when it comes to their sins and oppression we are considered full members. (And yes, pun here intended.)

For some women, gender always trumps race. So whatever discrimination or bias Asian men might face, when compared with women of any race, Asian men must have it better, must be more empowered, must be using their status as men to dominate women and dominate women successfully.[4] So in a consideration of an Asian American man on the one hand, and on the other, a white/Black/Latina/Native American/Asian woman, the Asian American man is always regarded as inherently part of the patriarchy and enjoying the rewards and power of the patriarchy.

But this is not the way white men regard Asian men; to white men, Asian men will never belong to the white patriarchy. Is it so far a stretch to posit that a white woman might also hold similar beliefs

4 Which is a different assessment from whether we do want such power or believe we have such power.

or assumptions? And what about the fetish many white men have for Asian women, which is also based on racist and colonial stereotypes?

Moreover, in any encounter who possesses more power, particularly in the realm of sexual attractiveness and desire—an Asian man or a white woman? Or, say, an Asian man or a Black woman?

Generally, given the history of African Americans, Black women writers like Mikki Kendall are less likely to view gender as always trumping race, especially when they are interacting with white women or regarding interactions between men of color and white women.[5]

Thus: a blanket statement that a man is a man is a man whether white, Black, Latino, Native, or Asian is both true and not true.

Again: must gender always be regarded as a far more determining factor than race?

To sum up: we Asian American men are not deemed sufficiently masculine by American society—that's simply a fact; again, that's why Asian men are the least chosen racial group on Tinder and Grindr. On these platforms, even Asian American women prefer white men the most and over Asian American men. Black women, also the least swiped right, are often deemed overly loud, aggressive, and assertive—-i.e., overly masculine. Again, traditional patriarchal definitions of masculine and feminine are at play here.

And yet for many feminists, white or Asian, the base assumption is that we Asian American men should be regarded as no different from other men when it comes to issues of gender and the patriarchy. I will never be viewed as masculine or alpha in the same way as John Wayne or Bradley Cooper or Donald Trump or George Clooney or Joe Rogan or Machine Gun Kelly or Ryan Gosling or Tom Brady, but I must still be regarded as part of *their* patriarchy? And it really doesn't matter if early on I realized I was never going to be John Wayne and began to

5 It was the Black woman writer Roxane Gay who tweeted, "We are never going to make progress if we cannot hold Aziz Ansari accountable without lumping him in with guys like [Matt] Lauer and C.K." Black writer ShaRhonda Knott Dawson has written probably the most cogent questioning of the allegations against Ansari.

seek other models of masculinity in the sensibilities and perspectives of women and gay writers.[6]

Even Asian American men can sometimes subscribe to this view. In *The Souls of Yellow Folks,* here's how Wesley Yang puts this conundrum/contradiction, in a perhaps more eloquent and complex summation:

> My interest has always been in the place where sex and race are both obscenely conspicuous and yet consciously suppressed, largely because of the liminal place that the Asian man occupies in the midst of it: an "honorary white" person who will always be denied the full prerequisites of whiteness; an entitled man who will never quite be regarded or treated as a man; a nominal minority whose claim to be a "person of color" deserving of special regard reserved for victims is taken seriously by no one. In an age characterized by the politics of resentment, the Asian man knows something of the resentment of the embattled white man, besieged on all sides by grievances and demands for reparation, and something of the resentments of the rising social-justice warrior, who feels with every fiber of their being that all that stands in the way of the attainment of their thwarted ambitions is nothing so much as a white man. Tasting of the frustrations of both, he is denied the entitlements of either.
>
> This condition of marginality is both the cause and the effect of his erasure—and perhaps the source of his claim to his centrality, indeed his universality.

I do appreciate Yang's focus on Asian American men and the intersections of race and sex; he's right that the white patriarchy doesn't accept us either as white or fitting its definition of a man. But so much here I find questionable, starting with Yang's presumed acceptance of, or refusal to fight against, our model minority status.

6 In various ways, Asian/Asian American men confound and complicate the white patriarchal view of masculinity both in our appearance and our cultural values. There's also a historical dimension to this: a Latino friend once pointed out to me that the two wars America lost in the twentieth century were to Asian countries, Korea/China and Vietnam, and he argued that white American masculinity has never gotten over those losses.

While Yang recognizes the stereotypes that Asian Americans face and the ways we sometimes aren't regarded as true/authentic people of color, he doesn't seem to realize he has a choice: we do not have to assent to these negative forces or designations; we don't have to give them the power to determine who we are and what we believe or how we act in the world. I can reject the "honorary white" or "model minority" labels just as I reject racist tropes about Asians. Beyond that, I wonder how much contact Yang has experienced with other BIPOC. I have engaged with countless BIPOC and their events and organizations, and other than on a couple of occasions, I can't ever remember someone telling me I wasn't a person of color because I was Asian. Instead, the attitude was more, "We're happy you're joining us."

As for Yang's contention that the Asian man must echo the resentment of the embattled white man—why would I want the white guy's entitlements to be a MAGA sexist jerk? It's not a path that's helpful either to me or others, including, I would argue, white men.[7] The critique of the white patriarchy by feminists is not only understandable and justified, but it points to a world I would much rather live in. If as an Asian American male I want to be recognized and given equal opportunities for my abilities, why wouldn't I want the same thing for women or other marginalized groups?

On the other hand, I don't desire whatever Yang seems to imagine the "entitlements" of a "social-justice warrior" might be. Certainly, the fight for social justice isn't about my ego or my personal ambitions; I'm not seeking some merit badge nor am I seeking to be viewed as a victim. I simply want our society to be fair and equitable for all. The personal may often be political, but the political starts with a focus on the group, not the individual's psychological motives. At the same time, Yang doesn't understand that activism can help us align our lives with something greater than ourselves. Anger at injustice, empathy, and compassion for others who have suffered injustice can release us from the prison of the self.[8]

7 A 2013 American Psychological Association report states that "Adherence to stereotypic masculinity" leads to "stress and conflict, poor health, poor coping and relationship quality, and violence."

8 I realize that this release doesn't always occur. Activism has become, in recent years, especially online, a social performance of virtue. Some have used this "performance"

This is not to say individual psychology doesn't come into play with politics. In the end, I can't believe, much less consent to, the bullshit Whiteness and MAGA America want me to believe—it's denial of our history, it's blind denial of our current racial and gender realities. Yes, I find it objectionable to my sense of morality and justice, but it also insults my intelligence. And because I have seen how other marginalized people can be erased and because I have learned to see more clearly their uniqueness and truths, I understand I can work against these erasures, both for myself and for those who have been similarly erased. Their fight is my fight. And if you fight along other BIPOC for their causes or our mutual causes, eventually that makes a difference in how they regard you. Look at Asian American activists like Yuri Kochiyama or Grace Lee Boggs, who were respected and renowned in the Black communities where they lived and practiced their activism (Yuri in Harlem, Grace in Detroit).

Let me repeat: the model minority is a myth. Originally used to critique the Black civil rights movement in the 1950s and '60s, the model minority label was concocted by white conservatives: *look how quiet those Asians are; they don't protest like those Negroes; they work hard, etc.* But this white-coined label doesn't have to define *our* relationship with other people of color. Moreover, when we join the fight for equity for all BIPOC, eventually whites stop regarding us as the model minority because we aren't acting according to *their* ideal of what a model minority should be.

the way self-righteous church members present themselves as holier than thou. In light of this, I feel the necessity to address what activism does not do: if you are active in an issue involving social justice, whatever you accomplish, you do not become infallible. Certainly, it does not make you instantly into a virtuous person; it does not make you correct in every judgment of other people or other causes.

So a certain epistemic humility ought to be part of any participation in social justice. Empowerment without humility or doubt can be dangerous both for you and others—and certainly for any movement; empowerment with skepticism and humility ought to be what we're striving for. For me, this means that our focus shouldn't be on shaming or guilting people or labeling them as racists or decrying them for their privilege. Instead, we are invoking the principles of fairness and justice; we are critiquing *systems* of oppression and inequality. By focusing on systems, we allow space for individuals to critique and opt out of those systems—which is much harder for an individual to contemplate if we are attacking them as individuals.

Believe me, I know this from experience. It's not just that I alienated white artist friends in arguments concerning *Miss Saigon* or race. In my career, I've experienced far more support and encouragement from Black writers than from white writers.

But then I am not an Asian American neocon. Unlike Yang, I don't want to become a member of a club I will never belong to.

IV. HEY GUYS, SEXUALITY AND SEXUAL DESIRE ARE NOT A MONOLITH (I.E., NOT EVERYONE SUBSCRIBES TO THE NEGATIVE STEREOTYPES OF ASIAN MEN)

Amia Srinivasan is a South Asian American/British writer who takes a more egalitarian stance toward the issues of sexual attraction.[9] In her comments on the incel movement,[10] she writes about how the negative sexual stereotypes of Asian/Asian American men work in the gay world, not just the straight world (*no fats femmes Asians*):

> "The beautiful torsos on Grindr are mostly Asian men hiding their faces," a gay friend of mine says. The next day I see on Facebook that Grindr has started a web series called "What the Flip?" In its first three-minute episode, a beautiful, blue-haired East Asian guy and a

9 Having lived in Taiwan, New York, Singapore, and London, Srinivasen explains that she "speaks with a hybrid English-American accent"; perhaps having lived in diverse places, she's experienced a variety of racialized sexual hierarchies and is thus more able to entertain and examine new or other possibilities or standards of sexual desire both for herself and others.

10 There are those who believe if men don't feel desirable, they generally revert to or try to become stronger in their reinforcement of traditional masculinity. Certainly, this is one of the critiques of the incel movement, where hetero men who feel that they are involuntarily celibate have expressed not only great anger about their lack of desirability but also a rageful hatred of women—which has led to acts of violence on their part. Here's Jia Tolentino on the incel movement: "Men, like women, blame women if they feel undesirable. And, as women gain the economic and cultural power that allows them to be choosy about their partners, men have generated ideas about self-improvement that are sometimes inextricable from violent rage. . . . In the past few years, a subset of straight men calling themselves 'incels' have constructed a violent political ideology around the injustice of young, beautiful women refusing to have sex with them. These men often subscribe to notions of white supremacy. They are, by their own judgment, mostly unattractive and socially inept. (They frequently call themselves 'subhuman.') They're also diabolically misogynistic."

> well-groomed, good-looking white guy trade Grindr profiles. The results are predictably grim. The white guy, now using the Asian guy's profile, is hardly approached, and when he is it's by men announcing that they're "Rice Queens" and like Asian men for being "good at bottoming." When he ignores their messages, abuse is hurled at him. The Asian guy's inbox, meanwhile, is inundated with admirers. Talking about it afterwards, the white guy expresses his shock, the Asian guy cheerful resignation. "You're not everybody's cup of tea, but you're going to be somebody's," the white guy offers, feebly, before they hug it out. In the next episode, a ripped Ryan Gosling–type switches profiles with a pretty-faced chubby guy. In episode three a fem guy trades with a masc guy. The results are as one would expect.

For Srinivasan, all of this calls for a variety of levels of intersectional thinking:

> Consider the supreme fuckability of "hot blonde sluts" and East Asian women, the comparative unfuckability of black women and Asian men, the fetishisation and fear of black male sexuality, the sexual disgust expressed towards disabled, trans and fat bodies. These too are political facts, which a truly intersectional feminism should demand that we take seriously.

Srinivasan believes that "our sexual preferences can and do alter." We can't necessarily always will them to alter, and yet that is a possibility. Certainly, our sexual desires can surprise us and go against our previous preferences or our firmly held beliefs about who we are as a person and whom we desire. And if we can't control whom we desire or love, that might also mean that the dictates of the society around us, its hierarchy of sexual desire, don't necessarily control us or others as completely as we might think. Or as Srinivasan writes, "Desire can cut against what politics has chosen for us, and choose for itself"—and here one can take *politics* for either what we deem politically correct *or* what we deem politically oppressive and incorrect.

In the real world, the one where we encounter actual people, our sexual desires can't be quantified and predicted. What attracts any two people to each other may involve certain cultural norms—however we define them, whichever ones we might accept—and yet, however prevalent those norms may be, they can't tell the whole story, they can't explain everything about our attractions, and they don't necessarily *determine* our attractions. Anyone can be attracted to someone they never expected to be attracted to—or vice versa.

This is good news for us all, and for Asian American men in particular. Again, in the real world the size of one's penis is generally not a determinant of who is attracted to you—after all, a person doesn't decide to go to bed with you by judging the size of your penis. Nor is penis size a decisive determinant of success in the bedroom. With the latter, there are again so many factors that go into mutual sexual satisfaction, and in the straight world an inordinate number of these have little to do with penis size. Some women, like Ali Wong, say they like the smooth skin of Asian men, the lack of hair for many of us (it's like stroking a baby seal, Wong coos). Others, like the porn star Adriana Chechik, say they like the way Asian men smell (many of us don't possess a strong body odor). Some like our work ethic, our education, our bicultural backgrounds, our strong attachment to family.

Beyond this, the huge dicks of porn are not common and are not commonly encountered by women outside of porn. Just as important, these huge penises are far more the projection of male fantasies than every woman's fantasy or desire. Yes, there are some straight women who prefer larger penises. But for many women, the huge cocks in porn are scary or off putting. There are straight women—and bi women—for whom the size of one's penis may not be a determining factor, or for whom a large penis is undesirable or physically painful, or for whom a smaller penis is preferable. (For some it better stimulates their G-spot.) There are women for whom penile penetration does not produce orgasms or only rarely, and so for these women the size of the man's penis is somewhat beside the point.[11] There are women who prefer to get off not by penises but manually or orally or by vibrators or toys, and any partner, with or without a penis, can use their tongue or fingers or a vibrator. And obviously, you can have a large penis and be

11 According to Professor Debby Herbenick et al., research suggests only 18 percent of women orgasm from penetration alone. https://www.tandfonline.com/doi/full/10.1080/0092623X.2017.1346530.

terrible in bed and leave your partners sexually frustrated or unsatisfied. Or you can have a large penis and be a total asshole. (Note: while you can't change the size of your penis, you can make yourself less of an asshole and a better person—so why not work on that rather than fret on something you can't change?)

In heterosexual encounters, knowledge of women's bodies and sexuality and an openness to asking your partner what is pleasurable to her are generally more crucial factors in her sexual satisfaction than penis size. Most important, there's emotional connection and love, which have a huge effect on any sexual connection. Sexual satisfaction takes place as much or more in the mind than in the body, and for many women, perhaps even the majority of women, the emotional connection is the most important factor in sexual pleasure—again, not the size of the man's penis.

Yes, stereotypes of Asian male sexuality do affect our lives, but they aren't a monolithic all-powerful force. Not everyone subscribes to these stereotypes or believes them or even knows about them. Even when people do know about stereotypes or believe them to a certain extent, contact with real individuals in the stereotyped groups can change people's beliefs and how they react to those in the stereotyped group.

In the end, of course, you have to be happy with who you are. And if you aren't, the biggest task you have is not worrying about stereotypes but, again, accepting yourself.[12]

12 The perception of Asian American men is changing, according to media figures like the Fung Brothers. Two Chinese American comedian/rappers who grew up in Kent, Washington, Andrew and David Fung center their podcasts on Asian American cultural and political issues (Jeremy Lin, hot pot, Andrew Yang), with a frequent focus on the sexuality and dating prospects of Asian American men. They pursue the latter topic with relentless detail from media representations to specific historic tropes of Asians by American society. Recently, some topics allude to a new shift in the perception of Asian American men: "Did BTS Make Asian Guys Hotter?"; "Asian Men Are FINALLY Getting the Girl"; "Is Dating Asian Men Finally Normal?" Watching their YouTube videos I have the feeling that I've been decades ahead of the curve—but perhaps progress is being made.

Even Jimmy Yang who first appeared on *Silicon Valley* as an Asian immigrant nerd is getting lead roles. Yang stars in the recent Hulu series *Interior Chinatown,* based on the National Book Award–winning novel by Charles Yu about a Chinese restaurant

V. THE ISSUES OF ASIAN AMERICAN WOMEN

During the Covid-19 pandemic, the alarming rise of anti-Asian hate crimes and microaggressions involved our whole community, but the majority of victims were Asian/Asian American women. Six of the eight people killed in the horrible Atlanta massacre were Asian women: Daoyou Feng, Hyun Jung Grant, Suncha Kim, Soon Chung Park, Xiaojie Tan, and Young Ae Yue. Since the killer's rage seemed to be focused on Asian sex workers and how his desire for them put him in conflict with his Christian fundamentalism, some portion of the public blindly did not see the connections in these killings between the race of these sex workers and the patriarchal structuring of white American male sexual desire. In general, Asian/Asian American women in America are subjected to stereotypes regarding their sexuality that go back to the roots of colonialism in Asia.

In an interview in the *Atlantic,* "Violence Against Asian American Women Is Rooted in More Than Just 'Hate,'" Nicole Chung and Connie Wun attempt to explore the structural roots of sexism, racism, and violence against Asian and Asian American women:

that serves as a frequent backdrop for films and television shows. The television series is set amid a quasi sci-fi landscape of media representations of Chinatown, and its protagonist, waiter Willis Wu, longs to break out of his minor role in American society—generic anonymous Asian man. In a world that at times feels structured like a video game, where Willis must always lose, his search for his missing brother eventually leads him both to a starring role as a television detective and a romantic connection with a beautiful *hapa* detective, Lana Lee. And so, as in the HBO series based on Viet Thanh Nguyen's novel *The Sympathizer,* or the Apple series based on Min Jin Lee's *Pachinko,* Asian American authors are also helping enlarge the range of roles for Asian American actors, thus moving all Asian Americans out of the rigid stereotypes created by Whiteness. That both *The Sympathizer* and *Interior Chinatown* dissect Orientalist stereotypes, particularly for Asian American men, is both symptomatic and heartening.

I binge-watched *Interior Chinatown* and finished it in two nights. As a way of showing how culture can change our unconscious, after watching the last episode I had a dream where I returned to college and was part of an Asian American student group. Such a group did not exist when I was in college many years ago, nor would I have joined one in college. But such groups exist now on college campuses across the country. Even my seventysomething unconscious is opening to a new vision of who we are and who we might become.

> Connie Wun: The violence against Asian women and girls and our nonbinary communities is deeply rooted in the legacy of patriarchal violence, too—this has been part of our histories here in the United States and abroad. Today is the anniversary of the My Lai massacre, in which hundreds of women and children were assaulted and killed by U.S. troops in Vietnam. Today is also the anniversary of the eight people who were killed in the Atlanta spa shootings. There is a long history of aggression against our bodies and communities, here and abroad. It is part of U.S. history.
>
> People need to understand that we experience racial and gender violence beyond the deaths. . . . this violence is an everyday experience—and by that, I'm talking about the racism and sexism Asian women experience in corporate America, at the hands of the medical industry, on the street. I've had men in my life say things like, "How's that moo shu going?" I've been asked, "Is your pussy slanted, too?"

In combating all this, Asian American men need to be supportive of Asian and Asian American women and speak out against the racist sexism they face, a racist sexism with many of the same roots as the negative stereotypes faced by Asian American men. We are fighting the same forces of oppression and marginalization and hate; we should be aligned with each other.

Acknowledgments

I want to thank my editor Erik Anderson, who has now worked with me on two of my books. I so appreciate his understanding of my work, his insightful critiques and the many ways he has helped me shape this manuscript. His encouragement and support have been invaluable and restorative. His assistant Emma Saks provided key administrative support.

I thank the staff at the University of Minnesota Press for their professionalism and hard work. Once again, Louisa Castner was particularly helpful as my copy editor and suggested excellent editorial advice. Agent Scott Edelstein again provided me with valuable expertise with my contract, even though he is in semiretirement.

Alexs Pate provided excellent criticism of the manuscript; his friendship of thirty-five years and our many collaborations together have been instrumental, not just to my career or psychological well-being but to my understanding of race in America. Similarly, my friend and colleague Garrett Hongo has been there with me almost from the start, and I so value his support and reading of this manuscript. His vast scholarship and knowledge of Asian American history and culture have been a constant source of reference for me. Steve Woodward provided a major critique of the book, and his input has been crucial in shaping both the content and structure. Other colleagues who have read the manuscript and provided key critiques are Ed Bok Lee and Alexis Paige.

I'd like to thank the many friends and artists who have supported and influenced me over the years: Carolyn Holbrook, Bao Phi, Sun Yung Shin, Shannon Gibney, Tim Seibles, Richard Hoffman, Maurice Carlos Ruffin, Lauren K. Alleyne, Dipankar Mukherjee, Meena Natarajan, David Henry Hwang, Gish Jen, Viet Thanh Nguyen, Randy Reyes, Kathy Haddad, Lana Barkawi, Marion Gómez, Arthur Jafa.

Director Rick Shiomi helped create Theater Mu and gave me the opportunity to play the King in *The King and I*. Producer Katie O'Rourke invited me to join in the Twin Cities Public Television documentary on the MIS Nisei, *Armed with Language*, and I am so thankful for being able to contribute to that project.

Sun Mee Chomet has been a constant and loving cheerleader for me for many years. Mat Johnson, Junot Díaz, and Ananya Chatterjea wrote valuable recommendations for me for the Guggenheim Fellowship, which helped me finish this book. I thank Ed Hirsch and the Guggenheim Fellowship for much needed support. Frank Wilderson's writings have been instrumental to my thinking, as well as the examples of Yuri Kochiyama and Grace Lee Boggs.

Valerie Lee joined with me and others to create the Asian American Renaissance; all of us in our local Asian American community owe her a great debt. My longtime friend Marlina Gonzalez was one of the original group.

Elmaz Abinader invited me to be part of VONA, and I would not be the writer or the person I am without that generous invitation. Diem Jones welcomed me to VONA with open arms. I learned so much from my VONA teaching colleagues and students, unfortunately too numerous to name, but they include M. Evelina Galang (fellow VONA board member), Willie Perdomo, Suheir Hammad, Chris Abani, Quincy Troupe, Tony Khalife, Zahir Janmohamed.

I want to thank my fellow members of the Don't Buy *Miss Saigon* Coalition, including Margie Andreason and Juliana Pegues.

I thank my parents, Tom and Terry Mura, who passed during the writing of this book, and my siblings, Susan, John, and Linda, for their love and support. Through their love, experiences, and perspectives, my children, Samantha, Nikko, and Tomo, along with their partners, Lance, Baydan, and Lariza, have taught me about the multiethnic, multiracial world here in the Twin Cities.

Finally, I owe countless and incalculable thanks to my wife, Dr. Susan Sencer, who has loved me and read my work since we first met in college. She is my heart and anchor. I would not be the writer or person I am without her.

Publication History

Previous versions of the chapters in this book were originally published in the following publications.

"Introduction: A Surrealist Asian in Minnesota" was published as "A Surrealist History of One Asian American in Minnesota" in *A Good Time for the Truth: Race in Minnesota,* edited by Sun Yung Shin, Minnesota Historical Society Press, 2016.

"Do I Belong Here?" was published in *Read America(s): An Anthology,* edited by Hari Alluri, Garrett Bryant, and Amanda Fuller, Locked Horn Press, 2016.

"Raising a Multicultural Daughter in a Multicultural World" was published as "Secrets and Anger" in *Mother Jones,* September/October 1992.

"Secret Colors" was published in *Some of My Best Friends: Writings on Interracial Friendships,* edited by Emily Bernard, Amistad Press, 2004.

"*Armed with Language*" was published as "Covid 19 and Asian Americans" in *We Are Meant to Rise: Voices for Justice from Minneapolis to the World,* edited by Carolyn Holbrook and David Mura, University of Minnesota Press, 2021.

"The Internment of Desire" was published in *Where the Body Meets Memory: An Odyssey of Race, Sexuality, and Identity* by David Mura, Anchor, 1996.

"Asian American Masculinity: Performing or Not Performing the Patriarchy" was published as "Performing *Prop 8* and John Wayne" in *Witness* 32, no. 1, Spring 2019.

"Fragments in Search of Asian American Masculinity" was published as "Further Statements in Search of Asian American Masculinity," in *Identity Theory*, by David Mura, February 4, 2022, and as "On Dr. David Dao, United Airlines, and the Model Minority Myth" in *Unmargin* 2017.

"Race, History, and My Marriage" was published as "Therapy (Couples): No Race Allowed," in "Open in Emergency: A Special Issue on Asian American Mental Health," *Asian American Literary Review* 2017.

"What VONA Taught Me (Part II): Teaching" was published in *A Stranger's Journey: Race, Identity, and Narrative Craft* by David Mura, University of Georgia Press, 2018.

"Owning My Asian American Body" was published as "The King and I: How We as Asian Americans Inhabit Our Bodies" in *Where Are You From? An Anthology of Asian American Writing*, CreateSpace, 2012.

DAVID MURA is a memoirist, poet, fiction writer, essayist, and literary critic. His books include *The Stories Whiteness Tells Itself* (Minnesota, 2023); *A Stranger's Journey: Race, Identity, and Narrative Craft in Writing*; the coedited *We Are Meant to Rise: Voices for Justice from Minneapolis to the World* (Minnesota, 2021); and the memoirs *Turning Japanese: Memoirs of a Sansei* (a *New York Times* Notable Book) and *Where the Body Meets Memory: An Odyssey of Race, Sexuality, and Identity.* He has also written four poetry collections and a novel, and he coproduced, wrote, and narrated the Emmy-winning documentary *Armed with Language.* Mura taught at the VONA writers' conference for writers of color and worked with the Innocent Classroom, a program designed by Alexs Pate to improve teachers' relationships with students of color.